# IN SILENT FORTITUDE

In memory of the men
of the North Tyne Valley
who fell in the Great War

Alan Isaac Grint

IN SILENT FORTITUDE

In Memory of the Men of the North Tyne Valley

Who Fell in the Great War

First Published by Ergo Press

5 St Mary's Chare

Hexham

Northumberland

NE46 1NQ

ergo.press@yahoo.co.uk



ISBN: 978-0-9557510-9-7

Cover graphics: Slim Palmer

Printed by ElandersHindson Ltd

Merlin Way

New York Business Park

Newcastle upon Tyne

NE27 0YT.

# CONTENTS

# ACKNOWLEDGEMENTS

I would like to acknowledge the help of the enthusiasts who responded with great clarity to my questions on the forum of the Long Long Trail website; the depth of their knowledge and understanding is humbling. Also thanks go to Neil Taylor of www.4thbnnf.com, who has provided me with details about a number of the Northumberland Fusiliers mentioned in this book. In particular I would like to mention Graham Stewart, as well as the staff of the Bellingham Heritage Centre, for permission to use some of their photographs. I am also grateful to local people who took the trouble to visit Cogito Books in order to offer information, photographs and memorabilia; they bring both warmth and humanity to enhance these pages. Finally,I would like to thank my wife, Julia, who provided support and editorial comment, without whom this book would never have been produced.

**Dedicated to my grandfathers who survived the Great War but with lasting injuries.**

## Editor's Note

This book was several years in the making. Researching the Great War yields far more information than a book of this kind can possibly use, so there has necessarily been liberal use of the editor's 'red pen'. What follows are concise overviews of the various theatres of war, with enough detail to put each soldier mentioned in his rightful place of action. I would recommend that the interested reader should use the references at the end of each chapter to find further reading, if needed.

The title of this book is taken from Rudyard Kiplng's poem
*For All We Have And Are*
written in 1914.

# FOREWORD

In *The Souldiers Catechisme* of 1644, the ordinary 'souldiers' are asked '*What hope have you from them that are ingaged in this warre?*' The Catechisme provides an answer: '*Because our men generally are so full of courage and resolution*'.

In this, his latest book, Alan Grint draws our attention to the 'courage and resolution' of the men of the valley of the North Tyne who gave their lives for their country. It is now, of course, customary to regard such deaths and sacrifice as ill-founded, the result not so much of courage and resolution, but of the crass and manipulative behaviour of sanctimonious politicians and incompetent generals. There is some truth in this view: and no one standing in front of any one of the thousands of memorials to our war dead can suppress that sad and haunting sense of the loss that they evoke. Yet, as Alan Grint shows, nothing, but nothing, can diminish the pride we take in the steady and ultimately successful way in which the ordinary 'souldiers' of the British Army fought their way through the years 1914-1918. Here, in Alan's pages, we meet the men and boys, from all walks of life, who left the loveliness of the North Tyne for the destroyed and oozing battle-sites of the Great War. The North Tyne is just as lovely now as it was then: and the battle-sites too have recovered from the terrible destruction visited on them: yet these young men will never see this loveliness, will never themselves enjoy the peace which was, other wars later, bought by their sacrifice. It is fitting indeed that we should remember them, in all the small and personal detail of their lives as men of Northumberland and as soldiers of the British Army. What more about the Great War do we need to know? Alan Grint's meticulous reading of the lapidary texts of the memorials of the North Tyne brings back with extraordinary vigour the realities faced by those young men who left Northumberland, never to return: they went to war: and we are the beneficiaries of the tomorrows they never had.

Jon Gower Davies, October 2011

Men of Humshaugh, Great War

Pte E Charlton: Cpl O Saint; Pionner R Bestford ?

Pte J Henderson; Serg G Robson

# CHAPTER ONE

# IN THE BEGINNING

*'My subject is War and the Pity of War'*
Wilfred Owen

The British Empire paid a terrible price for its participation and ultimate victory in the Great War. By 1918, when the bitter struggle finally ended, there was hardly a family in the land not burdened by grief for someone who had died during this worldwide conflict. Nearly a million men from Britain were killed, the vast majority died abroad; many were eventually laid to rest in the wonderful cemeteries now cared for by the Commonwealth War Graves Commission.

Although we tend to associate the Great War chiefly with the horrors of the Western Front and with the well-documented slaughter of men on the Somme and at Passchendale, along the North Tyne Valley from the confluence with the westerly flowing South Tyne to the northern reaches of Kielder, war memorials record the deaths of soldiers killed in many other theatres of the Great War. Local men died in Salonika, India and Mesopotamia.

Sadly, there remain a significant number of men who lost their lives but have no known grave; their names are to be found in seemingly endless lists on a number of magnificent edifices positioned throughout the length of the battlefields of the Western Front: at the Menin Gate (Ypres), Tyne Cot (Flanders), Arras and Thiepval (Somme). Further lists are to be found in more exotic locations in Turkey, Iraq, Egypt and Pakistan. To put this in context, on 21 March 1918, the first day of the German offensive on the Somme, of the 7,500 men killed, fewer than a 1000 have known graves.

Also to be found in a large number of the Western Front Cemeteries are graves containing soldiers with no identification; they are inscribed simply, 'Known unto God'.

The process of remembrance began even before the war had ended, with the development of small street shrines and rolls of honour. Many of the volunteers in the early part of the war were known as 'Pals', as they had volunteered *en masse* from tight knit communities or even from sporting clubs. After battles such as the *First Day of the Somme*, many of these communities were devastated by the loss of sons, husbands and fathers. In this area, men of the local Territorial Battalion, 1/4th Northumberland Fusiliers met such a fate at *Ypres* (April 1915), *Somme* (September 1916), *Passchendaele* (1917) and *Aisne* (1918). It is not surprising that the communities from which the men came responded by erecting their own immediate and heartfelt tributes to the dead.

After the war, every city, every town and nearly every village built a permanent war memorial, which altered the landscape of post-war Britain. There was no government direction in their erection, simply the desire by local people to remember those who had gone to war, who had paid the ultimate sacrifice and who had not returned. Their shape and form varies across the country, as does the manner in which the names and further details are recorded, but what they have in common is the great effort made to include all of the locals who lost their lives. Further to these memorials were the plaques erected in churches, sports clubs, schools and places of work, again to replace the temporary shrines that had been built during the course of the war all over Britain, Ireland and the British Empire.

In Great Britain, according to the last count, there remain over 36,000 memorials to the dead of the Great War. Sad to say, there are many instances where memorials have been lost or destroyed as buildings have been demolished or their function changed. The lack of any fixed template for memorials resulted in the country being embroidered with a plethora of monuments in many different styles; they have a dark and unaccountable beauty.

Falstone Cross

Mewburn Effigy
St John Lee

TO THE GLORY OF GOD, AND IN GRATEFUL
MEMORY OF THE MEN OF KIELDER, WHO
GAVE THEIR LIVES IN TWO WORLD WARS.
1914 - 1918.
DAVID JACKSON MATTHEW ROBSON.
1939 - 1945.
ANDREW FLETCHER. EDWARD FIDDLER.
ALEX P. WEIR. RAYMOND TERRY.
JOHN L. BIRD. GEORGE W. GLENDINNING.

Kielder Church

Stained Glass Window
St John Lee

Wall Cross

Not surprisingly, many of the memorials have Christian symbolism: crosses and angels in particular. Others are unadorned obelisks. Some have simply a list of names of the dead, usually incorporating a rank, whilst others incorporate regimental information; the year of death is also a common feature. Some war memorials incorporate the names not only of the local people who died, but also of those who served and returned home; these include the memorial at St Luke's Church, Greystead (now closed) and Wall Village memorial. The people recorded on the memorial would result from a public announcement inviting the community to submit the names of soldiers known to them. This call for names was generated by a committee who had taken on the task of securing the funds to build the memorial and to devise its shape and form.

In many cases, personal memorials were funded by the family to commemorate someone loved and sadly missed, for example the Spencer plaque in St Oswald Roman Catholic Church, Bellingham; the White family stained glass window at St Cuthbert Bellingham; the Robson family plaque and Hutchinson plaque and stained glass window at St Giles Birtley; the Cuthbert and Walton family memorials at St John Lee and the Leadbitter shrine at Warden, (now missing).

Some memorials have new homes, removed from their original positions. For example, the memorial from Plashetts, a village lost during the construction of the Kielder Reservoir, was removed to the Methodist and United Reformed Church Hall in Bellingham. One hopes that a new home can also be found for the two war memorials in St Luke's Church at Greystead, now closed.

Whatever the memorials commemorated, it was inevitable that errors were made in the final edition. In a number of cases initials were confused. A simple example of this is when the hero was commonly known by his nickname, thus 'Robert' might have been recorded as 'B' for 'Bob' etc. Many soldiers had their regimental and battalion affiliations included, but these were dictated by what was known at the time by those who submitted their names, but during the course of the war the 'where' and 'with whom' a man served could change considerably, so these details were subject to frequent alteration and therefore easily confused. If a man had been wounded and then returned to the Front after treatment, it was not always the case that he went back to the battalion and regiment of his enlistment; he may have been posted to another battalion of the same regiment, or even to another regiment altogether. Further, during the course of the war, battalions were sometimes virtually annihilated in action and were then amalgamated with another battalion to make them viable, and if battalions were lacking a core of experienced soldiers, men from battalions who had more than their share would be ordered to transfer a number of men. To make the situation even more complicated, in early 1918 the Army was so desperately short of manpower that the brigade system was modified; instead of each brigade containing four front line infantry battalions this was reduced to three. Thus, a man's service record is not always easy to trace. It is hardly surprising, therefore, that memorials sometimes have inaccuracies.

During my extensive research in writing this book on the men of the North Tyne Valley, I have happened upon a number of these inconsistencies, where the data on the war memorial is not consistent with that found in public records and the newspapers.

Not all of the men who are honoured on local war memorials may be found on the national database compiled by the Commonwealth War Graves Commission. This discrepancy is being rectified by the sterling work of the *"In from the Cold"* project. Along the North Tyne Valley there are at least two instances where their hard work has yielded dividends: the commemoration of Sergeant Andrew Cowan (Bellingham) now inscribed on the Pozières Memorial to the Missing and Able Seaman John Rae who is now commemorated in Bellingham Cemetery. However, there are a significant number of others, including Private Walter Rutherford (Wark); Private John English Urwin, (Wall); Driver John William Conkleton (St John Lee) and Corporal George Dalton, (Humshaugh), who remain unrecognised nationally.

In this book I have attempted to say, "Thank you, brave souls," to the men of the North Tyne who gave their lives in the Great War. I have, where possible, found out something about their civilian lives and also about what was going on in the field of war at the time they died. I would dearly like their names to resound along with the church bells on every Remembrance Sunday, and to live on in the hearts of the community for whom they gave their young lives. If I have missed any one of them, it was not for any lack of regard, but simply because no information about them was available when I was doing my research.

The last two surviving WW1 combatants died within a few days of each other in August 2009. In their honour, the poet laureate, Carol Ann Duffy, wrote a poem, *Last Post*, in which she wishes that as a poet she could "tell it backwards": reverse the horror of it all and bring the "thousands dead" home safely. She imagines them "shaking dried mud from their hair and queueing up for home", to fulfill their potential with lives "crammed with love, work, children, talent, English beer, good food". We all share this hopeless but beautiful thought - that the killing might never have taken place - but we are left, instead, with our memorials to those who died. I hope that this book adds in some small way to the written library that has been created as a tribute to those who entered a story that ended in death.

# CHAPTER TWO

# FOR KING AND COUNTRY

*Squire nagged and bullied till I went to fight*
*(Under Lord Derby's scheme), I died in hell ...*
From Seigfried Sassoon's, *Memorial Tablet*

In the years of the twentieth century before the Great War, the British army was regarded as a 'police service' for its extensive empire. It was recognised as a highly professional force, but it was overwhelmingly dwarfed in size by those of its continental neighbours; France had 2.75 million men and Germany 3.7 million men in their armies. By comparison the British Army was regarded as second to the Navy and had a total strength of fewer than 250,000 men, half of whom at any time were based overseas. Generally, each of the county regiments supported two battalions, with one of the two at any time based overseas.

**The Structure of the British Army**

A division is a large military unit, usually consisting of between 10,000 and 15,000 soldiers. In August 1914 the British Army was able to field only 5 divisions. A division is composed of several battalions, and in turn several divisions make up a corps. The division, with its artillery and engineers, tends to be the smallest unit capable of independent operations and is commanded by a Major General. In 1914, each division was divided into three infantry brigades, each of which was commanded by a Brigadier General. Until early 1918, each brigade was sub-divided into four infantry battalions of approximately 1000 soldiers each. Men in the infantry battalions came from several different county regiments of the time (some no longer exist, e.g. The Northumberland Fusiliers) and each was commanded by a Lieutenant Colonel. Every battalion was further divided into five companies commanded by either a Captain or a Major. Each division was supported by 3 to 4 artillery brigades, engineers, medical and veterinary support.

When the British Expeditionary Force landed in France it could only muster 5 divisions; in comparison the Germans could count on 72 divisions. Even Belgium could muster 6 divisions.

From 1908, in the years leading up to the war, the British Army obtained its recruits from three sources: regular professional soldiers, part time members of the Territorial force or soldiers of the Special Reserve.

A man enlisting in the regular army could do so as long as was able to pass a number of physical tests, was taller than 5 feet 3 inches and was aged between 19 and 38. He joined at either the Regimental Depot or the local recruiting office and could choose in which regiment he served. Of our local men, for example, William Armstrong Johnson (Bellingham) was a regular soldier with the Northumberland Fusiliers in India when the war broke out. Captain Mewburn (St John Lee) was on leave when war was declared and initially fought in France before returning to his original regiment (14th Hussars) in Mesopotamia.

At the end of a man's service he was assigned to the National Reserve and might be called back to fill the numbers of his regiment. At the beginning of the war, over 350,000 men were on the national reserve, many of whom immediately rejoined. Those doing so included Captains Taylor (Chollerton), Cuthbert and Allgood (St John Lee), David Sinclair Robson (Wark) and James Wylie (Plashetts).

In 1908 the Territorial Force came into existence as a result of the reorganisation of the former militia and other voluntary bodies by the Secretary of State for War, Richard Haldane, following the Territorial and Reserves Forces Act of 1907. This new force closely followed the model of the regular army, but was composed of volunteers who would train as soldiers on a part time basis and who would give up a night or two each

Courtesy of the Heritage Centre, Bellingham

week for training. They were also required to attend an annual camp. The majority of county regiments supported up to four battalions of Territorials with their associated support units such as transport, medical and artillery. The physical criteria for joining the Territorials were similar to that of the regular army but with the lower age limit of 18. Territorial soldiers were not obliged to serve overseas, but their enthusiasm for the war in the early days was evident; vast numbers signed up for active service overseas.

Many of these Territorial Battalions were under strength at the onset of war, but numerous volunteers came forward to make up the numbers, some with previous military experience, such as Andrew Cowan (Bellingham) who had fought with the local volunteers in the Boer War, and William Hartley (St John Lee) who had seen service in the South African War. Many educated men volunteered as privates, seeking commissions at a later date, such as George Walton (St John Lee). Territorial Battalions can be recognised by the use of a particular style of numbering, such as *1/4th Northumberland Fusiliers*

Field Marshal **Horatio Herbert Kitchener, 1st Earl Kitchener** (24 June 1850 – 5 June 1916), was an Irish-born British Field Marshal and proconsul who won fame for his imperial campaigns and later played a central role in the early part of the First World War. Kitchener made his name in 1898 for winning the Battle of Omdurman and securing control of the Sudan, after which he was given the title Lord Kitchener of Khartoum. As Chief of Staff (1900–02) in the Second Boer War he played a key role in Lord Roberts' conquest of the Boer Republics, then succeeded Roberts, by which time Boer forces had taken to guerrilla fighting and British forces imprisoned Boer civilians in concentration camps. As Commander-in-Chief (1902–09) of the Army in India he quarrelled with the Viceroy, Lord Curzon, who eventually resigned. Kitchener then returned to Egypt as British Agent and Consul-General (the *de facto* Viceroy). In 1914, at the start of the First World War, Lord Kitchener became Secretary of State for War, a Cabinet Minister. One of the few men to foresee a long war, and one in which Britain's victory was far from secure, he organized the largest volunteer army that Britain, and indeed the Empire, had ever seen and a significant expansion of materials production to fight Germany on the Western Front. His commanding image, which appeared on recruiting posters demanding, 'Your Country Needs You!' remains recognised and parodied in popular culture to this day. He was blamed for the shortage of shells in the spring of 1915, one of the events leading to the formation of a coalition government, and was stripped of his control over munitions and strategy. He died in 1916 near the Orkney Islands when the warship taking him to negotiations in Russia was sunk by a German mine. After his death, Kitchener was often dismissed as a great image, but not a great administrator. He was criticised by many who wrote about the war, including Lloyd George, who in his *War Memoirs* may have taken credit for some of Kitchener's achievements in the field of munitions. After many years' experience of commanding relatively small forces in imperial campaigns, Kitchener had harmed his reputation by his habit of secrecy; he had been unwilling to explain his actions to his colleagues and was reluctant to organise and delegate. Since 1970, new records have opened and historians have to some extent rehabilitated Kitchener's reputation. His strategic vision in World War I is now praised, especially his laying of the groundwork for the expansion of munitions production and his central role in the raising of the British Army in 1914 and 1915, which provided a force capable of meeting Britain's continental commitment.

It was with these Regular Soldiers, Reservists, Territorials (Northumberland Hussars) and troops from the colonies that the battles of the early months of the war were fought. A large number of these experienced soldiers would already be dead or badly wounded by the spring of 1915.

Field Marshall Earl Kitchener was reluctant to accept the Territorials as anything but a "town clerk's army of Saturday soldiers" and this was one of the reasons why, in early August 1914, that as Minister for War he issued orders for the expansion of the army, as he was convinced – contrary to popular opinion – that the war would *not* be over by Christmas. This new, larger army was to be composed of volunteers, who would sign up for three years or the duration of the war and who could be sent to fight anywhere. "Your King and Country need you. A call to Arms" was published on 11 August 1914, calling upon 100,000 men to enlist, a target that was achieved in two weeks. Army Order 324 created six new divisions from these volunteers,

and were numbered 9 through to 14, and referred to as "K1". These divisions moved to France in May 1915 or to Gallipoli in the August, (Serjeant Walter Dodd, Falstone).

On 28 August Kitchener asked for another 100,000 volunteers and by Army Order 382 created a further six divisions numbered 15 through to 20 and referred to as "K2", (John Stanley Allen, Bellingham, who volunteered as a Private and eventually rose to the rank of Major). A third 100,000 came forward and formed another six divisions numbered 21 through to 26, and were to referred as "K3", (George Charlton, St John Lee; George Hymers, Plashetts).

More volunteers came forward to form reserves and by December 1914 orders were given to create another six divisions, eventually numbered 30 through to 35 and referred to as "K4". Most of the units of "K4" were locally raised and often referred to as 'Pals'. All the battalions making up these volunteer divisions are referred to as 'Service Battalions'. Then came *Second Ypres, Neuve Chapel, Festubert* and *Aubers Ridge* and enthusiasm began to ebb. Following the horrors of *Loos* in September 1915 it could not be revived.

When Britain declared war on Germany on 4 August 1914, members of the British Empire were automatically involved. Canada declared war with Germany on the 5 August, and even though it had only a regular army of just over 300 men, within two months 32,000 men had volunteered to defend the mother country; the first division arrived in Flanders in February 1915 and another three followed, (William Little, Falstone; James Daley, Bellingham; William Dodds, Andrew Surtees, Charlton Richley, Chollerton; Walter Ridley, Robert Mews, St John Lee). Australia followed suit without hesitation, providing an all volunteer expeditionary force that initially saw action against the Ottoman Empire,

(William Dodds, Greystead; William Gilroy, Reed School; John Thomas Hutchinson and William Ernest Robson, Birtley; Albert Edward Dodd, Chollerton). India, New Zealand and even South Africa, which faced significant internal opposition by the Boers, all sent significant numbers of troops to fight Germany and its allies

In the UK, by the Spring of 1915 voluntary recruitment was not at the necessary level to provide the numbers of men required by the armed services and so, on July 15, the Government passed the National Registration Act, which was a step towards stimulating recruitment and was also designed to discover how many men between the ages of 15 and 65 were engaged in each trade. The results of this census became available in the middle of September 1915.

On 11 October, Lord Derby was appointed as Director-General of Recruiting and within a week had instigated a scheme, which is referred to as the Derby Scheme, for increasing the numbers of men available for military service. Men between the ages of 18 and 41 could continue to enlist voluntarily, or could *attest*, which formed an obligation to respond to being called up. All men who registered under the Derby Scheme were classified as either married or single, with both groups further sub divided into 23 classes, based on age. Coincidentally, a War Pension was introduced to entice men who were worried about supporting their dependents. The 15 December was chosen for the closing of the Derby Scheme and at this point a further 215,000 men had enlisted and 2,815,000 had attested under the scheme, many of whom were sent home until their call up came. However, it was estimated that over 615,000 unmarried men had evaded the call up. The 23 groups of unmarried men were the first to be called up, from the youngest to eldest, and they were followed by married men, (Edward Crisp, Chollerton).

The Military Service Act was introduced on 27 January 1916. The provisions of the Act concluded that all British males between the ages of 18 and 41, residing in Great Britain and unmarried or a widower on 15 November 1915, had enlisted in the armed forces. They were conscripted. The act was extended to married men on 25 May 1916. A series of tribunals was established to hear the cases of men who believed that they were exempt from military service on the grounds of ill health, occupation or conscientious objection. Initially the act delivered only 43,000 men for service, another 93,000 failed to appear and were chased through the courts, whist another 750,000 claimed some form of exemption in addition to the 1,400,000 already serving in war occupations or deemed to be ill. From September 1916 the conscripted men were assigned to training battalions, before going to front line units, (Robert Curry, Wall).

The Appeals Tribunal in Tynedale was presided over by Colonel Fenwick of Higham Dykes, with Mr C Riddell of Swinburne Castle, Mr John Robson of Bellingham and Mr James T Robb of Hexham, in attendance. Lieutenant Kinsley Taylor appeared as the military representative with Mr A W Hoyle (Prudhoe Military Representative) and Mr George H Waddilove (Hexham Military Representative) and Mr A M Allgood (Agricultural Representative). Mr Jasper Gibson acted as clerk.

A further extension to the Act was made on 10 April 1918 to offset a serious political crisis concerning the provision of men to the services, which along with a large extension of the British section of the Western Front, was cited as a prime cause of the defeat of the Fifth Army in March 1918. This act reduced the minimum age of recruitment to 18.

Conscription ceased on 11 November 1918 and all conscripts were discharged, if they had not already been so, by 31 March 1920. By the end of the war 8.5 million men had been recruited from Britain and they had become the most effective fighting force on the Western Front.

# CHAPTER THREE

# 1914: WAR OVER BY CHRISTMAS

*"The war was inevitable and justifiable. Courage remained a virtue ... I had serious aspirations to heroism ... My one idea was to be first in the field."*
From Siegfried Sassoon's *Memoirs of a Fox-Hunting Man*

Germany declared war on France and Russia in early August following the breakdown of diplomatic activity following the assassination of Archduke Franz Ferdinand in Sarajevo, on 28 June 1914. The subsequent invasion of neutral Belgium by Germany prompted Britain to enter the war against Germany. A week later, Britain landed in France with an Expeditionary Force of 103,600 men under Field Marshall Sir John French. Of this force, Kaiser Willhelm II decreed:

> " It is my Royal and Imperial Command that you concentrate your energies and the valour of my soldiers to exterminate the treacherous English and walk over General French's contemptible little army."

Thus the term *Old Contemptibles* was coined for the small British force which advanced north meeting a hugely superior force at *Mons* (23-24 August). Although the British gave a good account of themselves, all along the Front, the British and French forces were compelled to retreat; it was at the *First Battle of the Marne* (5-10 September) that the German onslaught was finally stopped. Following the subsequent *Battle of the Aisne* (12-15 September) both sides began to dig in and build a system of trenches. Each side attempted to outflank the other as the war moved progressively westwards towards the sea. In the autumn the Allied resolve was severely tested during the *First Battle of Ypres* (14 Oct-22 Nov). It was touch and go as to whether they would hold the line but they did inflict enormous losses on the Kaiser's troops. At the same time, British casualties were also high. Further, and unbeknownst to the Germans, British artillery batteries were down to their last few shells because of manufacturing problems in Britain.

On 6 December 1914 the 1st Battalion Royal Irish Rifles were returning to the Front Line trenches near Estaires for a three day tour of duty, relieving a battalion of the Lincolns. The battalion had opted to change its approach to the Front so as to avoid Laventie Station (three miles southeast of Estaires) which was under heavy artillery fire. They arrived under the cover of darkness and, during the change over, Captain Allgood was killed whilst escorting his men back to their positions [1].

**Captain Bertram Allgood, aged 40**
**1st Battalion Royal Irish Rifles**
**Died 6 December 1914**

Bertram was born in February 1874. He was the second son of Elizabeth and Major-General Allgood C.B., Indian Army and latterly Chief Constable of Northumberland. He was educated at Eton and received his commission into the Royal Irish Rifles in May 1897, becoming Lieutenant in the following year and Captain in 1904. He served in India and in Belfast until retiring in February 1914, when he joined the Reserve of Officers. Bertram was married in April 1913 to Isa Cochrane Bayley, daughter of the late Arthur Bayley and Mrs Herbert Lyde. He was also the father of a daughter Elizabeth, born in August 1914. At the outbreak of hostilities Bertram was called up from the Reserve list, eventually joining his old battalion [2,3].

Colonel G B Laurie wrote in his diary [4]:

> "I had ordered everyone to return, (to the trenches), wished them good luck, and was waiting to see that they were all in whilst the Germans were sniping at us, when someone came and reported to me that a man had been shot through the shoulder by the same bullet that killed Captain Allgood. The stretcher bearers brought the latter in, and I sent for the doctor at once, but he could only pronounce him to be dead also! He was shot through the heart, and fell down remarking: "I am hit, but I am all right", and never spoke or moved again. He looked so peaceful lying on the stretcher."

On 19 December the Hexham Courant published the details of a memorial service held at St John Lee.

**Bertram Allgood is buried in Estaires Communal Cemetery.**

The 2nd Battalion Scots Guards were in the Front Line trenches near Sailly for most of the early months of the war. On 18 December a serious attack (for the time) was planned by the Scots Guards on the trenches opposite, along with elements of the Border Regiments. The attack led by Captain Loder used 'F' (Lieutenant Sir F FitzWygram) and 'LF' (Captain Taylor) companies. The attack started at 6pm, but unfortunately the troops of the Border Regiment did not leave the trenches to support their attack. The Scots Guards managed to reach the German trenches before the enemy was able to open fire (there was no barbed wire as yet on this sector of the Front). Although in places the enemy trenches were captured by 3am on 19 December, later the position of the Scots Guards became untenable and they were forced to retreat to their starting trenches. During this attack it was reported that Captain Hugh Taylor was killed by shrapnel, on the parapet of the German Trenches. For his courage during this action he was mentioned posthumously for gallant and distinguished conduct in Field-Marshall Sir John French's despatch, dated 14 January 1915. On the next day the battalion was withdrawn to Divisional Reserve near Sailly, returning to the Front on 23 December [5,6].

On 25 December it appears that the fighting drew to a halt and a number of unarmed Germans walked into no-mans land to wish their enemy a Happy Christmas, an informal truce which was condemned by the high command of both sides even though the event has captured peoples hearts ever since. During this poignant lull in the fighting, Hugh's body, which had been lying near the German trenches, was brought over to the British lines by Saxon soldiers, their heads bared in respect. He was laid to rest in a British military graveyard.

**Captain Hugh Taylor, aged 33**
**2nd Battalion Scots Guards**
**Died 18 December 1914**

Hugh was the eldest son of Mr and Mrs Tom Taylor of Chipchase Castle. He was born in Newcastle in 1880 and was educated at Harrow and Balliol College, Oxford, where he obtained a Second Class Honours in Moderations. After leaving Oxford he joined the Army. In 1904 Hugh was granted a commission in the Scots Guards; he was promoted to Lieutenant in 1904 and became Captain in November 1914. Hugh was married in July 1907 to Mary Villiers Stuart, of Dromara, County Waterford; they had a son, Thomas Brian Geoffrey and a daughter, Katherine Mona Mary.

At the outbreak of the war Hugh was in London on military business and within days went out to France with his regiment, assuming the responsibility of Machine Gun Officer for his battalion. Hugh's grandfather, Hugh Taylor, had lived in Sunderland for a long time and had strong links with the mining trade in the town: he was the founder of Ryhope Colliery and a prominent member of the River Wear Commission. He was also president of the Coal Trade Association and helped to establish the Miners' Permanent Relief Fund. Although he made his early career in the army, his grandson Hugh was interested in politics and he had intended to follow in the footsteps of his grandfather and father into public life. Indeed, in the summer of 1914, just before the outbreak of war, he had already made a number of speeches within the Sunderland Parliamentary Constituency, as the potential Unionist canidate. The Hexham Courant reported that he was given an enthusiastic reception, the working men appreciating his political candour and his interest in industrial problems. The miners' executives for both Durham and Northumberland recorded condolences to the family "of Captain Hugh Taylor, on his death" [7,8].

His gravestone is inscribed with the following:

**KILLED IN ACTION**

**Hugh is buried at Le Trou Aid Post Cemetery, Fleurbaix.**

## REFERENCES

1. WO95/1730, *War Diary 1[st] Battalion Royal Irish Rifles.*

2. Clutterbuck, Col L. A. *The Bond of Sacrifice, Vol. 1, page 6.*
Pub:1915, Reprinted Naval Military Press 2002.

3. Marquis of Ruvigny and Raineval. *De Ruvigny's Roll of Honour 1914-1924, Vol. 2, page 5.*

4. Taylor, J. *The 1[st] Royal Irish Rifles in the Great War.*
Pub: Four Courts Press 2002.

5. WO95/1657, War Diary *2[nd] Battalion Scots Guards.*

6. Petre, F. L., Ewart,W. and Maj Gen Lowther, Sir C. *The Scots Guards in the Great War 1914-1918.*
Pub: 1925. Reprinted Naval Military Press 2002.

7. Clutterbuck, Col L. A. *The Bond of Sacrifice, Vol. 1, page 390.*
Pub:1915, Reprinted Naval Military Press 2002.

8. Marquis of Ruvigny and Raineval. *De Ruvigny's Roll of Honour 1914-1924, Vol. 4, page 207,*

# CHAPTER FOUR

# WESTERN FRONT 1915

*Soldiers are sworn to action; they must win*
*Some flaming, fatal climax with their lives.*
*Soldiers are dreamers; when the guns begin*
*They think of firelit homes, clean beds and wives.*
*I see them in foul dug-outs, gnawed by rats,*
*And in the ruined trenches, lashed with rain,*

From Siegfried Sassoon's *Dreamers*

## OVERVIEW

By the start of the year the two sides faced each other from entrenched positions along the whole length of the Western Front. After the serious losses incurred by the British Army in 1914, more of Britain's regular battalions returned from their overseas postings, (the 2nd Northumberland Fusiliers returned from Sabathu in India a few days before Christmas and having been allocated to the 28th Division, embarked for France on 18 January 1915). As the year passed, Territorial battalions found themselves fighting on the Western Front; four battalions from Northumberland embarked for France on 20 April. Also, later in the year battalions formed from the newly trained volunteers began to arrive in France (9th Service Northumberland Fusiliers arrived in July, whilst the 12th and 13th Service Northumberland Fusiliers arrived in September 1915). Although the army's strength began to rise, there was always a shortage of ammunition, which severely diminished the effectiveness of these troops.

1915 was the first full year of the war; it saw the British and the French striving with limited forces to break through the entrenched German

Forces along the whole length of the Western Front. Notable examples include the battles of *Neuve Chapelle* (10 March-22 April) *Auber* (9-10 May) *Festuberg* (15-23 May) and *Loos* (25 September-18 October). In late April the Germans launched their own attack on the Ypres Salient, which was notable for the use of poison gas, (see page 35).

In October 1914 the Ottoman Empire's rulers, Young Turks (Turkey), entered the war on the German side, declaring a Jihad. However, no other Arabic country supported the Ottomans. As a result, in 1915 the Allies launched a series of disastrous naval and land based attacks on the Gallipoli Peninsula.

Furthermore, Britain was now faced with fighting in a number of other theatres, for example Mesopotamia and the defence of the Suez Canal, a vital imperial artery. At sea the Germans began their submarine attacks on Allied and neutral shipping, in an attempt to blockade Britain; in turn the British Navy launched an effective blockade of German ports. The war continued against the Russians on the Eastern Front.

Italy entered the war on the Allied side and attacked Austro-Hungarian Troops at Isonzo, but the Russians, after some initial success, were defeated by the Germans who advanced to capture Warsaw.

Another Front was opened by the Allies at Salonika in Greece, the war now spreading out to become a global conflict with action in Belgium, France, Greece, Turkey, Mesopotamia and Africa.

On the Western Front after the calamitous *Battle of Loos*, Sir Douglas Haig replaced Sir John French as commander of the British Expeditionary Force.

Overall, 1915 proved to be a disappointing year for the Allies and a correspondingly positive one for Germany and her allies.

## ALONG THE WESTERN FRONT

Having recently arrived back from duty in India, on 2 February the 2nd Northumberland Fusiliers (NF), as its initiation to the Western Front, entered the line in Flanders to the south and south east of Zillebeke, spending the next few days improving the trench system; they were relieved on the evening of 11 February. During this nine day period the battalion lost 3 officers wounded, and other ranks 10 killed and 61 wounded [1,2].

**Corporal William Armstrong Johnson, aged 21**
**2nd Battalion Northumberland Fusiliers**
**Died 11 February 1915**

William was born in Bellingham and the 1901 census shows that he was living with his grandparents, William and Elizabeth Johnson. He attended the Catholic school in Bellingham. The 1911 census show that William, aged 17, was based at the Northumberland Fusiliers Barracks in Newcastle upon Tyne, where he would undergo basic training before being posted to one of the regular battalions. His regimental number shows that he attested in July/August 1911. William joined the 2nd Battalion based in Sheffield and during his time there was promoted to Lance Corporal on 1 December 1912. The battalion was posted to Sabathu, India, in early 1914, where it replaced the 1st Battalion. During this tour of duty he was promoted to Corporal. His medal records shows that his daughter's guardian, who was living in Sheffield, applied for her father's medals.

**The Menin Gate Memorial** was inaugurated by Field Marshall Herbert Plumer in1927. It was designed by Sir Reginald Blomfield, one of four principal architects engaged in directing the construction of over 1,200 British and Commonwealth cemeteries and memorials along the Western Front for the Imperial War Graves Commission (now named the Commonwealth War Graves Commission). Sculptures on the memorial were by Sir William Reid-Dick. The Menin Gate Memorial is one of four British and Commonwealth memorials to the missing in the battlefield area of the Ypres Salient in Belgian Flanders, and it bears the names of 54,389 officers and men from United Kingdom and Commonwealth Forces (except New Zealand and Newfoundland) who fell in the Ypres Salient before 16th August 1917 and who have no known grave. Their names are engraved in Portland Stone panels fixed to the inner walls of the central Hall of Memory and to the sides of the staircases leading from the lower level to the upper exterior level, and on the walls inside the loggias on the north and south sides of the building. The names of those missing after August 1917 are recorded on regimental panels at Tyne Cot Cemetery (34,940 men). Every night of the year, whatever the weather, visitors can attend a moving ceremony where the trumpeted 'Last Post' resonates around the huge arches of the memorial where the missing are commemorated with dignity. In his speech, Plumer said:

"One of the most tragic features of the Great War was the number of casualties reported as 'Missing, believed killed'. To their relatives there must have been added to their grief a tinge of bitterness and a feeling that everything possible had not been done to recover their loved ones' bodies and give them reverent burial. That feeling no longer exists; it ceased to exist when the conditions under which the fighting was being carried out were realized. But when peace came and the last ray of hope had been extinguished the void seemed deeper and the outlook more forlorn for those who had no grave to visit, no place where they could lay tokens of loving remembrance. ... it was resolved that here at Ypres, where so many of the 'Missing' are known to have fallen, there should be erected a memorial worthy of them which should give expression to the nation's gratitude for their sacrifice and its sympathy with those who mourned them. A memorial has been erected which, in its simple grandeur, fulfils this object, and now it can be said of each one in whose honour we are assembled here today: 'He is not missing; he is here'."

Memorials to the missing can be found throughout the length and breath of the Western Front: Ploegsteert (11,000), Loos (20,605), Arras (34,791), Vis-en-Artois (9,849), Thiepval (72,191), Pozières (14,655), Cambrai (7058) and Soissons (3,880). Wherever across the globe the Great War was fought, memorials to the missing were built: Gallipoli, Italy, Mesopotamia and Salonika.

Upon William's arriving back from India in late December 1914 the Illustrated News reported that he had visited Bellingham before being sent to France in mid January. The North Tyne Magazine reported of his death:

> "We commend his soul to Almighty God and his example to his countrymen."

**William is commemorated on the Menin Gate Memorial to the missing.**

By Soren Hawkes MA (see also p.18)
Passchendaele Prints and Drawings
www.passchendaeleprints.com

On 27 February 1915, the 2nd Battalion Northumberland Fusiliers moved as part of the 84th Brigade, into the Dranoutre sector, which was situated south east of Kemmel. The Front Line faced the Messines-Wytschaete ridge. On 5 March the battalion provided a working party of 100 men and 2 officers to dig a new line of fire. A Royal Engineers Officer was in charge of this exercise. The working party left at 4.30pm for Neuve Église and returned at 2.45am. During the night, the party dug over 200 yards of fire trench and 1 man was wounded, Lance-Corporal Eddy, who died of his wounds the following day [1,2].

**Lance-Corporal Edward Eddy, aged 41**
**2nd Battalion Northumberland Fusiliers**
**Died 6 March 1915**

Edward was born in 1874, the youngest son of Edward and Mary Eddy of Acomb. At the onset of war Edward lived in Birtley, Durham, a widower, with no children. Edward was a well known footballer, and whilst living in Acomb he played for Acomb United. He enlisted in the Hexham Company of the 1st Volunteers Battalion of the Northumberland Fusiliers and served throughout the South African War under Lieutenant Fisher. He returned to Hexham with the rank of Sergeant, and decided to retire from soldiering, but in 1914, at the outbreak of hostilities, he volunteered for active duty. Although he was offered his original rank, he thought it best to start at the bottom again. He was drafted out to France in January 1915, by which time three of his nephews were also serving with the forces: Wilson, Arthur and Joseph.

**Edward is buried at St Quentin Cabaret Military Cemetery**

Northumberland Fusiliers defending the Front Line near Ypres

As a result of the casualties sustained during April and May 1915, the $1/6^{th}$ and $1/8^{th}$ Durham Light Infantry (DLI) were amalgamated as a composite battalion $6^{th}/8^{th}$ until both battalions were brought up to strength in August 1915. From 20 June this amalgamated battalion moved into the

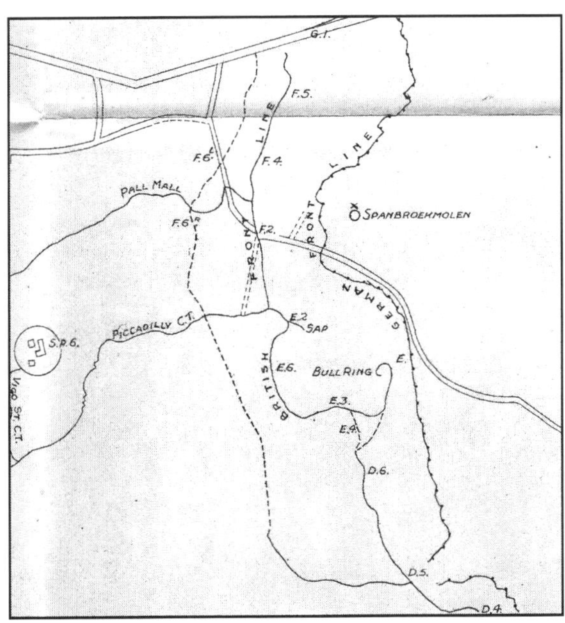


*Map showing the sector of the Front Line held by 1/8th Durham Light Infantry, June 1915*

area opposite Messines and Wytschaete, the Neuve Église sector. Each brigade of the 50th Battalion provided two battalions for Front Line duties. From 21 until 27 June the 6th/8th was in the Front Line, from trench E2 northwards to the barricade on the Wytschaete-Kemmel road. This sector included the Bull Ring, Pall Mall, and Regent Street Dugouts. Although regarded as a quiet sector, snipers were always active, a constant hazard to those involved in the daily toil of repairing and reinforcing the trenches [3,4].

The War Diary for the 1/6th Durham Light Infantry, which includes the 1/8th during the period of amalgamation, records for Saturday 26 June 1915:

> "In the trenches. There was some heavy shelling between 12 noon and 2pm especially in the support line. One man killed and wounded" [5] [persumably Lawrence Shortridge].

**Private Lawrence Shortridge, aged 26**
**1/8th Battalion Durham Light Infantry**
**Died 26 June 1915**

Lawrence was born in Lanercost, Cumberland, the eldest son of Robert and Hannah Shortridge. His father, Robert, later became the schoolmaster at Wark. Lawrence, like his father, trained and qualified as a teacher. The 1911 census shows that Robert held the position as an elementary school teacher at Castle Eden County School, living near Easington, County Durham. He embarked for France with his battalion on 19 April 1915 and as a result he would see a lot of action during a series of engagements known as *2nd Ypres*, (see page 35).

The North Tyne magazine October 1915 records the death of Lawrence:

"He has joined the great company of 'Golden Lads' who have made the great sacrifice. After all, it is a great death to die in a great cause and, sorely stricken as the hearts of the bereaved are, yet along with the ever present consolation that the parting is but for a time, there is the knowledge of a life well lived and then laid down for the safety of the dear homeland."

**Lawrence is commemorated on the Menin Gate Memorial to the missing.**

As early as November 1914, warfare tactics on the Western Front were based on a continuous network of defensive trenches. Tunnelling and the explosive destruction of these defences, as used in medieval times to destroy castle walls, was seen as a way to unlock the stalemate. Both sides employed specialist mining teams to dig tunnels under the enemy's trenches in order to explode mines which aimed to destroy their defensive positions and to disorientate the enemy, in support of an attack. When an enemy tunnel was discovered it was destroyed by explosive charges.

The 170th Tunnelling Company was formed in February 1915. In June 1915 it was moved from the Givenchy Sector to one further south and was attached to the 2nd Division for operations near Cuinchy and the Brickstacks [6].

The War Diary [7], records that:

"About 3pm on 6 August (1915) we restarted work on No 12 Listening Gallery. At about 8pm the Germans exploded a charge not far from this listening gallery. Second Lieutenant Dixon and Sergeant John McCarthy happened to be passing along the gallery and were killed instantaneously as were two men, Lance Corporal

Herbert Clarke and Sapper Walter Walker who were at work in the heading."

**Second Lieutenant George Dixon, aged 34**
**170th Tunnelling Company, Royal Engineers**
**Died 6 August 1915**

George was born in December 1881 at Snabdough, the eldest and only surviving child of James Gibson and Anne Dixon of Mantle Hill, Bellingham. He was educated at the Royal Grammar School, Newcastle, after which he attended the Newcastle and Durham Mining School and subsequently earned membership of the Institute of Mining Engineers.

He served his apprenticeship at Seghill Colliery and was later appointed Manager of High Park and Watnall Colliery in Eastwood, Nottinghamshire. George was an all round sportsman, an enthusiastic footballer who also played both cricket and tennis. He was a member of Nottingham County Cricket Club and captained Lamb Close Cricket Club, Eastwood.

At the outbreak of war George enlisted in the Coldstream Guards as a Private and embarked for France in early February 1915. In late April he was granted a commission in the Royal Engineers and was attached to the 170th Tunnelling Company, commensurate with his previous non-military experience [9].

The History of the Tunnelling Companies of the Royal Engineers reports that at many points the shafts of the coal mines connected galleries which could be accessed from both sides of the Front and many tales were told of spies passing from one to the other.

The history reports that a party from the 170th Tunnelling Company led by George Dixon entered some workings near Annequin; after much difficulty they succeeded in passing under the German Lines and reached the bottom of the shaft near Auchy, only to find that the Germans had blocked the upshaft. This uncharted maze of interconnected galleries and shafts was a constant source of concern for both sides. As a result the Germans often flooded a mine with gas, forming a defensive barrier [6]. His gravestone is inscribed with the following:

**BE THOU FAITHFUL UNTO DEATH**
**AND I WILL GIVE THEE**
**A CROWN OF LIFE**

**George is buried in Cambrin Military Cemetery.**

During the latter months of 1915 the 1/4th Northumberland Fusiliers (NF) as part of the 50th Division settled into the routine of service on the Western Front, taking its turn to man the trenches east of Armentières. On the evening of 1 October the battalion moved into the Front Line. The War Diary for 2 October reports that the day was quiet but noted that they faced 'better quality troops'. However, on 3 October the quiet was abruptly broken by an enemy artillery barrage which killed a man. Furthermore, the entry for 4 October reports that another man was killed during the morning; presumably Robert Steele. That night the battalion was relieved from its position, during which there were no further casualties [10].

**Private Robert James Steele, aged 23**
**1/4th Battalion Northumberland Fusiliers**
**Died 4 October 1915**

Robert was born in Hexham, the youngest son of James and Rebecca Steele of Anick Grange. He had been educated in Corbridge and before he enlisted in May 1915 was employed in agricultural work. He was a keen amateur photographer. Robert arrived in France in early September and had been at the Front for less than a month before he was killed.

Captain R Robinson wrote to his mother telling her that Robert had been shot in the head by a sniper whilst on sentry duty, and had died at a dressing station later that day.

**Robert is buried in Ferme Buterne Military Cemetery, Houplines.**

As part of the 21st Division, the 8th East Yorkshire formed part of the Reserves that saw action at *Loos* in September 1915. As these untested troops approached to support an attack on Hill 70, German artillery based in Cité St Pierre inflicted a large number of casualties on them. By the middle of October the battalion had returned to the Front, near Armentières. From the night of October 29 to the evening of 6 November they were based at L'Epinette, where they were employed in rebuilding and strengthening the trenches – a continuing task [11,12].

**Private George Hymers, aged 33**
**8th (Service) Battalion East Yorkshire Regiment**
**Died 1 November 1915**

George was born in Langholm, Dumfriesshire, the son of Robert and Frances Hymers later of Tile Row, Plashetts. He married Mary Ethel, (née Robson) in the latter quarter of 1906 and was the father of four daughters. The 1911 census shows that the family was living at Stone Row, Plashetts. However, they were living in Newburn, where George worked in the coal mine, when he enlisted as a volunteer in September 1914. He landed with the 21st Division in France in September 1915. His gravestone is inscribed with the following:

**THY WILL BE DONE**

**George is buried in Houplines Communal Cemetery Extension.**

## REFERENCES


1. WO95/2277. *War Diary, 2nd Battalion Northumberland Fusiliers.*

2. Sandilands, Brig H. R. *The Fifth in the Great War.*
Pub: 1921 reprinted Naval and Military Press 1998.

3, Wyrell, E. *The Fiftieth Division, 1914-1919.*
Pub: 1939, reprinted Naval and Military Press 2002.

4. Veitch, E. H. Maj *8th Battalion DLI 1793-1926.*
Pub: J H Veitch and Sons Ltd 1927.

5. WO95/2840. *War Diary 6th Battalion Durham Light Infantry (covering period of amalgamation with the 8th Battalion Durham Light Infantry).*

6. Barton, P. Doyle P. and Vandewalle, J. *Beneath Flanders Fields, The Tunnellers' War 1914-1918.* Pub: Spellmount 2004.

7. WO95/550. *Army Troops 170 Tunnelling Company, Royal Engineers.*

8. Grieve, W. G. Capt and Newman B. *Tunnellers, The Story of the Tunnelling Companies, Royal Engineers, during the World War.* Pub: Herbert Jenkins Ltd 1936, reprinted Naval and Military Press 2002.

9. Marquis of Ruvigny and Raineval. *De Ruvigny's Roll of Honour 1914-1924, Vol. 2, page 101.*

10. WO95/2828. *War Diary, 1/4th Battalion Northumberland Fusiliers.*

11.Wyrall, E. *East Yorkshire Regiment in the Great War 1914-1918.* Pub: 1928, reprinted Naval and Military Press.

12. W095/1424. *War Diary 8th Battalion East Yorkshire Regiment.*

# CHAPTER FIVE

# GAS, GAS, GAS!

Gas! Gas! Quick, boys! – An ecstasy of fumbling,
Fitting the clumsy helmets just in time;
But someone still was yelling out and stumbling,
And flound'ring like a man in fire or lime . . .
From Wilfred Owen's *Dulce et Decorum Est*

The war of attrition persisted along the Western Front, with both sides enduring limited attacks in Artois and Champagne. However, in late April, near Ypres, the Germans attempted to break the deadlock by the use of a new and inhumane weapon, chlorine gas, in spite of the fact that the Hague Convention of 1907 had banned the use of chemical warfare. Its deadly effects were delivered from large cylinders buried near the Front and the wind employed to deliver its deadly message. Within seconds of the vapour being inhaled it could destroy the victim's respiratory organs. Its creeping appearance on the battlefield would create mass panic.

**Chlorine Gas** destroyed the respiratory organs of its victims and this led to a slow death by asphyxiation. One nurse described the death of one soldier who had been in the trenches during a chlorine gas attack. "He was sitting on the bed, fighting for breath, his lips plum coloured. He was a magnificent young Canadian, past all hope in the asphyxia of chlorine. I shall never forget the look in his eyes as he turned to me and gasped: I can't die! Is it possible that nothing can be done for me?" It was a horrible death, but as hard as they tried, doctors were unable to find a way of successfully treating chlorine gas poisoning.

Later in the year the British, in their turn, used chlorine during their attack at Loos.

## SECOND BATTLE OF YPRES

By the end of 1914, the Germans had secured the height of Hill 60 to the south of the village of Zillebeke and were positioned only 2½ miles from the centre of Ypres, Belgium, allowing them to observe all the movements of the Allied armies occupying the salient. On 1 April 1915, a Canadian division arrived in France and two weeks later had replaced French troops at the Front, covering the head of the salient. To their left (east) were the 45th Algerian Division and beyond them troops of the French 87th Territorials, both of which were reserve formations [1].

## BATTLE OF GRAVENSTAFEL: 22 – 23 APRIL 1915

At 5pm on the 22 April the Germans released 160 tons of chlorine from 6000 cylinders, the gas from which drifted on to the French lines occupied by French colonial troops of the 45th (Algerian, Zouaves) Division. At low concentrations it causes extreme irritation to the eyes and lungs; at higher levels it fills the lungs with liquid and drowns the victim. The inexperienced French soldiers either fled or died and thirty minutes later the whole of the north side of the salient from Langemarck to Steenstraat was open to the German advance [2].

> " ...the German soldiers simply walked forward through the allied line, over the bodies of the dead, lying sprawled out, faces discoloured and contorted in the grimaces of agony. Within an hour the Germans had advanced more than a mile and they had hardly needed to fire a shot."

In desperation, the Canadians and small contingent of French Zouaves created a Front north of St Julien. As news of the gaping hole in the Front Line reached headquarters, whatever troops were available were rushed to the Front to stem the dangerous German advance. The newly arrived men of the 1st Canadian Division fought magnificently and at midnight they mounted a counterattack on Kitchener's Wood, but as they were unsupported on the right by the French, they had to withdraw, but were able to form a new line on the southern edge of the wood.

On 23 April another disparate force (known as Geddes Force) was quickly assembled and ordered to fill the gap between the French and the Canadians west of St Julien. The attack failed, partly owing to the French being unable to commit troops as they were needed further west near Steenstraat. At a meeting in Cassell between the French General Foch and Sir John French it was agreed that an attempt to regain all the ground lost in the last few days would be launched. As a result of this decision, the three brigades which made up the 50th (Northumbrian) Division, which had arrived on the continent on 20 April, were allocated to General Sir Horace Smith-Doreen's Second Army.

## BATTLE OF ST JULIEN: 24 APRIL – 4 MAY 1915

Early in the morning of 24 April the Germans once again attacked the Canadians with a mixture of more chlorine gas and high explosive shells. The Canadians fought bravely but had to yield ground to the advancing Germans, who by early evening had captured St Julien. The Allied front was under increasing pressure from the advancing enemy.

On 25 April a further scratch force was mobilized and tried to recapture St Julien and Kitchener's Wood, but was halted by a larger German force, although by these actions the Front (to a certain extent) was stabilized.

The next day (26 April) plans were set in motion once again to regain the lost ground, (a *sine qua non* of French Military tactics). The plan involved an attack in force by the French using their 152nd Division and parts of their 5th and 18th Divisions, with a significant force in reserve.

The plan for the attack would require men of the Lahore Division who had newly arrived from India and who had already marched thirty miles from Bethune, to attack northwards from St Jean and reoccupy the ridge west of St Julien. The attack would also involved elements of the four Northumberland Fusiliers (NF) Territorial Battalions, known collectively as 149th Brigade who had recently arrived in France on 20 April, with the 10th Canadian Brigade to their right.  For many men, their deaths would be known by their relatives before they had heard that they had left their home billets.

The 1/4th Battalion Northumberland Fusiliers marching down Loosing Hill on the way to Hexham railway station.

*Courtesy Graham Stewart*

The 1/4th Battalion Northumberland Fusiliers, (NF) had arrived in Boulogne on the evening of 20 April and moved forward during the next few days towards the intense fighting east of Ypres. Whilst passing through Ypres on the 24 April these raw troops experienced their first casualties. The 1/4th War Diary records that two men were wounded and a larger number of casualties were reported from the 1/7th Battalion [3,4,5].

On 25 April the Northumbrian Territorials were under the command of 10th Brigade and at 1.30am moved to a position near Wieltje to provide support to a planned counterattack. As they moved forward the 1/4th NF came under artillery attack. On arrival at the GHQ line the 10th Brigade discovered that there were only two gaps in the wire through which they could attack. General Hull realised that the York and Durham Brigade had not arrived in their position on the right flank of the Brigade. As a consequence he ordered up two battalions of the Northumbrian Territorials from Corps Reserve, (1/4th and 1/7th NF). The 1/4th and 1/7th NF set off in artillery formation but when they reached the wire entanglements Colonel Foster was informed that the attack had failed. He therefore attempted to stop the advancing battalion, but unfortunately he suceeded in preventing only the two companies at the rear of the attack (1/4th NF), the other two had passed out of sight in the rear of 1/7th NF.

The following report from an officer in the 1/4th NF, appeared in the Hexham Courant 15 May 1915:

> "We advanced in artillery formation and then extended into successive lines under machine gun fire, which appeared to be coming from our flank. This became so severe that eventually I had to change direction with the two platoons I had with me. It was here that Joicey and a number of men were hit, and we found it impossible to advance till they were located. This we did after some

trouble and were able to get the artillery directed on them, so we remained till dark and dug ourselves in. At 11pm we got the order to return to our original line where we again entrenched ourselves and got what sleep we could."

By the morning of 26 April, the 1/4th NF found themselves in good trenches to the east of Wieltje, but were under heavy artillery bombardment as German spotter plans flew overhead unmolested.

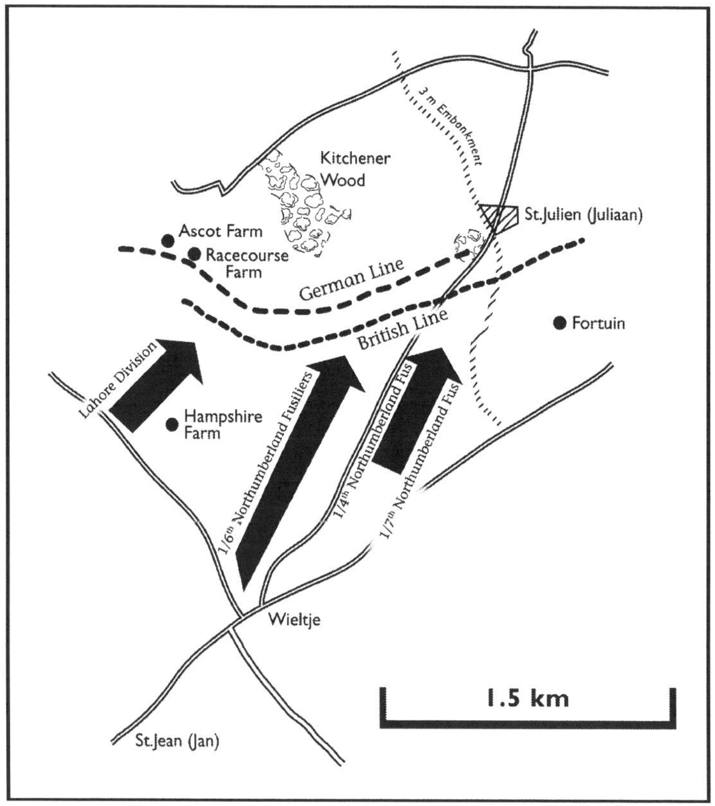


Attack of the 149th Brigade: 26 April 1915

Early in the afternoon the raw troops of 1/4$^{th}$, 1/6$^{th}$ and 1/7$^{th}$ Northumberland Fusiliers moved forward to take up positions for an imminent attack. This was to take place in a north easterly direction following the road between Weiltje and St Julien.

The 1/4$^{th}$ Battalion were to attack along the right side of the road, whilst the 1/6$^{th}$ were to attack on the left. Initially the 1/7$^{th}$ Battalion was held in reserve. As the battalions reached their attacking positions they came under heavy shell, machine gun and rifle fire. As the men passed through the narrow gaps in the protective wire in front of the British defences, they tended to bunch up and became easy targets.

In his diary, Lieutenant Bunbury wrote [6}:

> "Practically from the moment that we started off we had to face a perfectly hellish shelling, which increased in intensity as we advanced. Shells of every description literally raining upon us from our front, right and rear, while it seemed to me in the excitement of the advance that our artillery was giving no support whatever. The line of our advance lay for about a mile over open ground and after we had gone a short way, in addition to the inferno of shells in which we were, we became exposed to a very heavy rifle and machine gun fire from the German trenches, which were directly in front of us near a wood at the top of some rising ground, and in such a position that they could fire from right over what turned out to be our advanced trench, down on to us. The small arm fire was intense and the nearest thing I can liken it to is a gigantic swarm of angry bees buzzing around one. Men were falling on every side ..."

By 2.45 pm, what was left of the brave men of the 1/4th and 1/6th NF reached the trenches that formed the Front Line and were surprised to find it occupied by remnants of the 2nd Seaforth Highlanders. During the attack some of the 1/6th NF managed to enter the southern part of St Julien before being driven back. The War History of the 1/7th Northumberland Fusiliers records that from the start their casualties were very severe but worse was to come as they came under terrible machine gun fire ... in all, their casualties were ghastly [5].

Later, the brigade's commander, Brigadier-General Riddell, moved up to the Front to get a greater understanding of what was going on and, tragically, was shot in the head. Lieutenant-Colonel Foster, the next senior officer and battalion commander of the 1/4th, replaced him. By 7.30 pm the brigade was ordered to retire and spend the night near Wieltje.

In an article published in the Hexham Courant on the 29th May 1915, an officer of the 1/4th Northumberland Fusiliers wrote:

> "After the attack it was a strange sight when darkness fell that night. Although quite close to the German trenches both sides seemed to be tired of fighting for the present, and we were able to get up and walk about with comparative safety and get the battalions and companies sorted up ready for everybody else. We had a busy time after that gathering in wounded and burying the dead, and there were many things I saw that night I should be glad to forget. What disgusted me most I think was the way they fired on the wounded crawling back to shelter. There was a farm about half way up used as a dressing station, and this they shelled continuously and any party of stretcher bearers leaving it always came in for a hot time."

**Corporal William Edward Hartley, aged 33**
**1/4th Battalion Northumberland Fusiliers**
**Died 26 April 1915**

William was born in Newcastle. He had seen some seen action during the South African War, with the Northumberland Fusiliers Volunteers. He joined the Territorials following Lord Kitchener's appeal for volunteers and presumably his previous experience earned him his stripes. He married Margaret Nevins in the summer of 1908. The 1911 census shows that William was working as a hewer at Wall Colliery. William and Margaret were living at 2 Alma Cottages, Acomb, with Margaret's remarried mother, (Rose Johnson). His gravestone is inscribed with the following:

**BELOVED BY ALL**

**William is buried in Seaforth Cemetery, Cheddar Villa.**

**Private William Fox, aged 22**
**1/4th Battalion Northumberland Fusiliers**
**Died 26 April 1915**

William was the youngest son of James and Elizabeth of Heathery Hall. He was born at Thorneyburn, Bellingham.

2nd Lieutenant Robert Allen wrote to his parents:

" He was an excellent fellow, was very happy with his work, and was very popular with his comrades. He died a brave and unselfish death while attending to the wounds of his comrades."

**William is commemorated on the Menin Gate Memorial to the missing.**

**Private Thomas Brown, aged 20**
**1/4th Battalion Northumberland Fusiliers**
**Died 26 April 1915**

Thomas was born in Warden and was the second son of Joseph and Elizabeth Brown of Grindstone Law, Whittington; they had lived in the Barrasford area for a number of years. The 1911 census reports that Thomas was working as a ploughman at Shortmoor Farm, Wark. Thomas joined the local Territorials as a volunteer at the beginning of the war.

**Thomas is buried in Seaforth Cemetery Cheddar Villa, Ypres.**

**Private John Elliott, 38**
**1/4th Battalion Northumberland Fusiliers**
**Died 26 April 1915**

John was born in Allendale in the summer of 1878. The 1891 Census records that he was employed aged fourteen as a servant in Allendale. He married Hannah Bella (née Lishman) in the summer of 1901, and became the father of five children, ranging in age from five to thirteen.

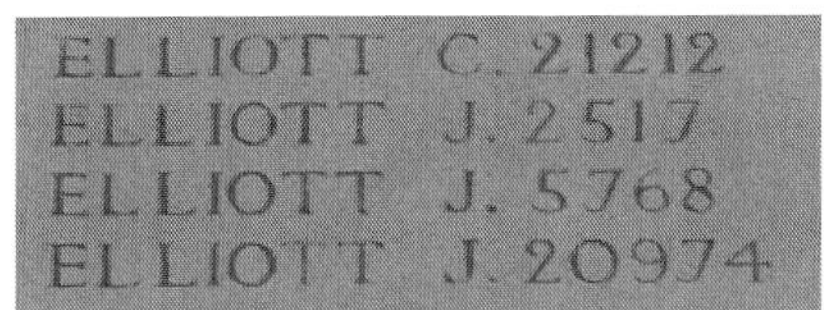


The family lived at Elwood Cottage in Barrasford. Before enlisting on 22 January 1915, he had been employed for over three years at the Barrasford Whinstone Quarry. Before this he had been employed at Gunnerton Sawmill for seventeen years and the 1901 census shows him lodging with the Hepple family in Gunnerton.

**John is commemorated on the Menin Gate Memorial to the missing**

**Private James Fenwick, aged 19**
**'B' Company 1/4th Battalion Northumberland Fusiliers**
**Died 26 April 1915**

James was the youngest son of James and Isabella Fenwick of South Farm, Gunnerton, Barrasford. The 1911 census reports that James was working on his father's farm. He joined the Territorials in March 1914 and was called up on mobilisation. His brother was serving with the Northumberland Hussars.

**James is commemorated on the Menin Gate Memorial to the missing**

**Private Arthur John Herdman, aged 23**
**1/4th Battalion Northumberland Fusiliers**
**Died 26 April 1915**

Arthur was born in Humshaugh, the eldest son of John and Annie Isabella Herdman of Hill House, Humshaugh. He was initially employed as a land agent's clerk in the Estate Office at Chesters. Later he worked for Mr

Vyner of Newby Hall, near Ripon. He was described as an all-round athlete, playing both cricket and football. He joined the Territorials following Lord Kitchener's appeal for more recruits

**Arthur is commemorated on the Menin Gate Memorial to the missing.**

**Private Thomas Forster, aged 22**
**1/4th Battalion Northumberland Fusiliers**
**Died 27 April 1915**

Thomas was the second son of Thomas and Jane Forster of Smalesmouth, Falstone. The 1911 census reports that Thomas was working as farm labourer at Donkin Ridge, near Cambo. Thomas died of wounds received during the previous day's fighting. A letter from an officer at the Front:

> "I feel that the death of Pte Thomas Forster of Smalesmouth … cannot be allowed to pass without some comment. Speaking to Forster before he joined the colours, I found that he had such a strong sense of duty and felt that unless he answered his country's call, he could never hold up his head in any company again."

His gravestone is inscribed with the following:

**THY WILL BE DONE**

**Thomas is buried in Vlamertinghe Military Cemetery.**

**Sir John French's Tribute to the Northumberland Infantry Brigade**

"Oficers, non commissioned officers, and men of the Northumberland Infantry Brigade, I want to say a few words to you this morning to tell you how much I appreciate the splendid work you have done in the last ten days in the fighting at Ypres. When the Northumbrian Division came out here in the ordinary course to settle down at Cassel, it was expected to have some little time to pull itself together, as every large unit which comes to this country is obliged to have, but we had this treacherous attack under cover of asphyxiating gases, which no soldiers have used yet, and men who use them are not worthy of the name of soldiers. We had this villainous proceeding, and I was obliged to send you up to reinforce the troops there. That would have been a high trial for any body of troops, even for a regular division with years of training at Aldershot, troops that had been fighting before, the highest trial.

The Hexham Courant of May 29 1915, under a heading of: **Splendid Gallantry of the County Territorials,** printed extracts from national daily papers whose correspondents were in France:

**North Mail**

> Of the performances of the Territorial battalions engaged it is impossible to speak too highly. In some cases the units had only been in the country a bare week before they had their first experience of trenches and yet they faced the enemy's gruelling fire like hardened veterans and never gave an inch. Every officer that I have spoken to of the subject expresses the same opinion and many are the stories of unflinching bravery displayed by these units.

**The Times**

The hardest task, perhaps fell to the men of North England. The others for the most part had been some time in the field and had been broken in gradually to war. But these had arrived from home only a short time before.

The Northumberland men were employed in an attack on St Julien on the 26th. There was no time to reconnoitre the position: they got into wire and were faced with a terrific shelling. Their 6th Battalion managed to advance 250 yards beyond our front trenches, but they could not maintain their position and had to retire in the evening. Brigadier-General Riddell falling with many gallant officers and men.

Consider what is meant by the fight of these Northern Territorials. Men only lately out from home, most of whom had never before seen a shot fired in battle, were flung suddenly into the most nerve-racking kind of engagement. They had to face one of the worst artillery bombardments of the war and the new devilry of the poison gas. There was no time for adequate staff preparation, the whole a wild rush, a crowding up of every available man to fill the gap and reinforce the thin lines. They were led by officers who a year ago had been architects and solicitors and business men. The result was a soldier's battle like Albuera where we escaped the annihilation which by all rules was our due by sheer dogged fighting quality of our men and their leaders. The miners of the north are a sturdy race in peace both in work and sport. The second battle of Ypres has proven them to be one of the finest fighting stocks on earth.

## London Daily Express

Equally gallant was the work of certain Northumberland Territorial Battalions during the bombardment of the 26th to 27th. They attacked St Julien on the afternoon of the 26th and after advancing steadily isolated parties of the 6th Battalion got 250 yards forward of the first line and occupied some small trenches that the enemy had abandoned. These they held until dusk when they retired to the first line.

Brigadier-General Riddell who was in command of these operations was killed about half past three. He was on his way to a farmhouse to get in closer touch with his men, and while walking along an exposed road was hit by a rifle bullet.

One German attack was frustrated by a battalion of Northumberland Fusiliers. The bombardment had been intensified - the usual prelude to a bayonet attempt - and when it suddenly ceased to allow the infantry to come on, our waiting reserves were rushed into the weakened first line.

"You should have seen the Northumberland Fusiliers come tumbling into the trenches" says an eye witness, "turning their machine guns on the enemy almost at the same moment and cutting great swathes in their ranks." The disordered column turned tail and sought cover again.

Thus we held what was seemingly an impossible line day after day, while men were being blown out of trenches and lying in hundreds on all sides.

## GAS, GAS, GAS

## BATTLE OF FRENZENBURG: 8 – 13 MAY 1915

From 8-13 May the two opposing armies fought for control of the Frezenberg Ridge situated between St Julien and Hooge, which the Germans won, although the defensive lines in front of Ypres held.

## BATTLE OF BELLEWAARDE: 24 – 25 MAY 1915

On 24 May at 2.45am the Germans signalled their attack along a four and half mile Front, using a series of red lights. This was immediately followed by heavy outbursts of artillery, machine gun and rifle fire from the German trenches. With the emergence of dawn, great clouds of gas were spotted floating towards the British Line. Where the lines of trenches ran together, the hissing of the discharge could be heard even above the roar of the guns. The German infantry attack was repulsed by withering fire from the British defenders, with a large number of casualties on both sides. Only at Mouse Trap Farm did the enemy over-run the defences. Eventually, the Germans succeeded in capturing Bellewaarde Ridge.

The 1/5th Durham Light Infantry (DLI), a Territorial battalion based in Stockton on Tees, arrived in France on 18 April 1915 and was part of 150th Brigade (50th Division). On the night of 23 May the 150th Brigade occupied the line with the Cavalry Corps from the south eastern corner of Armagh Wood to west of Bellewarde Lake. At this time the 1/5th Durham were attached to the Hussars and Lancers of 2nd Cavalry Brigade. However, at the onset of the attack they were not positioned in the Front Line, they were based on the north-eastern side of Sanctuary Wood. The War Diary and Battalion History records that some of their positions were engulfed in gas and that there were a large number of casualties. During the later part of 24 May the battalion manned the GHQ line, being in reserve to the 3rd Battalion Middlesex Regiment who were under orders to deliver a counterattack, which was later cancelled [7].

**Private John Nicholas Robson, aged 29**
**1/5th Battalion Durham Light Infantry**
**Died 24 May 1915**

John was born in 1886 in Humshaugh and was the second eldest son of Thomas and Jane Robson. Some time between 1901 and 1911 John moved to Darlington to live with his elder sister, Mary Jane Ibbotson. The 1911 census records that John was unmarried and that he was working as a labourer in the railway goods yard.

**John is commemorated on the Menin Gate Memorial to the missing.**

At the time of the attack on May 24 the 1/4th Northumberland Fusiliers (NF) were occupying dugouts near Chateau des Trois Tours, near Brielen and were immediately moved into a reserve position near the Ypres Canal, some three miles from the immediate action. Even in this position the threat from gas was formidable. At 10am they were ordered forward into a line west of the St Jean to Wieltje road. During the day, gas shells were falling amongst the Fusiliers' positions. Later that night the Fusiliers were instructed to deploy to right of the road and "to hold their position at all costs".

The next day, 25 May, the battalion was moved to a number of sectors along the Front to try and stem the German attacks. Although the men were not directly involved in any fighting, exposure to non-stop shelling and gas resulted in the death of six fusiliers and the wounding of a number of others.

## GAS, GAS, GAS

### Letter from Private J Moody published in the Hexham Courant (17 June 1915)

"On Sunday night a terrific bombardment started, and early on Monday morning (24 May) we got the order to leave our dugouts and advance. The Germans were using those gases so we had to use our respirators. I do not know how we could have come on without them, and we passed a lot of unfortunate soldiers making their way back, some very badly gassed. The effects of gas are too awful for words. The sweat was teeming down the men's faces and they are gasping for breath. Thanks to my respirator I was able to go on although I thought my head was going to split. Once as we advanced towards some trenches a German machine gun started to play on us and Lt. Bunbury, one of our officers, was wounded. Whenever we crossed a field it was ploughed up by "Jack Johnsons*." [*An Afro-American boxer who held the world heavyweight championship until 5th April 1915 and whose name was used as slang for a heavy German artillery shell that gave off a lot of black smoke.]

They were bursting all over, and how we got so far up with so few casualties is little short of a miracle. When night fell we went forward again and took our place in the firing line. Things were pretty quiet just then, only a few stray bullets flying about, but we had to keep a sharp lookout, as the German trenches were only 500 yards in front of us. We were only in the front line for two days and are now back in some reserve trenches not far behind the front line. I expect we will be going further back for a rest shortly and will give you further news then."

**William Milburn, aged 28**
**1/4th Battalion Northumberland Fusiliers**
**Died 24 May 1915**

William was born in Caldbeck, Cumberland, the eldest son of Isaac and Hannah Milburn of Church View, Caldbeck. At the age of 14 he was employed as a cattleman in Caldbeck. Before going to France on 20 April 1915, William was employed at Gunnerton Colliery.

**William is buried in Hop Store Cemetery.**

**James Albert Carr, aged 20**
**1/4th Battalion Northumberland Fusiliers**
**Died 26 May 1915**

James was born in Elsdon and was the eldest surviving son of Thomas and Barbara Carr of Colwell, Barrasford. He died from the wounds he received the previous day. Albert joined the Territorials following Kitchener's appeal for recruits. In a letter from Second Lieutenant Turner to Mrs Carr, he described how Albert was wounded:

"He was separated from the 'A' company during the fighting on Whit Monday [24 May 1915] and attached himself to 'B' company. This company had to dig trenches under fire on Whit Tuesday [25 May] and your son was struck by a shrapnel bullet while bringing up water. He was able to walk to the dressing station, but died some days after in hospital. Your son fell bravely doing his duty…"

**Albert is buried in**
**Bailleul Communal Cemetery Extension.**

## REFERENCES

1. Macdonald, L. 1915: T*he Death of Innocence.*
Pub: Penguin Books Ltd 1996

2. Keech, G. *St Julien, Ypres.* Pub: Pen and Sword 2001.

3. WO95/2828. *War Diary, 1/4th Battalion Northumberland Fusiliers.*

4. Wyrell, E. *The Fiftieth Division, 1914-1919.*
Pub: 1939, reprinted Naval and Military Press 2002.

5. Buckley, F. Capt *War History of the Seventh Northumberland Fusiliers.*
Pub: T. M. Greirson.

6. Bunbury, W.J. *A Diary of an Officer with the 4th Northumberland Fusiliers in France and Flanders.* Pub: J Catherall & Co, Hexham 1915.

7. WO95/2837. *War Diary, 1/6th Battalion Durham Light Infantry.*

# CHAPTER SIX

# GALLIPOLI CAMPAIGN

*Y Beach, the Scottish Borderer cried,*
*While panting up the steep hillside,*
*Y Beach!*
*To call this thing a beach is stiff,*
*It's nothing but a bloody cliff,*
*Why beach?*

Major John Churchill (brother of Winston)

By early 1915, progress on the Western Front had stagnated, and Winston Churchill, First Lord of the Admiralty, was keen to push for a new Front in the East. Turkey, allied to Germany, was fighting against the Russians in the Caucasus and against the British in the Middle East. Churchill envisaged a naval attempt to win the Dardanelles Straits, allowing a bombardment of Constantinople, which would, he hoped, lead to Turkish surrender. Furthermore, this would allow a passage along the Bosphorus from Constantinople for the supply of food and ammunition to Russia.

The Royal Navy made disastrous attempts in February and March to capture the Dardanelles Straits. It was the admission that these naval attacks had been a costly failure that brought about Churchill's political demise.

British and French fleets in the Dardanelles.

Even before the failure of the naval attacks, preparation had begun for an Anglo French landing on the Gallipoli Peninsula. Lord Kitchener appointed General Sir Ian Hamilton as regional Commander in Chief of a force of 75,000 men, consisting largely of untested Australian and New Zealand troops. The landings on 25 April 1915 were centred on two localities: Helles Point, where five sites were selected, called S, V, W, X and Y Beaches (using British troops from the 29th Division) and Gaba Tepe using Australians and New Zealanders, known collectively as *ANZACs.*

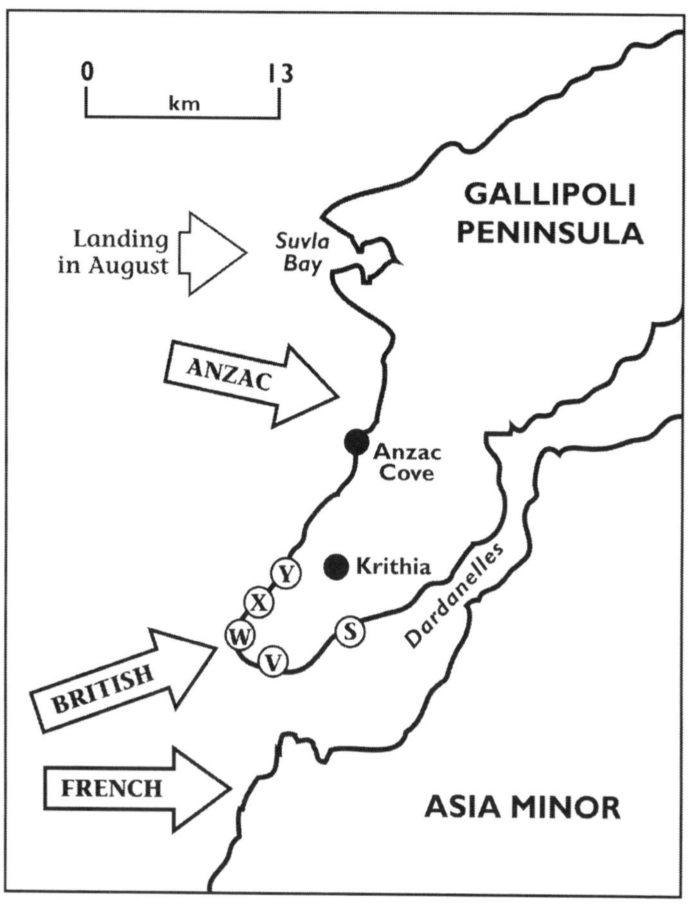

At X Beach the 2nd Royal Fusiliers landed, meeting minimal resistance; after securing the beach and cliff top they were reinforced by men from the 1st Border Regiment and the 1st Inniskilling Fusiliers. Regrettably, instead of moving inland, they dug in and waited for further orders, which unfortunately did not come.

At W Beach, which was better defended, the Lancashire Fusiliers suffered terrible losses, but thanks to the considerable bravery of those involved they were able to secure their position and were awarded six Victoria Crosses "before breakfast". Through supreme courage, Hill 114 was captured, allowing a link up with the troops on X Beach, as was Hill 138, allowing link up with Y Beach.

At V Beach, the Dublin Fusiliers were massacred as they reached the beach, with only a few survivors making it to the relative safety of a low ridge of sand. Disembarking from a specially adapted freighter, the River Clyde, the Munster Fusiliers met a similar fate. By afternoon the sea was lapping crimson with blood on the shore; only nightfall brought some respite from the slaughter.

At S Beach, the South Wales Borderers easily captured the lightly defended beach, but again the troops, lacking orders to the contrary, made no attempt to move inland.

Y Beach, the northernmost landing site on Cape Helles was allotted to the Ist Kings Own Scottish Borderers, supported by a company from the 2nd South Wales Borderers together with the Plymouth Battalion of the Royal Marine Light Infantry. The landing site had been chosen because of its narrow beach and high cliffs [1].

## THE SECOND BATTLE OF KRITHIA 6-8 MAY

By early May, large concentrations of Turkish troops were beginning to congregate on Gallipoli; if the Allies were to make any progress up the peninsula they needed to capture Krithia and the heights of Achi Baba. An attack was scheduled for May. The right flank was given to the French forces, supported by a brigade of the Royal Naval Division; the centre of the attack was carried out by the 87th and 88th Brigades, whilst the left flank was attacked using 125th Brigade (42nd Division). On leaving their trenches the attacking force was faced with heavy Turkish fire, making any progress impossible. The attack was renewed on the next two days without making any real gains and at the expense of considerable loss of life [2].

**Able Seaman David Rolfe, aged 23**
**Hood Battalion, Royal Naval Battalion**
**Died 6 May 1915**

David was born in 1891 and was the son of Robert Rolfe of Shilburnhaugh Colliery, Falstone. Before enlisting on 1 September 1914, he was employed as a miner at the local colliery. Robert was a well known preacher with the United Methodist Church and often preached in Bellingham.

He saw action during the desperate defence of Antwerp in 1914 and was part of the force that landed at Gallipoli in April 1915.

His family received a letter dated 21 September 1915 from Lieutenant Hughes:

> "During an advance made in rushes Rolfe was wounded and fell by my side. I spoke to him but received no reply. Immediately we made another rush and that was the last I saw of him. Rolfe was shot through the mouth and was totally unconscious. I believe that Rolfe was dead."

Shortly afterwards, Lieutenant Hughes was himself wounded.

**David is commemorated on the Helles Memorial to the missing.**

## THE THIRD BATTLE OF KRITHIA: 4 - 6 JUNE

For the third attempt to capture the village of Krithia and Achi Baba, a number of night advances were made in late May, which moved the Front forwards by half a mile at a cost of fewer than fifty casualties, in contrast to the six thousand casualties during the *Second Battle of Krithia* in which the Front moved forward by three quarters of a mile.

The attack across the width of the peninsula began on a sunny, breezy day with troops from the 29th Division on the left, (King's Own Scottish

Borderers) the 49th Division in the centre, with the Royal Naval Division to the right with French Troops to the extreme right.

The attack on the left was preceded by an artillery barrage from HMS *Swiftsure* and *Vengeance* lying offshore and at noon the Borderers left their trenches in Fir-Tree Copse. 'A' and 'B' companies were the first to advance and were met by withering fire; they took a lot of casualties. By this stage no Turkish trench had been captured and the remnants of the attack sheltered in small nullahs, (steep sided 'valleys' caused by flash flooding), still 100 yards from any enemy trench. Their position eased as Indian troops took a redoubt on the left and the Worcestershire Regiment made an advance on the right. At this point 'C' and 'D' companies, through a series of platoon rushes, captured the two forward Turkish Trenches, sending back sixty prisoners. Later in the day the battalion was able to move forward by charging down a communication trench. Eventually, over the next two days, the Turks forced the Borderers to retreat to the Turkish original Front Line [3,4].

**Corporal Walter Tait Ovens, aged 23**
**1st Battalion King's Own Scottish Borderers**
**Died 4 June 1915**

Walter, the eldest son of Walter and Isabella Ovens of Redesmouth, was born in Rothbury and was educated at the Reed Charity School in Bellingham. His father worked as a guard on passenger trains. Before joining the army in the winter of 1914/15, Walter worked as a booking clerk at Easter Road Station in Edinburgh. However, the 1911 census shows that previously Walter had been a serving soldier residing in the regimental barracks at Berwick upon Tweed, so he would be called up as a reservist.

At the onset of hostilities the Borderers were stationed at Lucknow in India and arrived back in England just after Christmas 1914. They landed on Gallipoli with the first wave of attackers at Y Beach on 25 April 1915.

**Walter is commemorated on the Helles Memorial to the missing.**

The 1/4th Battalion Kings Own Scottish Borderers (KOSB) arrived on the Gallipoli Peninsula on 14 June 1915. From 15 June the battalion's position was shelled frequently. On July 11 the KOSB moved into the firing line trenches in preparation for an attack the following morning. This attack was on a Front of 500 yards against three lines of Turkish trenches. To their right the Royal Scots Fusiliers also advanced, on a Front of 150 yards. The Borderers were selected to lead the attack and eventually to capture and consolidate captured positions.

The offensive took place on a gloriously fine summer day at 7.35am, preceded an hour earlier by an artillery bombardment. After advancing more than 500yds and capturing two trench lines the KOSB were not able to find any evidence of a third trench system. Casualties had been comparatively light during the advance, but as they turned back having not located any third trench system, the battalion had to pass through a zone of fire from their own artillery and that of the Turks, which resulted in heavy losses. Further, as the KOSB had broken through on a narrow front, and as they returned to consolidate the second trench line, they were caught in enfilade fire from Turks on both fringes of the attack and suffered many casualties. The remnants occupied and consolidated a position in the second trench system and came under a number of attacks from the Turks. Casualties for this attack by the 1/4th KOSB were 12 officers killed, 6 wounded and of other ranks 319 killed, 203 wounded and 13 taken prisoner. The History of the KOSB states, "In large areas between Tweed and Forth scarcely a household but mourned a son" [5,6].

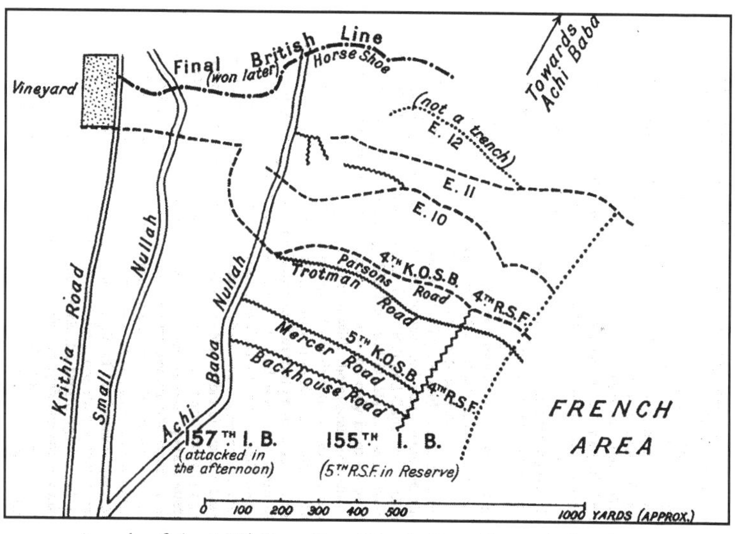


Attack of the 1/4th Battalion King's Own Scottish Borderers
12 July 1915

## Private William R Jeffrey, aged 38
## 1/4th Battalion King's Own Scottish Borderers
## Died 12 July 1915

William Jeffery is commemorated on the Reading Room Memorial, now hung in Wall Village Hall, although his name does not appear on Wall Village Memorial. However, the Roll of Honour published in the Wall, Bingfield and Hallington Parish Magazine for January 1915 records that a William Jeffrey of Wall had enlisted in the King's Own Scottish Borderers.

Census records do not record the Jeffrey family living in Wall and its surrounding area. The absence of his name from the main memorial would suggest he was a visitor to the area who used the Reading Room amenities.

The WW1 Medal Rolls Index Cards reveal that there were three William Jefferys serving in the King's Own Scottish Borderers, but only one has a regimental number consistent with a late 1914 enlistment and the record in the Wall Parish Magazine. This number 7459 belonged to William Restrick Jeffery, aged 38, of 'C' Company King's Own Scottish Borderers.

William Jeffrey was born in Glasgow and was the eldest son of William and Jessie Jeffrey who in 1891 lived in Dumfries. Data shows that William enlisted in Galashiels and lived in Maxton, Roxburgh. However, the Maxton War Memorial does not commemorate his death. Thus, Williams' relationship to Wall is slightly dubious.

**William is commemorated on the Helles Memorial to the missing.**

The repeated failure of the Allies to capture Krithia or to make any progress on the Helles Front, led Hamilton to pursue a new plan for the campaign which resulted in what is now called the *Battle of Sari Bair.* On the night of 6 August a fresh landing of two infantry divisions was to be made at Suvla, five miles (8km) north of what became known as Anzac Cove. Meanwhile, at Anzac Cove a strong assault would be made on the Sari Bair range by breaking out into the rough and thinly defended terrain north of the Anzac perimeter [7].

The landing at Suvla Bay was only lightly opposed but the British commander, Lieutenant-General Sir Frederick Stopford, had so diluted his early objectives that little more than the beach was seized. Once again, the Turks were able to win the race for the high ground of the Anafarta Hills thereby rendering the Suvla Front another case of static trench warfare. The offensive was preceded on the evening of 6 August by diversionary assaults at Helles and Anzac. At Helles, the diversion at Krithia Vineyard became another futile battle with no gains and heavy casualties on both sides. At Anzac, an attack on the Turkish trenches at Lone Pine by the infantry brigades of the Australian 1st Division was a rare victory for the ANZACs. However, the main assault, aimed at the peaks of Chunuk Bair and Hill 971, was less successful. The Suvla landing was reinforced by the arrival of the British 53rd and 54th Divisions along with the 10th (Irish) Division plus the dismounted yeomanry of the 2nd Mounted Division. The 29th Division was also shifted from Helles to Suvla for one more push. The final British attempt to resuscitate the offensive came on 21 August with attacks at Scimitar Hill and Hill 60. Control of these hills would have united the Anzac and Suvla fronts but neither attack succeeded. When fighting at Hill 60 ended on 29 August, the battle for the Sari Bair heights, and indeed the battle for the peninsula, was effectively over.

On 27 August. Charles Gilroy was ordered to deliver a despatch to an area near Chocolate Hill. It was later ascertained that he succeeded in delivering the despatch, but did not return from this mission. His route would not have taken him close eough to the Turkish lines for him to be taken as a prisoner, so it was concluded that he had been shot and buried without identification [8].

**Private Charles William Gilroy, aged 20**
**14th Battalion Australian Infantry**
**27 August 1915**

Charles, the son of Charles John and Annie Gilroy was born in Bellingham. Charles senior had been a member of the volunteer forces from Bellingham that fought in the Boer War. Young Charles was educated at the Reed School, Bellingham, after which the 1911 census shows Charles, aged 16, working as farm labourer for Alexander Taylor of Great Bavington. Charles emigrated, sailing for Australia on 5 December 1913, arriving in Adelaide aboard SS Omrah. Before joining the Australian Forces in Melbourne on 1 March 1915, he was working as a farm labourer. His younger brother, Gordon, serving with the Durham Light Infantry, was killed in April 1916 (see page 88).

**Charles is commemorated on the Lone Pine Memorial to the missing.**

Following the failure of the August Offensive, there was a hiatus in the Gallipoli campaign while its future direction was decided. Disaffected senior officers such as General Stopford contributed to the general air of gloom. The prospect of evacuation was raised on 11 October 1915, but Hamilton resisted the suggestion, fearing the damage this would inevitably cause to British prestige and morale. He was dismissed as commander shortly afterwards and replaced by Lieutenant-General Sir Charles Monro. Having reviewed the state of his command, Monro recommended evacuation. Kitchener disliked the notion of evacuating the peninsula and made a personal visit to consult with his commanders of the three corps, after which the decision to evacuate was confirmed. Evacuation of fourteen divisions, in winter and in proximity to the enemy, would be difficult; heavy losses were expected. The untenable nature of the Allied position was made apparent when a heavy rainstorm struck on 27 November 1915 which lasted for three days, followed by a blizzard at Suvla in early December. Rain flooded the trenches, drowning soldiers and washing unburied corpses into the lines. The snow that fell shortly afterwards killed still more men from exposure. Ironically, it was the *evacuation* that proved to be the greatest Allied success of the campaign. Suvla and Anzac were evacuated in late December, the last troops leaving before dawn on 20 December 1915. Troop numbers had been progressively reduced since 7 December 1915; cunning ruses, such as self-firing rifles, were used to fool the Turks and prevent them discovering that the Allies were departing. At Anzac Cove, the troops would maintain utter silence for an hour or more until the curious Turks would venture out to inspect the trenches, whereupon the Anzacs would open fire. The entire Allied force was evacuated, although at first Helles was retained in case the British wanted to resume the offensive. However, a decision to evacuate even Helles was made on 27 December. The Turks, now warned of the likelihood of evacuation, mounted an attack on 6 January 1916 but were repulsed. The last British troops departed from Lancashire Landing on 9 January 1916. Amazingly, only two soldiers were wounded during the evacuation, despite the dismal prediction of 50% casualties from Sir Ian Hamilton.

## REFERENCES

1. Carlyon, L.A. *Gallipoli.* Pub Bantam Books 2003.

2. Jerrold. G. *Royal Naval Division.*
Pub:1930, reprinted Naval Military Press 2002.

3. Gillon, S. Capt. *King's Own Scottish Borderers in the Great War.*
Pub:1930, reprinted Naval Military Press 2002.

4. WO95/4311. *War Diary,* 1st *Battalion King's Own Scottish Borderers.*

5. WO95/4320. *War Diary, 1/4th Battalion King's Own Scottish Borderers.*

6. Brown, W. S. *War record of the 4th Bn King's Own Scottish Borderers and Lothian and Border Horse.* Pub: John McQueen & Son 1920.

7. Bean, C.E.W. *Official History of Australia in the War 1914-1918 Vol. 11 Pub: 1946.*

8. AWM4 23/31/11. War Diary, *14th Battalion AIF,* August 1915.

# CHAPTER SEVEN

# BATTLE OF LOOS

*They took my boy to Loos ...*
*The boy we carved out of heaven's breath,*
*A boy with the powder of love*
*Now just a breath of lead, smell of steel.*
From Edna J Lacey's *Loos*

The *Battle of Loos* was the British part of a large offensive, conducted with the French, known as the *Third Battle of Artois*. The French attacked at Champagne and at Vimy Ridge. The British battle was launched on 25 September 1915 along a Front from the La Bassée Canal in the north to the town of Loos in the south. The day is infamous as the date on which the British first used gas as an offensive weapon; along the Front; 140 tons of chlorine gas were released, with mixed results – in some areas the wind blew the gas back into the British trenches, resulting in over 2000 casualties. The day is also remembered for the first use of Britain's citizen army, (the Volunteers). Further, 25 September saw the Royal

British Infantry advancing through gas at Loos 25 September 1915

Engineer tunnelling companies deploying mines underground which were detonated at zero hour [1].

In the south of the battlefield, the initial British advance broke through the German defences and captured Loos, then began to push forward towards Lens. The advance stalled due to lack of supplies and the need for fresh troops (reserves). Field Marshal Sir John French had taken the view that the reserves would not be needed until the second day of the fighting; this was pivotal to the failure of the enterprise. Earlier in the crucial first day, against the odds, the German first line had been pierced, but by the time French's decision had been revoked and the reserves released in the afternoon, it was too late for them to be of any use. This delay allowed the Germans to pour in reserves and strengthen their defences against the British who, by the 26 September, were unable to mount any effective artillery bombardment. Part of this British reserve was the 12th Battalion Northumberland Fusiliers, soldiers of the New Army, fit but untested in battle; probably with hindsight it would have been better to have used the newcomers for defensive operations, not for the inferno they would experience on 26 September [2].

The 12th Battalion Northumberland Fusiliers (NF) was formed in Newcastle in September 1914 as part of K3 (volunteers) and were attached to 62 Brigade 21st Division. These raw infantrymen landed at Boulogne on 9 September 1915 just over two weeks before their baptism of fire at Loos. After a series of marches and train journeys, the battalion arrived at Noeux Les Mines in the early evening of 24 September. As evening drew in, they moved through Loos and as they pushed forward towards Tower Bridge took their first casualties. By late evening a patrol was sent forward in case the battalion was called upon to reinforce an attack. On the morning of 26 September the NF came under heavy shell fire leading to more casualties, but by 9am they had formed up for an attack on Hill

70, using 'B' 'C' and 'D' companies. Initially, the attack progressed well, with reports of the enemy running. However, after the German Front Line trench had been taken the attack ran into devastating machine gun fire which caused appallingly heavy casualties making further progress impossible. The crest of the hill was held for some time but it was a dangerous place to be, under very severe machine gun fire. Eventually, the remnants of the attacking force retired to the German Front Line trench from where they easily repulsed a party of Germans following up on their retreat. By mid afternoon this position was under heavy enfilade machine gun fire from Hulluch. The order to retire to Loos was given, but it was not until the morning of 27 September that all the survivors of this ill-judged attack had been collected up and the extent of the casualties ascertained [3].

An eye witness described the horror these raw troops encountered on their first day under fire (Harry Fellows, 12th Battalion Northumberland Fusiliers):

> "After a few minutes I rose to my knees and should I live to be a hundred, I shall never forget the sight that met my eyes. The whole slope was one mass of prone figures some even lying on top of one another. The only thing I could liken it to would be one of the old fashioned fly-papers which used to hang in my mother's kitchen and which after a hot day were loaded with dead flys [sic].
>
> The Germans still held their fire and soon there was some movement. Men began to get to their feet, others rose only to fall back again, whilst others limped and some even crawled. Many, like the lad I had stumbled over, would never move again. He had been shot through the head!
>
> Some months later the German commander of this particular sector

was reported to have said, 'My machine gunners were so filled with pity, remorse and nausea at the Corpse Field of Loos that they refused to fire another shot.' This I do believe. On my return to our trenches a Scot handed me his water bottle and said. 'Ye nae had a chance!'"

**Private George Charlton, aged 32**
**$12^{th}$ (Service) Battalion Northumberland Fusiliers**
**Died 27 September 1915**

George was born in Acomb in 1879 and was the youngest son of John and Margaret Charlton of 30, Station Road, South Gosforth. The family left Acomb when George was very young and went to live in Ryton. After the death of his father in 1893, Margaret, his mother, moved to South Gosforth. George arrived in France on 9 September.

**George is commemorated on the Loos Memorial to the missing.**

**Private Adam Herdman, aged 24**
**$12^{th}$ (Service) Battalion Northumberland Fusiliers**
**Died 27 September 1915**

Adam was born in Simonburn in 1890, where his father was a tailor. He was the eldest son of Henry and Margaret Herdman of Simonburn. The official news of his death was received on October 17, ending a trying time of suspense and anxiety for his parents. At the time of his death, the family had three further sons serving with the forces, one with the Northumberland Fusiliers and two with the Army Service Corps.

**Adam is commemorated on the Loos Memorial to the missing.**

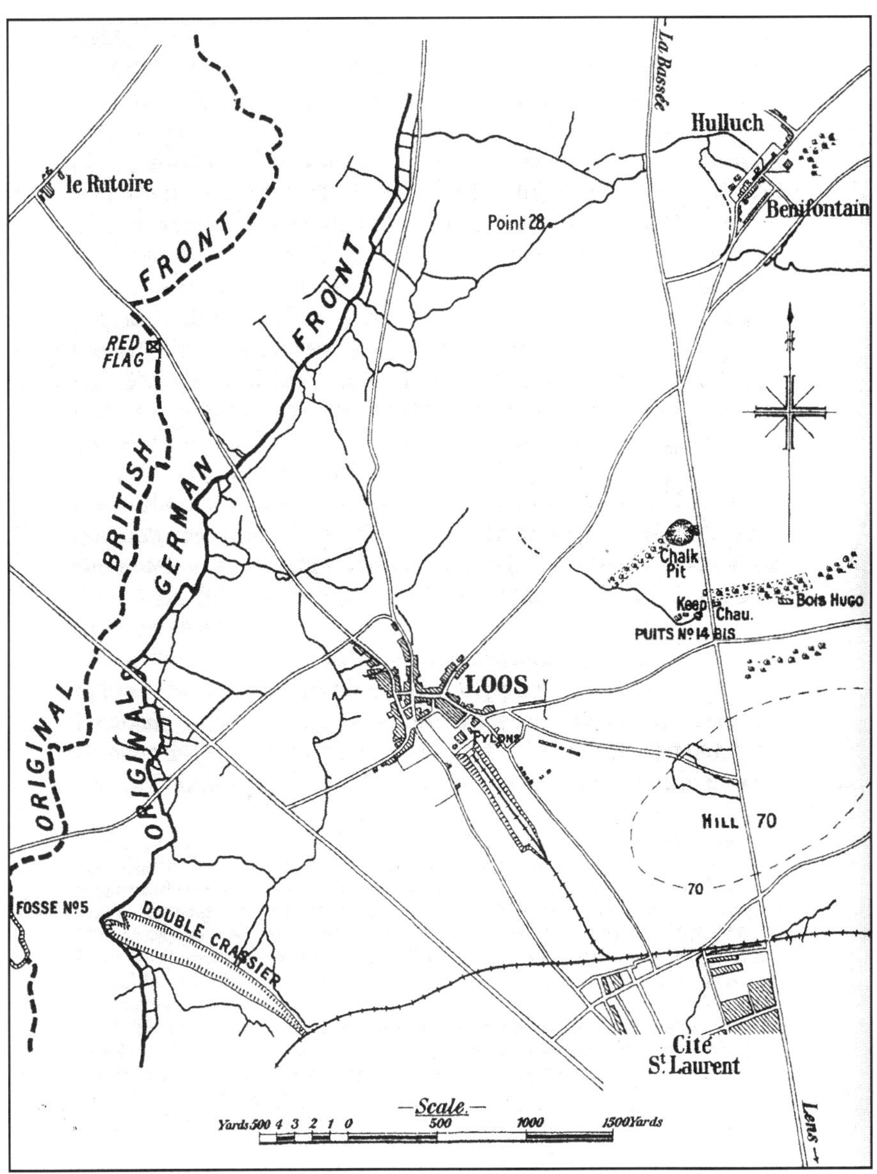


Southern Section of the Loos Battlefield showing the area fought over by the 12th Battalion Northumberland Fusiliers and 1st Battalion Scots Guards

On the afternoon of 27 September the 2nd Guards Brigade was ordered to attack Hill 70. However, two hours before the attack its objectives were scaled back, because of problems along the whole Front. The 2nd Irish Guards with the 1st Scot Guards on its right led the attack, which required the Guards to cross 1000 yards of ground before they would reach the German trenches [4,5,6].

Wartime panoramic picture of Loos showing the town and a puits (winding tower for the coal mine)

Following a 90 minute bombardment the attack began at 4pm. Initially the Guards sustained few casualities, but as they approached their objective – Puits No. 14 (winding gear for a coal mine) – they came under heavy fire; hundreds of men were mown down in murderous crossfire, from Bois Hugo, the 'Keep' and from the Puits. The History of the Guards Division relates:

> "... an assault on the Keep and the Puits was quickly organised. This attack was delivered with vigour and determination, but the enemy's positions were of exceptional strength and his machine gun

> fire was so effective and deadly that by the time the assaulting troops had reached the Puits their numbers were so reduced that sucess was no longer possible."

Lieutenant John Kipling of the Irish Guards, son of Rudyard Kipling, was one of those killed here. It was reported that a small party led by Captain Cuthbert reached the Puits. For a time they fought on, their strength increased by a platoon of Grenadier Guards, but without further support Cuthbert's men had to fall back. Initial reports from the Front stated that Captain Cuthbert had been wounded and was missing in action.

The **Distinguished Service Order** (**DSO**) is a military decoration of the United Kingdom, and other parts of the British Commonwealth and Empire, awarded for meritorious or distinguished service by officers of the armed forces during wartime, typically in actual combat. Instituted on 6 September 1886 by Queen Victoria in a Royal Warrant, the first DSOs awarded were dated 25 November 1886. It is typically awarded to officers ranked Major (or its equivalent) or higher, but the honour has sometimes been awarded to especially valorous junior officers. During the First World War, 8,981 DSOs were awarded, each award being announced in the London Gazette. The DSO was normally given in recognition of service under fire, or under conditions equivalent to service in actual combat with the enemy, although it was awarded between 1914 and 1916 under circumstances which could not be regarded as under fire (often to staff officers, which caused resentment among front-line officers). After 1 January 1917, commanders in the field were instructed to recommend the DSO *only* for those serving under fire. The medal itself is a gold (silver-gilt) cross, enamelled white and edged in gold. In the centre, within a wreath of laurel, enamelled green, is the Imperial Crown in gold upon a red enamelled background. On the reverse is the Royal Cypher in gold upon a red enamelled ground, within a wreath of laurel, enamelled green. A ring at the top of the medal attaches to a ring at the bottom of a gold suspension bar, ornamented with laurel. At the top of the ribbon is a second gold bar ornamented with laurel. The red ribbon is 2.86cm wide with narrow blue edges.

The Hexham Courant printed the following from the Daily Mail written by Mr G V Williams, a special correspondent in France:

> "The Guards were ordered to attack at 4pm on Monday September 27th. The Irish Guards advanced down the valley, calm and cool and in good order, and gained the lower edge of the wood about the chalk pit without many casualties. It was the baptism of fire of this battalion. Behind them came the Coldstreamers. The Irish men established themselves in the wood and with their machine guns and rifles opened a heavy covering fire against Pit 14a, to check the enemy and to enable the Scots Guards to reach Pit 14a, which was their objective.
>
> With their scrap of red Stewart tartan on their caps as their distinguishing badge, the Scots Guards advanced. A perfect inferno of fire was loosed from machine guns which could not be seen, but which rapped out their nerve racking note high above the thunder of the guns. The Scots Guards suffered heavily, their Colonel was wounded and other officers dropped, but "the Kiddies" as they call them in the army kept on.
>
> Pit 14a was ours to all intents and purposes. Captain Cuthbert DSO of the Scots Guards, who displayed splendid gallantry, went boldly in among the houses round about the pithead, leading a party of his men in the desperate hand-to-hand struggle with bomb and bayonet against the Germans still residing there.
>
> Brave men all, Scots Guards and Grenadiers hung on in the position they had won with their dead and dying comrades all around them. Men were falling fast. Rain came on as the shades of night crept over. Cuthbert and Ritchie held on to Pit 14a until practically no-

one was left, waiting for the support which was impossible to send them owing to the deadly German machine gun fire in enfilade. It must have been with bitterness in their hearts that they recognised that their position was untenable.

In this desperate and bloody fighting in which the Guards Division made its heroic debut, fitly carrying on the high traditions already established by the Guards in this war, many gallant officers fell. Captain Cuthbert DSO, who distinguished himself in the attack on Pit 14a, is missing. He was last seen to enter a house with some men. It is feared he was killed by a shell."

**Captain James Harold Cuthbert DSO, aged 39**
**1st Battalion Scots Guards**
**Died 27 September 1915**

James, of Beaufront Castle, was born on 21 July 1876 in South Africa and was educated at Eton and Sandhurst. He joined the Scots Guards in August 1896 and served as a Lieutenant in South Africa (1899-1902). During the Boer War he was involved in the advance on Kimberley and was present at the actions of Belmont, Enalin, Modder River, Magersfontein and others, including one in which his horse was shot from under him. He held the Queen's and King's medals with eight bars. In recognition for services during operations in South Africa in 1901 he was awarded the DSO. Before this he had been mentioned in despatches. He won the Army shooting championship in 1902 and served as High Sheriff of Northumberland in 1904. James was also the author of a definitive History of the 1st Battalion of the Scots Guards in South Africa, 1899-

1902. James married Anne Dorothy Frederica Byng, the third daughter of the Earl of Strafford, in September 1903, who died in a shooting accident in January 1907. He was remarried in October 1909, to Kathleen Alice Straker of Stagshaw, in Hexham Abbey.

James was recalled to the Colours from the Reserve Officers list in 1914 and went to France in April 1915. Two months before his death, whilst in trenches south of La Bassée where the Scots Guards were responsible for sending out digging parties, he was wounded in the hand whilst rescuing a wounded Scots Guardsman. This injury was caused by a grenade thrown by a German soldier. After his death at Loos in September, James left a widow, three sons and a daughter, who waited over a year for his death to be confirmed [7].

**James is commemorated on the Loos Memorial to the missing.**

**Guardsman Frank Steele, aged 21**
**1st Battalion Scots Guards**
**Died 27 September 1915**

Frank was born in Canobie, Dumfriesshire, the eldest son of William and Bridget Steele of Stable Row, Plashetts. Like his father and other brothers he worked underground at Plashetts Colliery. He volunteered for military service, joining the Guards in December 1914. He undertook his basic training at Caterham where he was punished for going absent for six days during late June 1915. Frank embarked for France in July 1915 and was reported 'missing presumed killed' on 27 September. His body was recovered three weeks later by soldiers from 18th London Regiment and was buried near the right section of the Loos trenches. However, after years in the battlefield his body was lost, as were many others. His younger brother, David, was killed on the first day of the Somme (see page 97).

**Frank is commemorated on the Loos Memorial to the missing.**

The fighting had all but subsided by 28 September. During the following days the Germans made several attempts to recapture the Hohenzollern Redoubt and on 3 October their efforts were rewarded. On 8 October the they launched a major offensive along the whole Front, but by nightfall this was abandoned due to heavy losses. Although this date marked the official end to hostilities, the British attempted an attack on 13 October which failed due to the lack of hand grenades.

Of the Battle of Loos, Major General Richard Hilton later wrote:

> "A great deal of nonsense has been written about Loos. The real tragedy of that battle was its nearness to complete success. Most of us who reached the crest of Hill 70 and survived were firmly convinced that we had broken through on Sunday 25th September 1915. There seemed to be nothing ahead of us but an unoccupied and incomplete trench system. The only two things that prevented our advancing into the suburbs of Lens were, firstly the exhaustion of the 'Jocks' themselves (for they had undergone a bellyful of marching and fighting that day) and secondly the flanking fire of numerous German machine guns, which swept the bare hill from some factory buildings in Cité St Auguste to the south of us. All that we needed was more artillery ammunition to blast these clearly located machine guns, and some fresh infantry to take over from the weary and depleted 'Jocks'. But, alas, neither ammunition nor reinforcements were immediately available, and the great opportunity passed.

## REFERENCES

1. Corrigan, G. *Loos 1915, The Unwanted Battle.* Pub: Spellmount, 2006

2. Rawson, A. *Loos Hill 60.* Pub: Pen and Sword 2002.

3. WO95/2182. *War Diary, 12th Battalion Northumberland Fusiliers.*

4. WO95/1219. *War Diary, 1st Battalion Scots Guards.*

5. Petre, F. L., Ewart,W. and Maj. Gen. Lowther, Sir C. *The Scots Guards in the Great War 1914-1918.*
Pub: 1925. Reprinted Naval Military Press 2002.

6. Headlam, C. DSO. *History of the Guards Division in the Great War 1915-1918.* Pub: 1924. Reprinted Naval and Military Press 2002.

7. Marquis of Ruvigny and Raineval. *De Ruvigny's Roll of Honour 1914-1924, Vol. 2, page 89.*

# CHAPTER EIGHT

# WESTERN FRONT 1916

*... and nations great in reputation of the arts*
*that bind the world with hopes of Heaven*
*sink to the state of brute barbarians ...*

From Robert Palmer's *How Long O Lord*
Killed in action 1916

## OVERVIEW

During the early months of 1916 the British Forces were engaged in maintaining the status quo along the Front Line, providing troops to man the trench systems, now well developed. Those battalions selected to be involved in the big thrust on the Somme on July 1 were busy with their preparations.

In February, the Germans had launched a massive attack on the French around Verdun with the aim of bleeding them dry. In the end, Verdun and the gateway to Paris remained secure, although the cost had been high: the battle had raged for over ten months and had caused the deaths of around half a million men.

Further afield the Italians, who had entered the war initially only against Austria-Hungary in 1915, after some fifteen months finally declared war on Germany. The Russians inflicted defeats on both the Turkish and Austro-Hungarian armies. In Mesopotamia the British advanced in their quest to occupy Baghdad; T E Lawrence fomented rebellion against the Turks. At home, what became known as the 'Easter Rising' against British rule in Ireland further added to the Government's difficulties.

At sea the Navy fought history's biggest sea battle, *Jutland*, which although there was no clear victor, the British were able to claim as an important strategic victory as the German Fleet never left their bases for the rest of the war, relying on their increasingly successful submarine menace.

## ALONG THE WESTERN FRONT

During the first days of February 1916, the 1/4th Northumberland Fusiliers were manning the trenches on Hill 60 [1]. The War Diary reports that "during last night (February 1) Pte Hedley of 'B' Company was killed, [2,3]. The enemy were very active with grenades". Further fusiliers were to die during the next two days. Buckley a 2nd Lieutenant with the 1/7th Battalion Northumberland Fusiliers wrote [2]:

**Hill 60** was a low rise on the southern flank of the Ypres Salient and was named after the 60 metre contour which marked its bounds. It was a modest 'hill' that had been formed from the debris created when a local railway cutting was built, but in the surrounding low lying area its height was of strategic importance. It was initially captured from the French by the Germans in December 1914. Throughout the initial months of 1916 a great deal of effort was expended in trying to recapture this position.

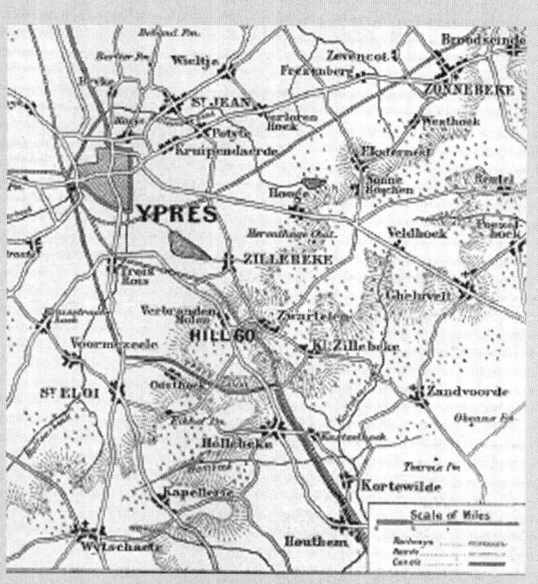

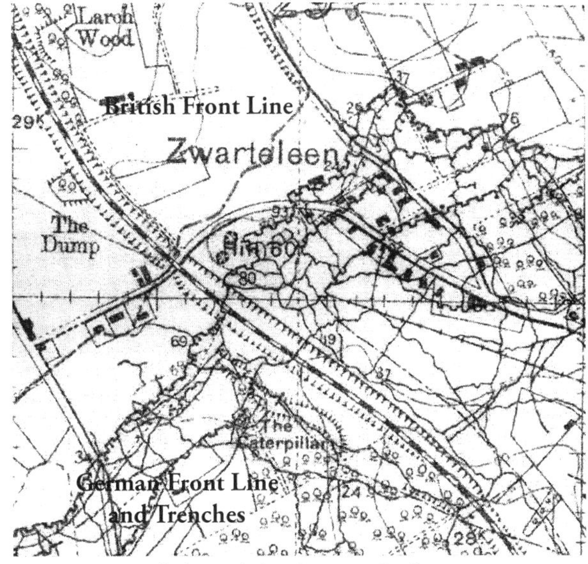


Hill 60 and the German Defences
note the craters from the explosion of underground mines

"Hill 60 was one of the hottest corners of the British Front. Owing to their vantage ground on the hill the enemy had little difficulty in sniping and shelling our trenches effectively. Whilst the German line ran solid along the top of the ridge, there were two complete gaps in the British trenches between Hill 60 and Mount Sorrel on the left. On paper it looks as if there were nothing to stop the German from walking across and behind our lines whenever he chose. But I imagine that these empty spaces were covered by machine gun posts and that the artillery were ready.

Another feature of the place was the awful nature of the ground outside the trenches. It was a morass filled with partially buried bodies. During a dense mist, about seventy identity discs were recovered from the ground behind our support lines. And it was worse in front between the opposing trenches."

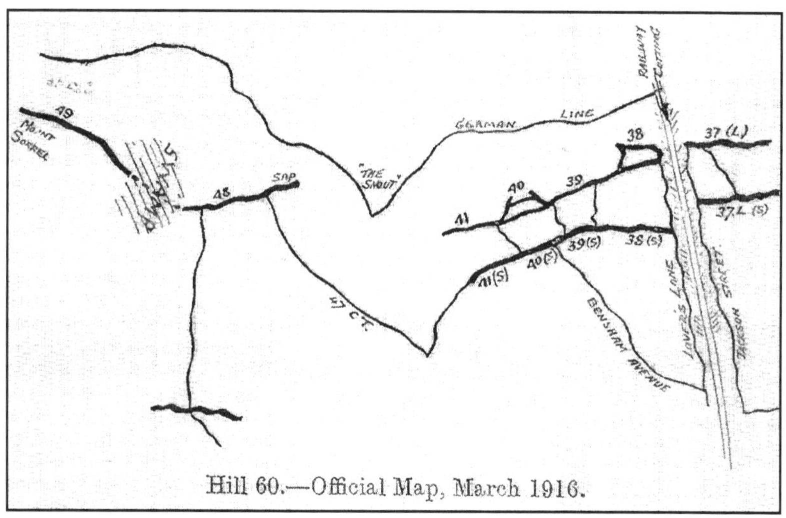

Hill 60.—Official Map, March 1916.

**Private Edward Riddle Hedley, aged 20**
**1/4th Battalion Northumberland Fusiliers**
**Died 1 February 1916**

Edward, the son of George and Jane Hedley, was born in Corsenside. The 1911 census shows that the Hedley family were living at Broomhill Cottages, West Woodburn, and that Edward was working with his father, who was a stone mason. At the start of the war Edward was a serving member of the local Territorials. He embarked for France with the first draft of the Northumberland Fusiliers in late April 1915 and saw action during April and May around Ypres (see page 35).

**Edward is buried in Railway Dugouts Burial Ground.**

On the night of 12 February the 1/4th Northumberland Fusiliers (NF) relieved the 1/9th Durham Light Infantry who were manning Sanctuary Wood Trenches. During the morning of 13 February the Germans began the shelling of Hooge Ridge, just to the left of NF's position; throughout the day Sanctuary Wood received some direct hits, injuring a number of soldiers.

On the afternoon of the 14 February the Germans once again shelled Hooge Ridge and followed up with an attack against the sector held by Rifle Brigade, but were beaten back. Again, a number of shells landed amongst the trenches held by the Fusiliers, killing four soldiers and injuring another dozen or so [2,3].

**Corporal Christopher Inglis, aged 22**
**1/4th Battalion Northumberland Fusiliers**
**Died 14 February 1916**

Christopher, the second son of Hector and Agnes Inglis, was born in Castleton, Roxburghshire. He was locally known as 'Kit'. Agnes, his mother, died when he was a small boy. His father remarried and was the Station Master at Falstone. Christopher was educated at Plashetts School and won a county scholarship to Hexham Secondary School, which he attended for three years. Before the war, Christopher worked at the electric winding engine at Plashetts Colliery. As a serving Territorial he embarked for France with the first batch of the Territorials in April 1915 (see page 35). Christopher was killed by shrapnel from a bursting shell. His older brother Thomas was serving with the Army Service Corps in Egypt.

One of his officers wrote:

> "He was one of the coolest and most gallant of soldiers I have ever seen, and whenever the transport had a dangerous duty to perform he was the first to volunteer to carry it out."

**Christopher is buried in Vlamertinghe Military Cemetery.**

**Private James Grieve, aged 19**
**1/4th Battalion Northumberland Fusiliers**
**Died 14 February 1916**

James, the oldest son of James and Janet Grieve, was born in Jedburgh. After the war Janet lived in Hawick. James went out to France in September 1915 as part of a new draft of fusiliers to increase the ever-depleting strength of the battalion.

**James is commemorated on the Menin Gate Memorial to the missing.**

The 1/4th Northumberland Fusiliers (NF) took up position in trenches on the night 6/7 March, at Hill 60; the War Diary reports that the trenches were in a bad state due to recent heavy snow and a partial thaw, which caused in many places the collapse of the side of the trench. It also reports that on 9 March two sergeants were killed and that the trenches came under heavy shelling and needed continuous repair. The morning of 10 March started quietly, but later the enemy strafed the trenches with artillery during the day and 4 men were killed and 13 wounded. That night the battalion was relieved by the 1/5th NF and moved to Square Wood [2,3].

**Sergeant Wilfrid Marshall Henderson, aged 20**
**1/4th Battalion Northumberland Fusiliers**
**9 March 1916**

Wilfrid was the eldest son of Henry, an invalided lead miner, and Elizabeth Henderson of Lanthorn Cottage, Acomb. From the age of fifteen he was employed at Black Pastures Quarry and was in charge of a compressed air drilling machine. Wilfrid was an esteemed member of the 'West Acomb Tent of the Independent Order of Rechabites'. He was also a chorister at St John Lee Church. He was a serving member of the Territorials at the onset of war and embarked for France in April 1915 with the rank of Private (see page 35). He was a highly proficient marksman and had won the Stewart Trophy for marksmanship before he left for France. As a result he had trained to be a sniper and it is ironic, therefore, that he was killed by a sniper's bullet. Four of his fellow Acomb Territorials were in attendance at his burial: Corporal J Davison, Lance-Corporal J Horne and Privates T Horne and T Hawkins.

The Roll of Honour, published in the Hexham Herald contained the following:

He is gone, but not forgotten,
He was always kind and true;
Never murmured in his sufferings,
No one knew what he went through,
For King and Country he did his best,
May God grant him eternal rest.

**Wilfred is buried in Railway Dugouts Burial Ground.**

The War Diary for the 1/4th Northumberland Fusiliers reports that on 11 March two sergeants were wounded and one man was killed when their position was heavily shelled by the Germans in retaliation for British shelling. Also, it states that the battalion transport was shelled as it passed through the Kruisstraat, killing a corporal and wounding two further men. The rest of this duty until the night of the 14/15 appears to have passed relatively quietly [2,3].

**Private Archibald Wark Bell, aged 24**
**1/4th Northumberland Fusiliers**
**Died 11 March 1916**

Archibald, the son of Archibald and Alice Bell, was born in Corsenside. The 1901 census shows that Archibald was living with his brother and two sisters. Alice, his mother, had died in the winter of 1899. The 1911 census shows Archibald working as groom gardener for the Reverend Rhum Augustine Price and living at the Rectory in Falstone.

He went to France with the initial batch of Territorials in April 1915 and saw action on the 26 April at St Julien (see page 35). His gravestone is inscribed with the following:

**REST IN PEACE**

**Archibald is buried in Railway Dugouts Burial Ground.**

On the night of 2/3 April the 1/4th Northumberland Fusiliers moved into the Front Line in the Wytschaete sector for the next six days.

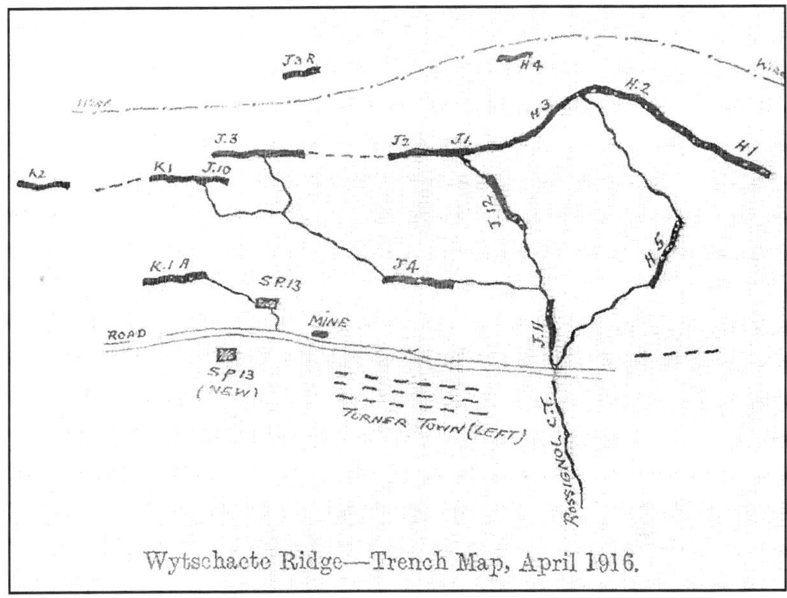

Wytschaete Ridge—Trench Map, April 1916.

Buckley [4], describes the Wytachaete Ridge sector:

> "Instead of the high narrow trenches of Hill 60, they were mostly mere breast-works with little or no back protection. And the communication trenches were hardly deep enough to afford protection from sniping or indirect fire. Fortunately the Germans did not snipe these trenches. There were two gaps in the Front Line and two small posts in No Man's Land."

The Battalion Diary [2,3], records that "in the first three days casualties were about eight men wounded, but they were slight from splinters which could have been avoided had the trench been a proper one". However, on 8 April a dugout received a direct hit from a heavy shell, killing two men (one of these was James Hedley) and wounding four others.

Later that night the battalion was relieved by the 1/5th Northumberland Fusiliers.

**Private James Hedley, aged 22**
**1/4th Battalion Northumberland Fusiliers**
**Died 8 April 1916**

James, the oldest son of George and Jane Hedley, was born in Corsenside. The 1911 census records that he was working as an apprentice joiner. At the outbreak of war James, like his younger brother Edward, was a serving member of 'B' Company of the local Territorials. He saw action and was wounded at the Battle of St Julien in April 1915. His younger brother Edward was killed two months earlier, (see page 82).

**James is buried in La Laiterie Military Cemetery.**

The 1/8th Durham Light Infantry were part of 151st Brigade 50th Division and on the evening of 8 April 1916 moved forward to the Front Line occupying M and N trenches in the Wytschaete Sector. After a relatively quiet first night, the Germans continually shelled this sector until the battalion was relieved on 14 April [5].

**Private Gordon Gilroy, aged 19**
**1/8th Battalion Durham Light Infantry**
**Died 12 April 1916**

Gordon was born in Bellingham, the son of Charles John and Annie Gilroy. Charles Gilroy had fought as a volunteer in South Africa at the turn of the century. Gordon was educated at the Reed Charity School. The 1911 census shows that the Gilroy family were living at the Mires, Capheaton. At the outset of hostilities Gordon was living in Newcastle, from where he volunteered to join the Colours. He arrived in France at the end of October 1915, aged 18. His brother Charles was killed in 1915 whilst serving with the Australians (see page 64).

**Gordon is buried in Ridge Wood Military Cemetery.**

From 2 December 1916, the 39th Battalion Australian Infantry was out of the line and positioned in reserve near Armentières. However, for three days from 3 December the battalion provided working parties to work at the Front. Some time during the 4 December, Basil was accidentally wounded. He was initially admitted to 10th Field Ambulance with gun shot wounds to the abdomen, right arm and left foot and was transferred to No 2 Casualty Clearing Station, where he died on 6 December.

An inquiry conducted on 12 December found that Basil had died as the result of wounds received by the premature explosion of a grenade during a fracas with the enemy in no-man's land. His death was deemed to be accidental.

**Second Lieutenant Basil White, aged 35**
**39th Battalion Australian Infantry**
**Died 6 December 1916**

Basil was born in Bellingham, the son of Arthur Robson and Louisa White of Barton House, Barton-under-Needwood. Basil was born in Charlton House, Charlton, Northumberland. His father was described as a 'landed proprietor'. However, soon after Basil's birth the family moved to Staffordshire. The 1901 census shows Basil, aged 19, living with his family in Barton-under-Needwood; his occupation is recorded as 'Lieutenant in the Militia'. He left London on board the SS Sussex in November 1908 and landed in Melbourne, Australia.

Basil volunteered for the Australian forces in November 1915. His papers show that he was single and working as a labourer. They also show that he had significant experience in the army; he claimed to have had three years' experience with the militia and served six years with the regular army in England, prior to emigrating. He was formally accepted into the 39th Battalion in May 1916. He left Melbourne in late May 1916, arriving in the UK in mid July. In the following month he was promoted to Second Lieutenant. On 23 November he proceeded to France. His gravestone is inscribed with the following:

**ORA PRO NOBIS**

**Basil is buried in Bailleul Communal Cemetery Extension (Nord).**

REFERENCES

1. Cave. N. *Hill 60 Ypres.* Pub: Pen and Sword, 1997.

2. Wyrell, E. *The Fiftieth Division, 1914-1919.*
Pub: 1939, reprinted Naval and Military Press 2002.

3. WO/95/2828. *War Diary, 1/4th Battalion Northumberland Fusiliers.*

4. Buckley, F. Capt. *Q. 6. A. and Other Places.*
Pub: Spottiswoode and Ballentyne 1920.

5. WO/95/2840. *War Diary, 1/8th Battalion Durham Light Infantry.*

6. AWM4 23/56/8. *War Diary, 39th Battalion Australian Infantry December 1916.*

# CHAPTER NINE

# BATTLE OF THE SOMME

*They left their homes in perfect health,*
*They looked so strong and brave;*
*And side by side they fought,*
*Their country's flag to save.*

For Pte Fred Mead and Cpl Henry Mead (died 15 and 22 September 1916)

## 1 JULY - 18 NOVEMBER 1916

The *Battle of the Somme* was the British Army's major offensive on the Western Front in 1916. General Rawlinson's Fourth Army, which included thousands of confident citizen volunteers (Pals Battalions), was entrusted with the task. The main line for the attack ran for 25,000 yards from Serre in the north to Maricourt in the south. A diversionary attack was to take place at Gommecourt, a further two miles to the north. South of the British attack the French mounted a limited offensive using only three divisions. The focus for the French was the defence of Verdun. An intense artillery barrage of the German positions began a week before the attack, an overture that sustained its crescendo as a number of mines were exploded under the German Line [1,2,3].

## FIRST DAY OF THE SOMME: 1 JULY 1916

At 7.30am on a clear Saturday morning the confident British infantry emerged from their positions and advanced, as ordered, at a slow, steady pace across No Man's Land. They were met with intense machine gun and rifle fire from the German defenders. This, in tandem with accurate artillery fire, inflicted enormous casualties on the unprotected waves of advancing infantry. Through extraordinary gallantry, immeasurable suffering and a notoriously high number of casualties, the British broke the German Line at a number of points, some of which were lost again in the bloody ebb and flow of the day, although permanent gains were achieved by the end of the day along the southern end of the battlefield with the capture of Montauban and Mametz [4].

Explosion of the Hawthorn Ridge mine
7:20am, 1 July 1916

## BEAUMONT HAMEL, 'Y' RAVINE AND HAWTHORN RIDGE

The Scottish Borderers were part of 87 Brigade (29th Division). The Division's aim for the day was to capture the German strongpoint of 'Y Ravine'. The initial attack was carried out by the 1st Inniskilling Fusiliers and by the 2nd South Wales Borderers. Both battalions suffered heavy casualties. The two support battalions, the 1st King's Own Scottish Borderers and the 1st Border Regiment fared no better as they entered No Man's Land, which was tragic because their involvement was initiated by a misinterpretation of a flare signal: a German white artillery flare was mistaken for a similar British signal that the German line had been breached [5].

**Private Roger Hall, aged 33**
**1st Battalion King's Own Scottish Borderers**
**Died 1 July 1916**

Roger was born in Acomb, the son of Robert and Ann Hall of Ivy Cottage, Acomb. The 1901 census shows Roger living with his parents and working as a miner, below ground. However, at the time of enlisting, Roger lived at Chichester Road, South Shields and was employed by the South Shields Gas Company. Roger enlisted as a volunteer in North Shields on 6 June 1915. After basic training Roger arrived on the island of Imbros in late September 1915, and joined his battalion on Gallipoli as part of a new draft of 400 men in early October 1915. He would serve on the peninsula until the withdrawal of Allied forces during the night of 8/9 January 1916. The battalion arrived in France on 18 March 1916.

**Roger is buried in Ancre British Cemetery, Beaumont Hamel.**

## SCHWARBEN REDOUBT, ST PIERRE DIVION AND BEAUCOURT STATION

The 11th Inniskilling Fusiliers (IF) was part of the 109th Brigade (36th Division). The Ulster Division's task for 1 July was the capture of the

Schwaben Redoubt (a system of trenches and deep underground bunkers) situated on the crest of the Thiepval Spur. The redoubt was part of complex, interconnected defences which provided a network of enfilading fields of fire; these were a daunting and dangerous obstacle for the attacking troops of the Ulster Division. The 109th Brigade's attacks began at 7.30am with the 9th and 10th Inniskilling Fusiliers dashing forward under the cover of a dense smoke screen from their position in Thiepval Woods. They were easily able to overrun the German First and Support trenches. Although by now they had taken a significant number of casualties, they managed to enter the southern end of the redoubt. Following in their wake, the 11th Inniskilling Fusiliers and 12th Irish Rifles were immediately caught in machine gun fire from the German position known as 'the crucifix': "The dead and wounded lay thick in No Man's Land". By early evening the remnants of the 109th Brigade had exhausted their supply of ammunition and bombs and so were forced to give up the ground that had cost them so dearly. They retreated to the German First Line, taken earlier in the day [6,7].

**Private Thomas Alsopp Rutherford, aged 22**
**11th (Service) Battalion Royal Inniskilling Fusiliers**
**Died 1 July 1916**

Thomas was born in Great Lumley, County Durham. He was the second son of John and Phyllis Rutherford of West View, Acomb. Before he moved with his parents to Acomb in 1913 he was employed as an electrical engineer at his local coal mine. At Acomb he was employed at Black Pastures Quarry. He was also a long serving member of the Independent Order of Rechabites, who had a 'tent' in West Acomb. He enlisted as a volunteer in Newcastle in December 1914 and was sent to Ireland for his basic training. He arrived in France in early October 1915. The 11th Inniskilling Fusiliers had been on the Somme since February 1915.

**Thomas is buried in Connaught Cemetery, Thiepval.**

The Independent Order of Rechabites was a Friendly Society founded in England in 1835 as part of the temperance movement to promote total abstinence from alcohol. It gradually transformed into a financial institution which still exists, and still promotes abstinence. From the late 18th century a number of Friendly Societies had been set up to help working class people with such things as health insurance, death benefits, etc. Generally these held their meetings in public houses. In the 1830s a group of Methodists in Manchester became concerned that by encouraging working men to attend public houses to pay their friendly society dues, the societies were harming the men's health, their financial situation and threatening their moral welfare. To counter this they set up a new Friendly Society called the Independent Order of Rechabites, named after the nomadic, abstemious Rechabites of the Old Testament.

A branch may be known as a 'Tent', since the biblical Rechabites lived exclusively in tents. Before one could join the Rechabites and benefit from their insurance and saving scheme, a document had to be signed swearing that the proposed member and his family would not drink any alcohol. This document was known as The Pledge and represented a solemn promise. The initials "IOR" on a tombstone may indicate that the deceased was a member of the organisation.

## LA BOISSELLE

The 34th Division comprising the 101st, 102nd (Tyneside Scottish), 20th, 21st 22nd and 23rd Battalions Northumberland Fusiliers (NF)) and 103rd (Tyneside Irish), 24th, 25th, 26th and 27th Battalions Northumberland

Fusiliers (NF) Brigade where allotted the sector from Mash Valley, north of the Albert to Bapaume road to 'Sausage Valley', one mile south of the road. The Divisional commander (Major-General Ingouville-Williams, known to his men as 'Inky Bill') decided to use all his battalions in this attack, leaving no reserves. The division's twelve battalions formed up as four attacking columns moving forward as three distinct waves. The NF (Tyneside Scottish) formed the first two waves immediately north and south of the road. The four battalions of the NF (Tyneside Irish) formed up as the third wave for all four columns.

North of the Albert-Bapaume road the column was headed by the 20th NF followed by the 23rd NF (both Scottish) and then by the 25th NF (Irish). To the immediate south of the road the attack was led by 21st NF followed by the 22nd NF (both Scottish) and followed by the 26th NF (Irish). Units of the 101st Brigade formed the first two waves of the two columns to the south, followed in the third wave by 24th NF and 27th NF (both Irish).

The attack in this area began at 7.30am, preceded at 7.28am by the explosions of mines at 'Y' Sap and, famously, at Lochnagar, north and south of the road [8,9,10,11,12,13,14,15].

Cecil Lewis, then an officer in the Royal Flying Corps, witnessed the explosion of the mine on 1st July from his aircraft high above La Boisselle:

> "The whole earth heaved and flared, a tremendous and magnificent column rose up into the sky. There was an ear-splitting roar, drowning all the guns, flinging the machine sideways in the repercussing air. The earth column rose higher and higher to almost 4,000 feet."

To the north, where the distance to the German Front Line was 800 yards, the advancing lines of the 20th and 23rd NF were practically wiped out.

**Private James Ormiston Elliott, aged 22**
**20th (Service) Battalion (Tyneside Scottish)**
**Northumberland Fusiliers**
**Died 1 July 1916**

James was the eldest son of John and Barbara Elliott of Far Colliery, Plashetts. Like his father, James worked at Plashetts Colliery. He volunteered to join up in November of 1914 and after a short period of training embarked for France. His parents, as others, had to wait until the middle of November 1916 before receiving official notification that their son had been killed on 1 July.

**James is buried in Orvilliers Military Cemetery.**

South of the road, where No Man's Land was narrower and the mine at Lochnagar shook not only the landscape but also German morale, the 21st and 22nd NF fared slightly better reaching the German second line of defence.

**Private David Steele, aged 19**
**22nd (Service) Battalion (Tyneside Scottish)**
**Northumberland Fusiliers**
**Died 1 July 1916**

David was born in Canonbie, Dumfriesshire, the second son of William and Bridget Steele. Before volunteering to join the Colours in January 1915, David, like the rest of the working family, worked underground at Plashetts Colliery. He was the second son from the Steele family to die

in France. His elder brother Frank, a Guardsman, was killed during the *Battle of Loos* in 1915 (see page 76). In their book on the Tyneside Scottish, Stewart and Sheen list David's rank as 'Piper'.

**David is commemorated on the Thiepval Memorial to the missing.**

**Private George Smith, aged 29**
**22nd (Service) Battalion (Tyneside Scottish)**
**Northumberland Fusiliers**
**Died 1 July 1916**

George was born in Hexham, the fourth child of John and Cassey Smith. The 1891 census reports that they lived in Back Street, Hexham. After the death of his father, John, aged 13, worked as an apprenticed painter. Later he worked as a butcher for Mr John Dodd of Hexham. Before he volunteered to join the Colours, George had worked for over six years as a groom at Chipchase Castle. At the time of his death his mother lived at Whorlton, near Newcastle. His older brother, Harry, was undergoing military training in Canada.

**George is commemorated on the Thiepval Memorial to the missing.**

The Tyneside Irish Battalions fared no better, each of the four battalions recording between 140 to 150 men killed and over 350 wounded.

**Lance Corporal John Hymers, aged 31**
**23rd (Service) Battalion (Tyneside Irish)**
**Northumberland Fusiliers**
**Died 1 July 1916**

John was born in Langholm, Scotland, the son of Robert and Frances Hymers of Tile Row, Plashetts. Like the rest of his family he worked in Plashetts Colliery. Initially, at the age of fifteen, he worked above ground in the coal washery, but by twenty five he was working underground as a hewer along side five of his eight brothers.

His brother George had been killed in the previous November, (see page 32). The North Tyne Magazine of June 1915 records that from the Hymers family, the father and three sons were serving in the forces.

**John is commemorated on the**
**Thiepval Memorial to the missing.**

**Private Matthew Robson, aged 20**
**24th (Service) Battalion (Tyneside Irish)**
**Northumberland Fusiliers**
**Died 1 July 1916**

Matthew was born in Elsdon, the son of Roger and Jane Robson of Oakenshawburn, Plashetts, where his father and some of his older brothers worked as shepherds. The 1911 census shows that at fourteen Matthew was still attending school.

**Matthew is commemorated on the**
**Thiepval Memorial to the missing.**

**Private Robert Andrew Bonas, aged 31**
**24th (Service) Battalion (Tyneside Irish)**
**Northumberland Fusiliers**
**Died 1 July 1916**

Robert was born in Islington, London. At the outbreak of war he was a married man, and on his death Mary, his wife, was left to care for their five children. Before enlisting Robert, who was of Greek descent, was living in Brookside Place in Bellingham and working at Carriteth Colliery. It is known that he had a beautiful, high tenor voice of great sweetness which he used willingly in aid of charity. Robert volunteered to join the army in January 1915, opting to train as a bomber. He was reported missing after participating in a bombing attack on the German Front Line. His brother Alexander (also with the Tyneside Irish) made an exhaustive search but sadly could find no trace of his brother's body.

In a letter to his widow, one of Robert's officers spoke very highly of her husband's courage and devotion to duty:

> "In his high courage and noble patriotism
> he has set us all a great example."

**Robert is commemorated on the**
**Thiepval Memorial to the missing.**

The 2nd Battalion Yorkshire Regiment (YR) as part of 21st Brigade (30th Division) was in action on the southernmost sector of the British assault on the 1st Day of the Somme. The 21st Brigade was involved in successfully breaking through the German lines and the subsequent capture of the fortified village of Montauban. The attacking troops came under very accurate artillery fire, but it bore no resemblance to the deadly deluge faced by men further to the north.

During the evening of 4 July the YR was relieved and spent the next three days resting and cleaning their gear after the exertions of the previous few days. However, on 7 July the battalion moved back in heavy rain to the Front, in preparation for an attack scheduled to capture the southern portion of Trones Wood on 8 July. Before the start of the attack, the YR came under severe shell fire which caused a number of deaths and injuries. As they approached Trones Wood the Germans laid down very intense and accurate machine gun fire from the edge of the wood. The Battalion History records, "the front line was practically hit to a man". Eventually they were forced to withdraw to Bernafay Wood, but here they came under a heavy high calibre bombardment, which caused numerous casualties. The bill for 8 July was 3 officers killed and 4 wounded; other ranks 19 killed, 116 wounded and 17 missing, many of the missing would be confirmed as killed in the days to follow [16].

**Lance Corporal William Stephen Hepburn, aged 23**
**2nd Battalion Yorkshire Regiment**
**Died 8 July 1916**

William was born in Monkton, Durham, the son of William and Fiona Hepburn. The 1911 census shows that Stephen was working as an under gardener for Charles Duncombe Shafto at South Bailey, Durham. Although no details of his connection to Wall are known, he is mentioned in the Wall, Bingfield and Hallington 'Roll of Honour' published in the Parish Magazine for January 1915. It is highly likely that William volunteered for army service not long after the beginning of hostilities. He enlisted in

Sunderland and arrived in France in early October 1915. The Wall parish magazine for September 1916 recorded his death on 8 July 1916.

**William is commemorated on the Thiepval Memorial to the missing.**

## BATTLE OF BAZENTIN RIDGE 14 – 17 JULY 1916

On 11 July the 12th Northumberland Fusiliers (NF) received a draft of 142 other ranks from the 15th Reserve Battalion and moved from Meaulte to Mametz Wood to relieve the positions of the 115th Infantry brigade which were within the wood during 11/12 July. During this operation the enemy shelled heavily the area between Fricourt and Mametz Wood, resulting in a large number of casualties during the relief and during the digging in. On 12 July orders were issued to clear the wood as far north as possible which was achieved by the battalion; the Germans in this sector offered only half-hearted resistance. However, the enemy constantly bombarded the wood with "great violence", plastering the terrain with high explosive, shrapnel and gas shells causing an ever increasing list of casualties. By midnight the list was estimated to be one officer wounded and over 80 other ranks killed or wounded. The battalion stayed in the Line until 17 July, during which they were involved in the capture of Bazentin-Le-Petit Wood [17].

**Private Richard James Grossick, aged 20**
**12th (Service) Battalion Northumberland Fusiliers**
**Died 12 July 1916**

Richard was born in Simonburn, one of twins born to James and Mary Grossick of Nunwick, Humshaugh. The 1911 census shows that Richard at fourteen was working as a groom at Nunwick Hall. There is a curious anomaly in the circumstances surrounding the news of Richard's death. The Hexham Herald of 30 June 1917 published the following under the by-line: "Nunwick Parents' Anxious Time"

> "Now after experiencing nearly twelve months of anxiety, they have received official notification that the gallant young fellow (son) is presumed to have been killed in action."

This report implies that even a year later, Richard's body had not been found, but the CWGS states that his date of death was 12 July 1916, and that he was buried along with his comrades.

**Richard was buried at Flatiron Copse Cemetery, Mametz.**

## BATTLE OF DELVILLE WOOD
## 15 JULY – 3 SEPTEMBER 1917

The 50th Brigade Royal Field Artillery (RFA) was attached to the 15th (Scottish) Division from its inception in September 1914. Although the division was not involved in the first day of fighting on the Somme, they saw action on July 3 during the capture of Bernafay Wood near Montauban. Although the wood had been easily taken, it proved costly to hold. After action to capture Trones Wood, on the 14 July the battalion pushed forward in an attempt to take the village of Longueval and beyond.

The initial attack was carried out by 27th Brigade on the left and by 26th Brigade on the right, supported by the Divisional Artillery, 50 Brigade RFA. They fired a programme of eight separate barrages, using high explosive shells. The infantry was supported throughout their advance by the shelling of each successive portion of the enemy's Line just in front

The brigade was the basic tactical unit of the field artillery of the British army in the Great War. In 1916, Divisional Artillery would be made up of brigades of the Royal Field Artillery. Each infantry division would be supported by four brigades. It was composed of a brigade headquarters and four batteries of guns or howitzers. These would be designated A, B, C and D. A battery would consist of six of either 18-lbr field guns or 4.5in howitzers. Each of the brigades would be supported by its own ammunition column. One Divisional Artillery was described by its chaplain as consisting of 3,000 men dispersed over 40 locations, from the trench mortars at the extreme front to the ammunition column eight miles to the rear. Each battery had its gunners and drivers living in separate locations, the drivers holding the horses in the rear.

of the oncoming troops. As a preliminary to the attack the supporting artillery provided a resounding cacophany allowing the infantry to move undetected into No Man's Land near to the German Front Line. By the end of the day the Germans still held part of Longueval and Waterlot Farm. Delville Wood still needed to be taken. The next day the majority of Delville Wood was taken after heavy fighting. By 9.00am on 17 July, Waterlot Farm was taken after a preliminary artillery bombardment.

During the night of 17/18 July the Battalion History records that, "during the hours of darkness, in addition to their usual artillery fire, the Germans poured thousands of gas shells into our artillery positions and back areas. At the same time the Germans counter-attacked from the north-west, towards Delville Wood, penetrating the British line to some depth before being driven back" [18,19].

**Gunner George William Crozer, aged 24**
**'B' Battery 50th Brigade Royal field Artillery**
**Died 18 July 1916**

George was born at Seaton Hirst, Ashington, the eldest son of Robert and Jane Crozer. The available censuses show that the Crozer family were farm labourers who appeared to lead a nomadic existence, moving from farm to farm. The 1911 census shows that they were living at Norwoods Farm, Acklington and after the war were living at Otterburn. The North Tyne Magazine for September 1916 reports that the Crozer family were resident in Chollerton at the start of the war and that another of their sons was serving with the army overseas.

George volunteered to join the forces in Newcastle and arrived in France in May 1915 as part of the 9th (Scottish) Division. In September the men of 9th division and its artillery would be blooded at the *Battle of Loos,* where they eventually liberated the town of Loos.

**George is commemorated on the Menin Gate Memorial to the missing, Ypres.**

Although this appears slightly illogical, as he died fighting on the Somme, there are a number of similar cases.

## BATTLE OF FLERS-COURCELLETTE 15 – 22 SEPTEMBER

This major attack was launched on 15 September 1916 across an eight-mile Front using twelve infantry divisions along with a small number of tanks and extensive artillery support. The Front stretched from south of the village of Courcellete, west of Albert-Baupame road, eastwards to the south of Combles.

This date is famous for the introduction of the tank to warfare, although this was a very primitive beast compared to those that we know today. By the day of the attack, Britain had built forty-nine tanks, but only fifteen

managed to roll into action, at a speed of 1mph. Apart from the dangers of the raging battle, the tank crew faced extreme heat and high carbon-monoxide levels, together with metal splinters erupting from the tanks' armour, which was impervious to small arms and machine gun fire but which was susceptible to artillery shells. However, the tank was effective at crushing barbed wire and giving supporting fire to infantry. Further, on this first day their sinister appearance and size made them an effective psychological weapon [20,21,22,23,24,25].

In preparation for the battle, the artillery fired over 800,000 shells, a greater intensity than that fired on 1 July, but fewer than at some of the other battles during the Somme campaign.

A local Humshaugh lad with the 3rd Battalion Coldstream Guards wrote to his father whilst in hospital in Worcester:

> "I got wounded in the first advance. We cleared the first line of German trenches, and were making for the second when I got a piece of shrapnel through my left arm. They gave us hell till we got

into their trenches: then up went their hands, and 'mercy kamarades' was shouted on all sides. None of us, however, were in the humour to show much mercy, and we let into them right and left … The first trench was heaped with dead. We had two new 'caterpillars' [i.e. tanks]."

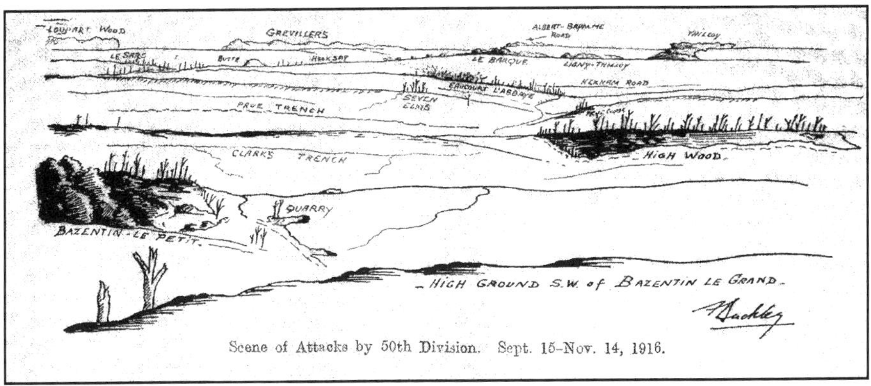

Scene of Attacks by 50th Division. Sept. 15–Nov. 14, 1916.

Along this eight-mile Front the 50th Division were to be found to the west of High Wood. Until September 1916 this Division had not been involved in the momentous struggles on the Somme. This was to change dramatically. By September 9 the 1/4th Battalion Northumberland Fusiliers (149th Brigade) was deployed on the Front Line between the village of Martinpuich and High Wood.

On 12 September the preliminary bombardment began in preparation for the attack on 15 September. By Thursday 14, the attacking units had taken up their positions as shown in the map. The initial attack on the 149th Brigade front was to be undertaken by the 1/7th Northumberland Fusiliers on the left with the 1/4th Northumberland Fusiliers (NF) on the right, nearest to High Wood. From left to right the company designation was 'D', 'B', 'A' and 'C'. Three objectives had been assigned to the 50th Division sector. First was the capture of Hook Trench which ran westwards from High Wood. Second was an advance of a further 500 yards and the capture of Martin Trench, the Bow and part of the Starfish Line. Third was the capture of Prue Trench and the capture of a further section of the Starfish Line. The attacking front was initially 1000 yards wide increasing to 1800 yards as the successive objectives were achieved.

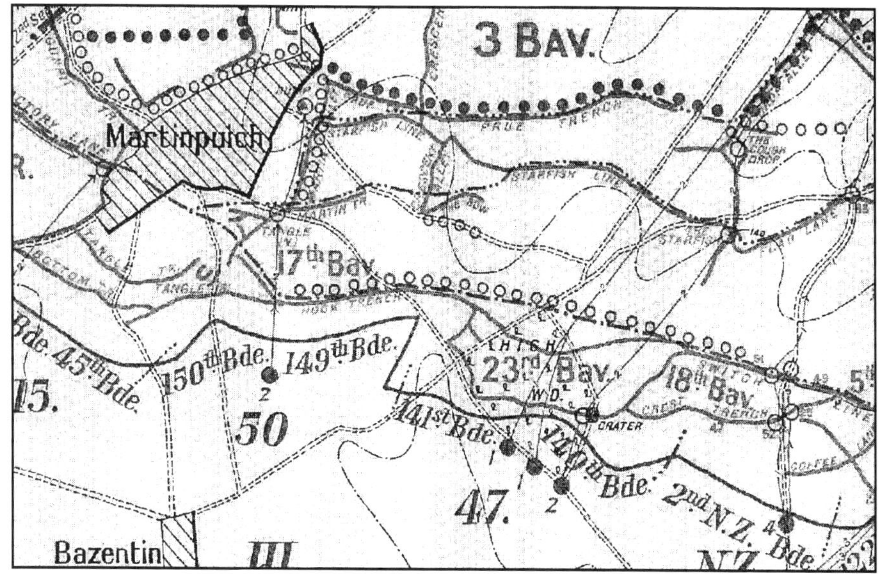


The position of the 50th Battalion on the morning of 15 September 1916

The position of the 1/4th NF was ominous. Earlier fighting had left a dogleg in the Front, thus their position was 300 yards ahead of the 47th Division position (to the east). If for any reason the 47th Division's attack was held up, then the attacking Fusiliers would be exposed to a murderous enfilade fire from the corner of High Wood (Bois de Fourneaux). This fire would rake the ground between the wood and Martinpuich. Since the middle of July repeated unsuccessful attacks had been carried out against the nemesis called High Wood.

The assault started at 6.20am; no tanks were available on the 149th Brigade's

Front. At 7am it was recorded that 'B' company had taken Hook Trench with very little opposition and had established contact with 'D' company on its left flank. Shortly afterwards they came under intense machine gun and rifle fire from High Wood.

At 7.27am the 1/4th NF began their advance towards their second objective. At the same time, news was received that 47th Division's attack on High Wood had met with severe opposition and had stalled. In spite of this, 1/4th NF captured their second objective and entered the Starfish Line.

The failure of 47th Division's attack left the Northumberlands' right flank murderously exposed to enemy fire, which exacted heavy casualties. This forced a retreat to Hook Trench, which was also in the line of fire from High Wood.

During the morning, companies from the 1/5th and 1/6th NF were moved forward to support the attack and by noon it was reported that the Martin Trench had been recaptured, but a determined counterattack forced the 1/4th to retreat to Hook Trench. High Wood was captured during the early afternoon. Fighting continued next day with all elements of 50th Division involved and the eventual capture by the 1/4th of both the second and third objectives.

On 15 September the 1/4th Northumberland Fusiliers attacked with 22 officers and 695 men. A roll call three days later recorded that 10 officers and 110 men had been killed, 7 officers and 229 men had been wounded and 143 men were classed as missing.

Later records would confirm a monstrous butcher's bill for this attack: 180 fusiliers were killed during the foray and many more would die of their wounds in the days to come.

The Hexham Herald fittingly reported of one of the dead:

> "... B Company of the 1/4th Northumberland Fusiliers and fell on September 15 (1916), that sad and memorable day when our brave troops achieved such notable success, no small part of which was earned by our own lads."

Although *Flers-Courcellette* was regarded by High Command as a triumph, so great was the death toll during this bloody advance that there are few memorials in Northumberland which do not commemorate a soldier who fell during this momentous battle.

**Serjeant John William Cocker, aged 35**
**1/4th Battalion Northumberland Fusiliers**
**Died 15 September 1916**

John was born in Scotland and was the youngest son of James Cocker, of Chesters Gardens, Humshaugh. Like his father he worked in the gardens at Chesters. John, an unmarried man, joined the forces with his brother at the outbreak of hostilities and was sent to France in April 1915. The Hexham Herald reported that he had been wounded during the attack of 26 April1915 (see page 35). It is reported that John was shot through the heart during the advance on 15 September.

**John is buried at Delville Wood Cemetery, Longueval.**

**Serjeant James Hamilton, aged 39**
**1/4th Battalion Northumberland Fusiliers**
**Died 15 September 1916**

James was born in West Linton, Peebleshire, the son of George and Marion Hamilton. He was married in 1904 to Elizabeth Jessie (née Hardy) and was the father of at least four children, a son and three daughters, who lived in West Woodburn. Before he volunteered for service in France, he worked as a freestone quarryman. The North Tyne Magazine for October 1916 reported James' death, stating that he was an old soldier who re-enlisted at a recruiting meeting held at West Woodburn on 3 July 1915; consequently he was quickly promoted to Serjeant. James arrived in France in November 1915.

**James is commemorated on the Thiepval Memorial to the missing.**

**Corporal Robert Armstrong, aged 22**
**1/4th Battalion Northumberland Fusiliers**
**Died 15 September 1916**

Robert was born in Simonburn, the second son of Robert and Elizabeth Armstrong, formerly of Park End, who had a family of five daughters and two sons. At the time of his death his parents were living at The Office, Whitfield. Robert attended the Presbyterian Church in Wark where he won book prizes for regular attendance. At Christmas 1907, whilst still at school, he was awarded a prize for Religious Knowledge. The 1911 census shows that Robert was working as a domestic gardener and the family lived at Through Gates, Wark. When he enlisted in the army with his brother, George, in October 1914, he was working for Mr Pumphrey of Hindley Hall, near Stocksfield.

Robert arrived in France in April 1915 (see page 35). In June 1915 it was reported that he had suffered a minor wound. According to the local newspaper, Robert was on home leave in January 1916 and was wounded again in April 1916, only to be killed in September.

**Robert is commemorated on the Thiepval Memorial to the missing.**

IN LOVING MEMORY OF

ROBERT,

SECOND AND DEARLY BELOVED SON OF ROBERT AND ELIZABETH ARMSTRONG, THE OFFICE, WHITFIELD, LATE OF PARK END, WARK-ON-TYNE,

CORPL. 4TH N.F.,

Who was killed in the battle of the Somme, in France, on 15th September, 1916.

BORN 7TH MARCH, 1894; IN HIS 23RD YEAR.

"Greater Love hath no man than this: That a man lay down his life for his friends."

"Till the day breaks and the shadows flee away."

Official card sent from Robert's battalion to his parents.

**Lance-Corporal Matthew Martinson, aged 23**
**1/4th Battalion Northumberland Fusiliers**
**Died 15 September 1916**

Matthew was born in Capheaton, the son of Charlton and Sarah Jane Martinson of the Post Office, Bellingham. Before enlisting he had been employed as an auxiliary postman, but by the time of voluntarily enlisting on 3 September 1915, he was employed as a groom by Mr Carter of The Glen, Slaley.

He attended the United Methodist Church where he was a Sunday School teacher. He was also the secretary of the Christian Endeavour and sang in the church choir at Slaley. In his leisure time he played football, cricket and billiards as member of the Bellingham Mechanics' Institute. In 1912, Matthew won a gold medal for billiards, and was the proud holder of a silver cup in that sport.

Matthew travelled out to France with the first contingent of the Northumberland Territorials and was wounded at Ypres on 26 April (see page 35), returning to his battalion late in 1915. In June 1916 he was on home leave.

His parents received a letter from Major Robinson, his company commander, who wrote that he "knew him well and he was a good soldier". Just before Matthew left to go back to the Front after his home leave, he left the following words with his parents; a premonition of forthcoming events?

"He died that all he loved might live,
And man his mission might achieve;
He died for those he held most dear,
He died to save the world from fear.
For Faith and Liberty and Truth.

He offered up his stalwart youth:
He fell in strife that peace may reign
Throughout the tortured world again,
And we who loved him should rejoice
Though never more we hear his voice,
That he has joined the glorious land
Who perished for the Motherland
He died, if it were death to give
His life that all he loved might live."

**Matthew is commemorated on the Thiepval Memorial to the missing**

**Lance-Corporal Edwin Armstrong, aged 21**
**1/4th Battalion Northumberland Fusiliers**
**Died 15 September 1916**

Edwin was the son of Thomas and Mary Ann Armstrong of Armstrong Square, Bellingham. The 1911 census shows that Edwin aged 15 was working for Mr Robert Thompson of Wood Park, Bellingham, as a general farm servant. However, before he volunteered to join the forces in September 1914, Edwin was working at Hareshawhead Colliery. Edwin was one of four brothers who were serving in the forces.

His brother Robert, who was in the same battalion as Edwin, was also wounded on 15 September. At the time of Edwin's death, another brother, John Ridley, was in the Northumberland Fusiliers and, after recuperating from being wounded, he served with the Royal Engineers. George, the eldest brother, was under training with the Northumberland Fusiliers at Catterick Camp. About a month before the end of the war George was killed, (see page 290). In correspondence with Edwin's parents 2nd Lieutenant J W Robinson wrote:

> "It may be of some consolation to you to know that he died a soldier's death in a charge which we will remember for ever."

**Edwin is commemorated on the Thiepval Memorial to the missing.**

**Private Frederick George Beattie, aged 23**
**1/4th Battalion Northumberland Fusiliers**
**Died 15 September 1916**

Frederick was born at Simonburn, the son of William and Thomasina Beattie of Simonburn. Before enlisting he was employed, like his father, as a joiner on the Simonburn Estate. The following is found on his headstone:

**FROM DEATH UNTO LIFE**

**Frederick is buried in Adanac Military Cemetery.**

**Private George Davidson, aged 19**
**1/4th Battalion Northumberland Fusiliers**
**Died 15 September 1916**

George was born in Morpeth, the son of Thomas and Ursula Davidson. The 1911 census shows the family living near Amble and the father and his eldest brother working in the local mines. It is likely that at the onset of hostilities the Davidsons were living and working in the Falstone area, probably at Stannersburn. Ursula Davidson died during the spring of 1917. At the time of George's death his older brother James was serving with the Royal Naval Division in France. James had been wounded twice whilst serving in the Dardenelles.

**George is commemorated on the**
**Thiepval Memorial to the missing.**

**Private Archibald Rutherford, aged 23**
**1/4th Battalion Northumberland Fusiliers**
**Died 15 September 1916**

Archibald was born in Bellingham in 1893. The 1901 census shows he was living with his grandparents, Archibald and Annie, in Percy Street. Before enlisting on 2 September 1914, he was employed at Messrs Armstrong Whitworth's steel proofing grounds. He was an enthusiastic footballer who played in goal. He joined up on 2 September 1914 and saw action on 26 April 1915. Archibald was wounded during this attack, (see page 35). His mother (Mrs Mason) was sent a letter of condolences from Lieutenant J H Long:

"Your son was killed on 15 September, in an attack, the success of which has considerably enhanced the reputation of the battalion, and I trust it will be of some consolation to you to know that only such brave lads could have made success possible ..."

**Archibald is buried in Adanac Military Cemetery.**

**Private Thomas William Nevin, aged 26**
**1/4th Battalion Northumberland Fusiliers**
**Died 15 September 1916**

Thomas was born in Whitfield, the son of Thomas William and Hannah Nevin of Colwell. Before enlisting in September 1914, he worked as a labourer at Knowsgate Quarry. After having been stationed at Blyth, Hexham and Ripon he went out to France in June 1915 as part of a draft of replacements.

Captain Hope Wallace wrote to Mrs Nevin confirming that her son had been killed:

"One of our stretcher bearers saw him on that day (15 September 1916) lying on the parapet of the German trench. He was shot in the head, and death would have come upon him instantaneously. He was lying on his face as he fell facing the enemy."

Although Thomas's body was recognised and his death reported, during the course of the war it was either buried without record or lost into the battlefield.

**Thomas is commemorated on the**
**Thiepval Memorial to the missing.**

**Private Thomas Welsh, aged 22**
**1/4th Battalion Northumberland Fusiliers**
**Died 15 September 1916**

Thomas was born in Langholm, Dumfriesshire, the son of Thomas and Jane Welsh of Kemera Bank, Langholm. He went to France with the first draft of the Territorials and fought at the Battle of St Julien in April 1915 (see pages 35). The North Tyne Magazine for June 1915 reports that Thomas Welsh of Tile Row had been wounded in the shoulder. As his sacrifice is commemorated on the Plashetts Memorial it is highly likely that he worked at Plashetts Colliery.

**Thomas is commemorated on the Thiepval Memorial to the missing.**

**Private John Dodd, aged 31**
**1/4th Battalion Northumberland Fusiliers**
**Died 15 September 1916**

John was born in Chollerton and was the eldest son of John and Ann Dodd of Chapel Row, Plashetts. The 1901 census shows that the family were living in Barrasford and John, aged fifteen, and his father were working at the local quarry. Later the family moved to Plashetts where the father and John's younger brothers worked in the coal mine. John, however, remained in Barrasford, lodging with George Pearson and his wife, continuing to work at the local quarry. He joined the Northumberland Fusiliers in December 1915 and went out to France on the last day of March. He was assigned as one of the battalion's bombers. Thomas, one of his younger brothers, was serving with the same battalion, but at the time of the attack he was in hospital suffering from trench fever. Second Lieutenant J H Long (officer commanding the bombers), wrote to his parents:

> "I trust it will be some consolation to you to know that had it not been for such brave lads the success which attended the battalion could not have been possible … your son did much excellent work and I am only too sorry to lose him."

**John is buried in Adanac Military Cemetery**

**Private Alfred (Fred) Armstrong Dodd, aged 22**
**1/4th Battalion Northumberland Fusiliers**
**Died 15 September 1916**

Fred was the youngest son of Robert and Dorothy Dodd of Swinburn Park Cottage, Barrasford. Before enlisting in November 1914, he worked at Knowsgate Quarry. The Dodd family had two further sons serving with the forces in France, one of whom, Albert, was killed in August 1918 (see page 269), while serving with the Australians.

Fred was posted to France in April 1915, (see page 35). He was wounded in October 1915 and spent time at home during the early months of 1916. The chaplain wrote to his parents:

> "… they feel the poorer by the passing of a good friend and a true soldier."

His parents wrote the following words of tribute for Fred:

Could we but see his smiling face,
As he bade his last good-bye,
And left his home forever,

In a foreign land to die.
Beloved in life, lamented in death.

**Fred is commemorated on the Thiepval Memorial to the missing.**

**Private Edward (Tailford) Charlton, aged 31**
**1/4th Battalion Northumberland Fusiliers**
**Died 15 September 1916**

Edward was a married man who lived at The Square, Humshaugh. The Hexham Courant reports that he was formerly known as Edward Tailford. An obituary appearing in the Hexham Herald (28 October 1916) further confirms this duality of names. The censuses for 1901 and 1911 show him living with his grandmother, Mary Tailford, which helps to explain his other name.

Before enlisting in November 1915, he was employed as an assistant gardener at Haughton Castle, although he had worked as a labourer in the local quarry. He was a keen angler, a member of the Humshaugh Angling Association and spent a lot of his free time at the river. He was posted to France in March 1916.

**Edward is commemorated on the Thiepval Memorial to the missing.**

It seems to me that the Edward *Tailford* who is commemorated on the St Peter's Church plaque at Humshaugh and on the Humshaugh memorial obelisk, and Edward *Charlton* who was on the memorial plaque at the Methodist Church, now closed, (and the plaque rededicated, also in St Peter's) were the same person.

**Private Robert Armstrong Smith, aged 30**
**1/4th Battalion Northumberland Fusiliers**
**Died 15 September 1916**

Robert was born in Wark, the son of John and Dorothy Smith of Wark. The 1911 census reports that Robert was working as a groom and living with his married sister, Mary Carr, in Wark. At the outset of war he was living in Corbridge and immediately volunteered to join the local Territorial Battalion. He saw his first action with the Fusiliers in late April 1915, (see page 35).

**Robert is commemorated on the Thiepval Memorial to the missing.**

**Private Frederick James Mead, aged 26**
**1/4th Battalion Northumberland Fusiliers**
**Died 15 September 1916**

Frederick was the son of Henry and Jane Mead of Fern Hill, Hexham. He was a single man and worked on Mr Herdman's farm on Acomb Fell. He went out to France with the first batch of Hexham Territorials in April 1915, (see page 35). Two other brothers were also serving at the Front. Frederick's brother, Henry, was with the same battalion and died a week later (see below). His other brother, Charles, was serving with the Argyle and Sutherland Highlanders and was also wounded during this action.

**Frederick is commemorated on the Thiepval Memorial to the missing.**

**Corporal Henry John Mead, aged 24**
**1/4th Battalion Northumberland Fusiliers**
**Died 22 September 1916**

Henry was the son of Henry and Jane Mead of Fern Hill, Hexham. He was a single man who had worked for Captain James Cuthbert as a groom (see page 75) and at the start of the war was employed by Mr Straker of Stagshaw in a similar capacity. Before going to France he was attached to the transport section of the battalion. He was the brother of Frederick (died 15 September 1916, see immediately above) and Charles Mead, who was serving with the. Argyll and Sutherland Highlanders.

**Henry is commemorated on the**
**Thiepval Memorial to the missing.**

At 8.25am, as news of the failure of troops from the 47th Division to penetrate their objective of High Wood became known, two companies from the 1/5th Northumberland Fusiliers were ordered forward to help the 1/4th NF maintain their forward momentum. As the apocalyptic day progressed, further companies of the 1/5th NF were committed to the attack. By mid morning one of these companies was involved in bombing around Hook Trench to its right and attempted to make contact with Bethel Sap [26].

**Private William Errington, aged 22**
**1/5th Battalion Northumberland Fusiliers**
**Died 15 September 1916**

William was born in Acomb, the eldest son of William and Elizabeth Errington. The Errington family lived in Acomb for a number of years before moving near to Brampton in Cumbria. The 1911 census shows William living and working as a cowman at West Deanraw Farm, Langley.

William was initially drafted into the 1/4th, but was later transferred into a sister Territorial battalion, the 1/5th Northumberland Fusiliers. Although the CWGC records William's death as 11 September 1916, an inscription on the family headstone in Farlam Churchyard, Brampton, records his death as 15 September.

His younger brother George was also serving with the army and died in 1920 in Whalley Hospital, Lancashire, (see page 386).

The Hexham Herald printed the following memoriam:

One year has passed since that sad day,
When one we loved was called away;
No morning dawns, no night begins,
But what we always think of him.

**William is commemorated on the Thiepval Memorial to the missing.**

There appears to be some confusion about the date when Private Alexander Hutton died. The *CWGS* and *Soldiers who Died in the Great War* have the date as 1 October 1916. However, in a letter published in the Hexham Herald, Captain Robert Allen wrote to Alexander's parents and reported Alexander as 'missing presumably dead' on 15 September 1916. Based on the letter I am using the date of 15 September as being more realistic.

**Private Alexander Hutton, aged 22**
**1/5th Battalion Northumberland Fusiliers**
**Attached 1/4th Battalion Northumberland Fusiliers**
**Died 15 September 1916**

Alexander was born at Warden in 1894. He was the seventh and youngest son of William and Margaret Hutton of the Steel, Bellingham. The 1911 census shows that William was working as a horseman on a farm near Stamfordham. Newspaper reports show that when he enlisted at the start of the war, Alexander was working as a groom for Mr Harry Bell of Bavington Hall. He did not embark for France until 1916. His parents waited three agonising months for official notification of their son's death. In a letter to Mrs Hutton, Captain Robert Allen (1/4th Northumberland Fusiliers) wrote:

> "I am very sorry indeed to have to inform you that your son was missing after the action of September 15 when the battalion had so many casualties. This went through the ordinary casualty list and should have been communicated to you by the War Office. I am afraid there is very little doubt that he was killed as the battalion have had no information of any prisoners being taken and the shell fire on the day was terrific. All the ground was searched on September 16 and 17 and all wounded brought in. I knew your son well and he was highly respected by all officers and men and will be a great miss to his company. I am afraid this is a very sad war and there are very few of the North Tyne lads left ..."

**Alexander is commemorated on the Thiepval Memorial to the missing, although his death is officially recorded as 1 November 1916.**

From 28 October the 1/4th Northumberland Fusiliers were in the Front Line near Butte de Warlencourt where two companies occupied the Flers Line. The War Diary reported that the British Artillery was active practising an SOS barrage which precipitated a German reprisal especially on the Hexham Road (a communication trench) [23].

**Private John Elliott**
**1/4th Battalion Northumberland Fusiliers**
**Died 29 October 1916**

John was the third son of George and Helen Elliott of the Peel, West Woodburn. He volunteered to join the army at Alnwick in September 1915 and as two of his brothers, Eddie and Willie, were with the Northumberland Fusiliers in Hexham, he began training with them there in November 1915, and subsequently went to Redcar. John was a crack shot with the rifle and soon won the coveted 'cross guns', an honour also held by his brothers. His draft left Redcar on 25 May 1916 for France. He was involved in the fighting of the 15 and 16 September (see pages 105) but luckily seems to have come through that ordeal unharmed, alas to die only six weeks later. A comrade wrote to his parents saying that he was killed by a British shell which fell short, killing him as he sat in his dug-out. A further seven fusiliers died in action on this day. The Battalion War Diary failed to mention these deaths. At the time of his death, his brother Harry was in France and his other brothers, Corporals Eddie and Willie Elliott, were based in England.

**John is commemorated on the Thiepval Memorial to the missing.**

On 5 November the 28th Battalion of the Australian infantry was involved in an attack on part of the German defences called Gird Trench. The attack took place on a 2000 yard front, using three Australian battalions. The battalion opposite the Maze, a German strongpoint which jutted into No Man's Land, was a composite force, made up of the reserve companies of 26th, 27th and 28th Battalions. Elements of the 50th Division (Durham Light Infantry) formed up on the left [27].

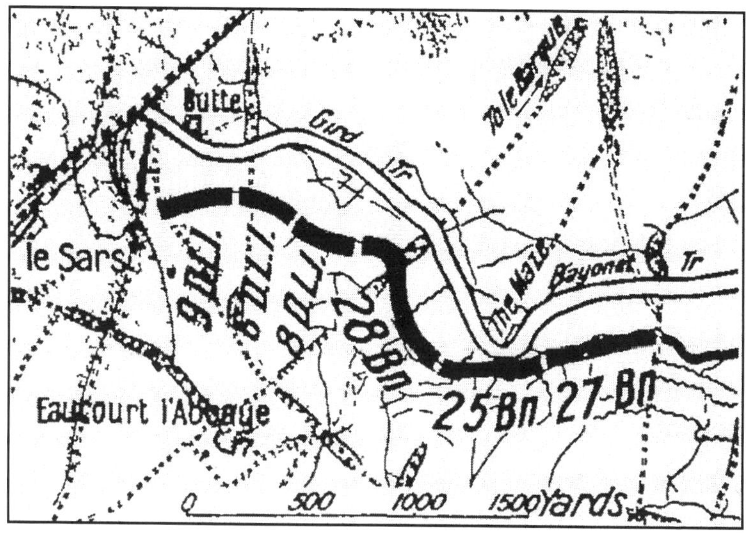


The War Diary for the 28th Battalion stated, "Owing to the inaccuracy of our artillery fire through lack of observation, the enemy were not kept down in their trenches by our barrage and the advancing troops were subjected to very heavy rifle and machine gun fire which prevented them reaching their objective of 'Gird Trench,. Furthermore, the inability to take the Maze allowed the Germans to directly enfilade into the advancing 28th Battalion [28]. Casualties for the attack were 1 officer killed and 3 wounded, for other ranks they were 58 killed, 166 wounded and 50 missing presumed dead, of which one was William Robson.

**Private William Ernest Robson, aged 35**
**28th Battalion Australian Infantry**
**Died 6 November 1916**

William was born in Birtley, Northumberland, the third son of Thomas and Lydia Sarah Robson (Lydia died in 1888) of Lowshield Green, Wark. The 1911 census shows that William, aged 30, was still single and working on his father's farm, as a shepherd. He regularly attended church and held the office of sidesman. In May 1913 he left England aboard the White Star Line's *The Belgic* landing in Freemantle, Western Australia. William worked as a station [large ranch] hand, and enlisted into the Australian Forces in August 1915; his enlistment was accepted on 7 September at Blackboy Hill and he was assigned to a draft of reinforcements for the 28th Battalion. William sailed from Australia in February 1916, arriving in Marseilles in late March; he had joined his battalion in June.

Captain Craig wrote to his sister, Dagmar Robson:

> "... during the preparations for the attack William was one of [my] runners and was at [my] side constantly except when delivering messages to the rear. He was a brave lad with a high standard of conduct. ... When I asked the sergeant-major for his most reliable man he sent me your brother."

**William is commemorated on the**
**Villers-Bretonneux Memorial to the missing.**

On 5 November the 151st Brigade, 50th Division attacked the Butte and Gird line of the German defence system. Although the 7th Northumberland Fusiliers were ordered to be prepared to support this attack, they were not required. During 6 and 7 November the 7th Northumberland provided over 160 men as stretcher bearers who worked under fire recovering the wounded from the previous day's attack. Also, other men were used by the Royal Engineers on the mending and extending of roadways. A number of casualties were recorded.

**Private Henry Vaas, aged 33**
**1/7th Battalion Northumberland Fusiliers**
**Died 7 November 1916**

Henry was born in Humshaugh, the youngest son of John and Ellen Vass. The 1911 census shows that Henry was living at New Stables, Chesters, and working as a groom. By 1914, however, his occupation had changed; the Hexham Courant reported that Henry was working as a grocer in Denton at the onset of war. The North Tyne Magazine reported that his many friends in Humshaugh deeply sympathised with his sister Miss J Vass in her loss.

**Henry is commemorated on the Thiepval Memorial to the missing.**

## THE 149TH BRIGADE ATTACK ON GIRD TRENCH AND HOOK SAP: 13 – 19 NOVEMBER 1916

In preparation for an attack on Gird Trench and Hook Sap, the 1/4th NF took over the Front Line on 12 November with 'B' and 'C' companies occupying Snag Trench and Snag Support, 'A' company in Abbaye Trench and 'D' company in the Flers Line. Due to incessant rain, these positions were waterlogged and in the case of Snag Trench it was almost impossible

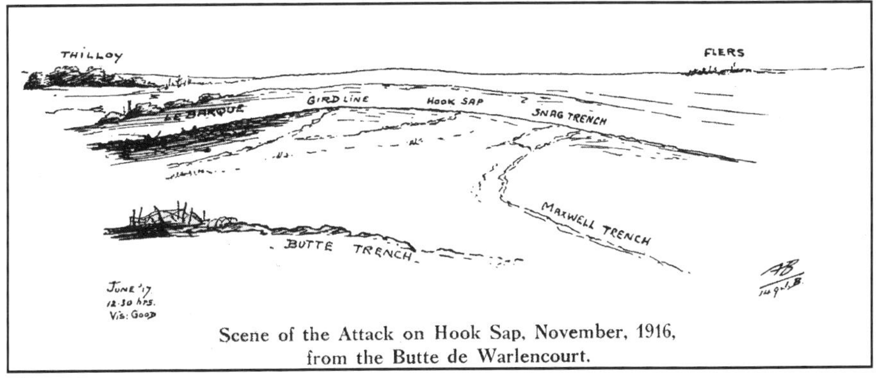


Scene of the Attack on Hook Sap, November, 1916, from the Butte de Warlencourt.

to negotiate. Incoming rifle fire was fairly heavy as the German 5th Battalion Grenadier Guards were now occupying the Front. This attack was postponed to 14 November and was carried out instead by their sister battalions, the 1/5th and 1/7th Northumberland Fusiliers.

During the night of 12/13, the 1/4th NF dug a new support trench and laid duck boards in Snag Trench. At 5.30am, supporting artillery laid down a Chinese barrage on Hook Sap and Gird Line, suddenly opening up and steadily creeping forward to give an impression that an infantry attack was in progress. Enemy retaliation was very severe especially on Hexham Road (communication trench). The 1/4th suffered a number of casualties. On 15 November the 1/4th Battalion was brought into the attack but was caught in the open by intense machine gun and artillery fire and failed to make any headway. Lt Colonel B D Gibson was wounded during this attack (see page 256).

**Private Harold Hiscock, aged 23**
**1/4th Battalion Northumberland Fusiliers**
**Died 13 November 1916**

Harold was born at Escrick, near York, the son of Richard Arthur and Ann Elizabeth Hiscock of Plantation Cottages, Cloughton, near Scarborough.

The 1911 census shows that Harold was still living with his parents and working, like his father, as a woodman on an estate near Cloughton. When war broke out, Harold was working in the Humshaugh area and was a serving member of the local Territorial battalion. He went out to France in April 1915, (see page 35).

**Harold is commemorated on the Thiepval Memorial to the missing.**

**Private William John Crisp, aged 22**
**1/4th Battalion Northumberland Fusiliers**
**Died 14 November 1916**

William was the youngest son of Robert and Mary Ann Crisp of the Crags, Barrasford. Like his father he worked in the local Whinstone Quarries. His elder brother Edward, who was with the Durham Light Infantry (see page 311), died in February 1917.

**William is buried in Cayeux Military Cemetery.**

## BATTLE OF ANCRE: 13 - 18 NOVEMBER 1916

The aim of this assault was the removal of a German salient between the Albert to Bapaume Road and Serre, with Beaumont Hamel as its head. (Since 1 July the capture of Beaumont Hamel had been an ongoing objective. Over the months some small gains near the Ancre River had been obtained but for a great loss of life.)

The 24th Battalion Royal Fusiliers took part on the first day of this attack. The Front for their attack was between Serre and Beaumont Hamel. They formed the left battalion of the 5th Brigade's attack, with 2nd Highland Light

Infantry to their right. They left their trenches at 5.15am in dense fog and reformed in No Man's Land for a general advance at 5.45am. The creeping barrage was within twenty yards of the advance all along the battalion front. It was noted that some shells fell short and these caused some casualties to the advancing troops. However, the men followed at walking pace and were able to capture the German Front Line trenches, taking a large number of prisoners. By 6.15am they had taken the major part of their objective, the Green Line, the German third trench system. On their left flank the attack was unsuccessful, (13th Essex). On 14 November the Royal Fusiliers were relieved by 2nd Oxford and Bucks. The short story writer H.H.Munro, pen-name 'Saki', a lance-sergeant in the 22nd Royal Fusiliers, was killed by a German sniper during this operation.

**Corporal Norris Ridley Johnson, aged 25**
**24th (Service) Battalion Royal Fusiliers**
**2nd Sportsman Battalion**
**Died 13 November 1916**

Norris was born in Simonburn, the youngest son of John and Isabella Johnson of Parkside, Wark. His father was a well known auctioneer. Norris was educated at Wark School and at Battle Hill School, Hexham. Before volunteering to join the forces, immediately following the onset of hostilities, Norris was employed by Barclay's Bank in Morpeth. Before this he had held positions at the Ponteland and Ryhope branches. He was a very able sportsman and played golf, bowls and football. He represented Morpeth in the Chronicle Cup and another one of his numerous sporting trophies was the Charlton Cup which he won at Bellingham Golf Club in 1912. He travelled to London to join the Sportsman Battalion of the Royal Fusiliers in 1914 and after basic training landed in France in November 1915. The Hexham Courant reported that he had a number of lucky escapes; on one occasion he was one of a party of five men when a shell burst, killing three of them. His company commander wrote to his widowed mother:

> "On the 13th inst. [November], our battalion took part in the recent successful operations during which your son was seen to fall. He was struck by a shell and death was instantaneous. It may be some relief to you to know that he died bravely and doing his duty ..."

**Norris is commemorated on the Thiepval Memorial to the missing.**

The Official History of the Great War recognises that the Battle of the Somme ended on 18 November 1916 with the capture of Beaumont Hamel. However, the war of attrition continued during the cold wintry months. The Front Line continued to be manned and during January 1917 the 50th Division reported that "casualties (killed or wounded) averaged 12 per diem".

## REFERENCES

1. Hart, P. *The Somme.* Pub: 2005, Weidenfield and Nicolson.

2. Sheffield, G. *The Somme.* Pub: 2003, Cassell.

3. Lynch, E. D. F. *Somme Mud.* Pub: 2008, Doubleday.

4. Middlebrook, M. *The First Day on the Somme, July 1916.*
Pub: 1971 Penguin.

5. WO95/2304. *War Diary. 1st Battalion King's Own Scottish Borderers.*

6. Shooter, W. A. Lt Col. OBE. *Ulster's Part in The Battle of the Somme.* Printed by The Northern Whig Ltd.

7. WO95/2510. *War Diary, 11th Battalion Royal Inniskilling Fusiliers*

8. Shakespear, Lt Col. J. *Thirty Fourth Division 1915-1919,* Pub: 1921 reprinted Naval and Military Press 1998.

9. Stewart, G. and Sheen, J. A. *History of the Tyneside Scottish.* Pub: Pen and Sword, 1999.

10. Terman, Brig-Gen. T. *History of the Tyneside Scottish.* Pub: 1919 reprinted Naval and Military Press 2003.

11. Sheen, J. A. *History of the Tyneside Irish.* Pub: Pen and Sword, 1998.

12. WO95/2462. *War Diary, 20th Battalion Northumberland Fusiliers.*

13. WO95/2463. *War Diary, 22nd Battalion Northumberland Fusiliers.*

14. WO95/2463. *War Diary, 23rd Battalion Northumberland Fusiliers.*

15. WO95/2466. *War Diary, 24th Battalion Northumberland Fusiliers.*

16. WO95/2329. *War Diary, 2nd Battalion Yorkshire Regiment.*

17. WO95/2182. *War Diary, 11th Battalion Northumberland Fusiliers.*

18. Farndale, M. Gen. KSO. *History of the Royal Regiment of Artillery,*

*Western Front 1914-18.* Pub: the Royal Artillery Institution, 1986.

19. Stewart, J. Lieut-Col. DSO. and Buchan J. *The Fifteenth (Scottish) Division.* Pub: 1926 reprinted Naval and Military Press 2002.

20. Norman, T. *The Hell they called High Wood, The Somme 1916.* Pub: 2003 Pen and Sword.

21. Pidgeon, T. *The Tanks at Flers.* Pub: Fairmile Books 1995

22. Wyrall, E. *The Fiftieth Division, 1914-1919.* Pub: 1939, reprinted Naval and Military Press 2002.

23. WO95/2828. *War Diary, 1/4th Battalion Northumberland Fusiliers.*

24. Buckley, F. Capt. *War History of the Seventh Northumberland Fusiliers.* Pub: T. M. Greirson.

25. Buckley, F. Capt. *Q. 6. A. and Other Places.* Pub: Spottiswoode and Ballentyne 1920.

26. WO95/2828. *War Diary, 1/5th Battalion Northumberland Fusiliers.*

27. Bean C. E. W. *Official History of Australia in the War of 1914-1918, Vol 3.*

28. AWM4 23/45/20 *War Diary, 28th Battalion Australian Infantry, November 1916.*

29. O'Neill, H. C. OBE. *The Royal Fusiliers in the Great War.* Pub: 1922 reprinted Naval and Military Press 2002.

# CHAPTER TEN

# WESTERN FRONT 1917

*We are the Dead. Short days ago*
*We lived, felt dawn, saw sunset glow,*
*Loved and were loved, and now we lie*
*In Flanders fields.*

From *In Flanders Fields* by John McCrae, died 20 January 1918

## OVERVIEW

In February 1917 Germany declared unrestricted submarine warfare (see Chapter 18) which nearly brought the Allies to their knees, but it was the effects of this policy that brought the USA into the war on the Allied side.

On 16 April, the French under General Robert Georges Nivelle launched a disastrous offensive along the Chemin des Dames ridge *(Second Battle of the Ainse),* a week after the British attack at Arras. Even though the Germans knew intimately the plans for the attack, Nivelle would not countenance any change. By 25 April the French Army had sustained over 96,000 casualties and by the end of the conflict on 9 May this had risen to 187,000 casualties, totally overwhelming their medical facilities. Mutinies occurred within the ranks, reducing the effectiveness of the French Army for at least the rest of 1917. Consequently, the British had to shoulder more of the fighting along the Western Front, concealing this weakness from the Germans.

During 1917 British troops fought a number of actions after the *Battle of Arras* in April, which extended into May to cover up the deficiencies in the French Army. This was followed by the battles of *Messines Ridge* and *Passchendaele,* June to November and finally the *Battle of Cambrai,* in November. All of these actions produced an ever increasing number of dead and wounded soldiers.

In late October a combined Austrian and German force launched the *Battle of Caporetto.* By sunset on the first day of fighting the Italians had been driven back by 12 miles to the Tagiamento River. As a result, much needed British troops were sent from the Western Front to Italy to support their Allies.

In the Middle East, where the British were fighting against the Turks, Baghdad was captured by the British in March. Lawrence and his Arab Irregulars captured Aguaba. Further reversals were suffered by the Turks with the British entering Jerusalem in December.

In the melting pot of Russia, Tsar Nicholas II abdicated following the revolution which eventually brought Lenin and the Communists to power. Following a succession of German victories on the Eastern Front, the Russians opened peace negotiations with Germany, which would take Russia out of the War. The consequences of this Brest-Litovsk peace would have serious consequences for the British during the early months of 1918.

## ALONG THE WESTERN FRONT

At the end of the *Somme Offensive* the French held the Bouchavesnes-Bergen sector, north of Peronne. However, on 12 December 1916 the British Fourth Army took over responsibility for this section of the Front Line. Later, the British took responsibility for another section of the Front Line from the French, southwards to the Somme River.

### Trench Mortars

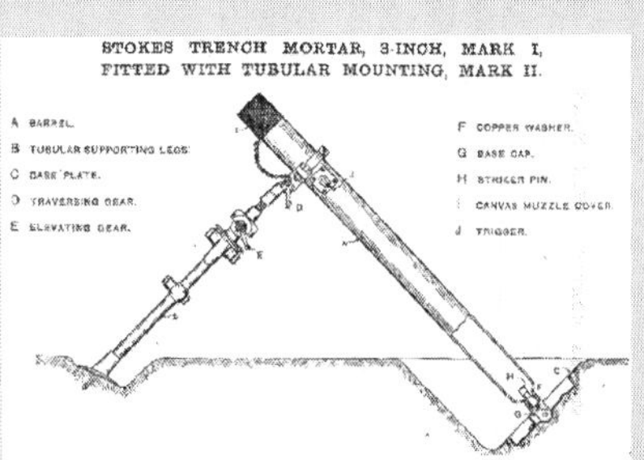


A 2 inch medium mortar was bigger than the Stokes 3 inch mortar. In the case of the Stokes the 3 inch was the size of the bomb. In the case of the 2 inch it was the size of the 'stick' that went into the weapon, its much bigger bomb stayed on the outside. The mortar consisted of a steel tube of 2-inch internal diameter mounted upon a wooden base and supported by a bipod fitted with elevating and traversing gears. Elevation was applied by means of a clinometer, while for line a 'tall periscope sight attached to the piece' was supplied.

Propellant charges consisted of packets of cordite, used to make up charges of 1½, 2½, and 3½ ounces, giving ranges of 100-220, 180-340, and 300-500 yards respectively. Owing to the nature of the bomb, the charges were loaded separately by dropping them down the barrel. Ignition was by 'T' friction tube inserted into a vent at the breech or by a rifle mechanism. The mortar was fired using a long lanyard because sometimes the packets of cordite did not burn completely and the bomb fell short – occasionally dangerously short!

The mortars were transported over short distances on 'frames with perambulator wheels' and over longer distances by vehicles.

## Gunner William Goodfellow, aged 23
## 'Z' 4th Trench Mortar Battery
## Royal Garrison Artillery
## Died 2 January 1917

William was born in Bellingham in 1894, the eldest son of William and Jane Goodfellow. Successive census records show that the family earned their living by working as farm labourers. In 1891 they were living in the Walbottle area and by 1911 were living at Grange House, Morpeth; William was working as a farm labourer. However, by 1915 William was living with his mother Jane in Blackhill, Durham. His younger brother, Howard, was serving with the Agricultural Branch of the Labour Corps in Perthshire.

William enlisted into the forces at Newcastle on 1 November 1915 and was posted overseas in January 1916, to 'Z' company Trench Mortar Battery which was attached to the 4th Division. Z Company was responsible for the firing of the 2 inch medium mortar. William was wounded in the arm on 2 January 1917 and died of his wounds that day.

William's name does not appear on any of the memorials to the dead in the North Tyne Valley, but he is mentioned on both Greystead's and Wark's Rolls of Honour.

**William is buried in Combles Communal Cemetery Extension.**
**During the battlefield clearances after the war**
**his body was exhumed from its initial resting place.**

The 11th Battalion King's Royal Rifle Corps (KRRC) went into the Front Line on 5 March, relieving their sister battalion the 10th KRRC. The part of the Front to be manned was on the right hand side of the Lesboeufs Sector. Towards midnight, during the changeover, Second Lieutenant Leadbitter was shot in the forehead by a sniper [1].

**Second Lieutenant Francis John Graham Leadbitter, aged 36**
**11th Battalion King's Royal Rifle Corps**
**Died 5 March 1917**

Francis was the eldest son of Thomas and Matilda Leadbitter of Warden, Northumberland, and Auckland House, Brondesbury, London. Francis was educated at Mostyn House School and between 1895 and 1899 at

Shrewsbury School. Whilst at Shrewsbury he rowed bow for the school. After leaving school it is reported that he became a valued member of Shrewsbury's old boys network, the Old Salopians. He also rowed in the Thames Rowing Club VIII at Henley. The 1901 census shows Francis was working as a solicitor's clerk. He was admitted as a solicitor in 1904.

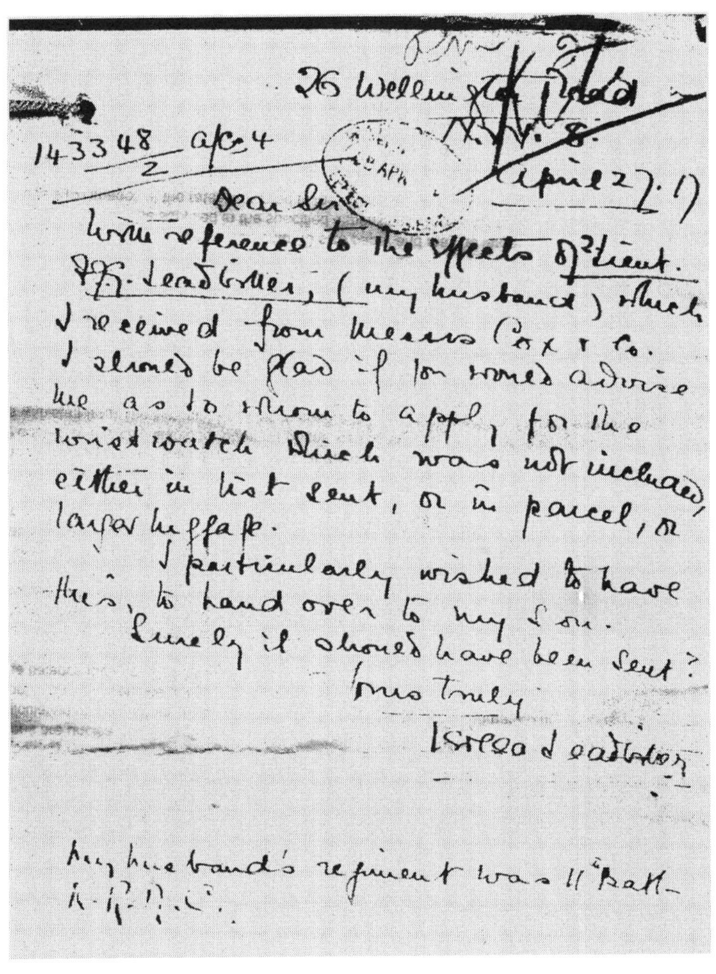

26 Wellington Road
N.W. 8.
April 27.17

143348/2 AC4

Dear Sir

With reference to the effects of 2nd Lieut. F.J. Leadbitter, (my husband) which I received from Messrs Cox & Co. I should be glad if you would advise me as to how to apply for the wristwatch which was not included either in list sent, or in parcel, or larger luggage.

I particularly wished to have this, to hand over to my son. Surely it should have been sent?

Yours truly

Teresa Leadbitter

My husband's regiment was 11th Batt. K.R.R.C.

Letter from Teresa Leadbitter about the loss of her husband's watch, see p.140

He married Teresa Clotilde (née del Riego) in the spring of 1908. They lived at Wellington Road, St John's Wood, London. Francis was the father of a son, Jasper. Francis joined the Inns of Court OTC in December 1915 and obtained a commission one year later. He embarked for France in January 1917. It is known that after his death Teresa received a number of her husband's possessions, but was dismayed that his watch was not returned, as she wished to give it to their son. His gravestone is inscribed with the following:

**IN PROUD AND LOVING MEMORY**

**Francis is buried at Guards Cemetery, Lesboeufs**

The 10th Battalion Northumberland Fusiliers moved to Dickebusch Camp (about 2 miles southwest of Ypres) on 12 June 1917 to provide working parties for the burying of cables. During the morning of 20 June the camp was shelled and both Major W Clifford DSO and the Adjutant Captain G L Bland were killed. Both were buried that day at Dickebusch Military Cemetery. At the same time, Lieutenant Savage was badly wounded and died later at 6.30pm in a Casualty Clearing Station. More men were killed during the day [2].

**Lieutenant Cuthbert Farrar Savage, aged 26**
**'A' Company 10th (Service) Battalion**
**Northumberland Fusiliers**
**Died 20 June 1917**

Cuthbert was born in Barrow in Furness and was the only son of Canon Edwin Sydney and Sibyl Savage of the Priory, Hexham; his father was the well known vicar of Hexham Abbey. He was educated at Aysgarth School, and Rugby School. At the age of 14 he won the Alpine Public

Schools Skiing Competition and at the same time passed the international skiing test. From Rugby he went up to New College Oxford, where he studied Law. After leaving Oxford he travelled to Vancouver to further his studies at Messrs Martin, Griffin and Co. At the onset of hostilities he enlisted with the Seaforth Highlanders of Canada, arriving in England with the 1st Canadian Contingent. In January of 1915 he obtained a commission with the Northumberland Fusiliers and was posted to France in the August.

Cuthbert was wounded at *Bully Grenay* in early April 1916. The Hexham Herald (15 April 1916), stated that Cuthbert had been wounded in the back of the head and in the right arm from grenade fragments, but although he spent some time in hospital these wounds were not considered serious. With his battalion, he took part in a number of actions on the Somme during the rest of 1916.

On 20 June 1917, Cuthbert was wounded by a shell which burst at his feet outside Battalion Headquarters at Dickebusch, near Ypres. He was admitted to No. 10 Casualty Clearing Station at Poperinghe with multiple shrapnel wounds and compound fractures of the humerus and the knee. He died that evening [3].

His Major wrote:

> "We shall miss him dreadfully. In the old days before he was wounded he was the best Platoon Commander in my Company, and I thought the Battalion, and latterly, during his Staff courses,

he turned out to be even more efficient. He was very popular with us all, as he was always cheery and only thought of others and not of himself at all."

Another who knew him well wrote:

"And what a gallant lad – handsome as a Greek god, courteous, charming, gifted. I have many memories of him skiing down steep slopes with grace and skill, and dancing and laughing and jesting with his friends or discussing serious matters with earnestness and intelligence."

His gravestone is inscribed with the following:

**SO** [*SIC*] **HE PASSED OVER THE TRUMPETS SOUNDED FOR HIM ON THE OTHER SIDE**

**Cuthbert is buried in Lijssenthoek Military Cemetery.**

## FLANKING OPERATIONS TOWARDS LENS 3 JUNE - 26 AUGUST 1917

From 3 June to 26 August 1917, battalions from the 1st Army commanded by General Horne undertook a number of flanking operations towards Lens. The aim of these attacks was to give the impression that the next major attack would be to capture Lille.

During 26-29 June, Canadian troops from 3rd and 4th Divisions (78th Battalion, 4th Division) captured the outskirts of Avion, which today is a suburb in the southwest part of Lens and was then part of the Hindenburg

Line defence. Further actions would capture Oppy Wood and Hill 70 (north of Lens).

Late in June 1917, the 2nd Battalion Sherwood Foresters (SF) was attached to 139th Brigade (46th Division) to take part in the attack to capture Lens. On the evening of 30 June the battalion moved up from Calonne, marching along the Lièvin to Lens road.

Owing to the darkness and the lack of guides, sections of the battalion were unable to reach their start positions for the attack. Accordingly, the time of the attack was changed, but not all the attacking troops received these orders and they went forward at the original time, and many were injured by their own artillery barrage as they advanced. On the right of the attack the SF moved forward but were hampered by severe fire coming from highly defensible positions in derelict houses.

However, they eventually consolidated a position in Alarm Trench. As they moved forward the SF met with further intense German opposition from their left, again from enemy forces who had taken up positions in derelict houses. 'D' Company lost 3 officers and 76 other ranks from a total of 4 officers and 116 other ranks that went into action. The centre company also faced heavy German opposition from strong points, again positioned in derelict houses [4].

The commanding officer of the 6th Division received the following message from the Commander of the 46th Division dated 3 July:

> "I desire to thank you most heartily for the assistance given by the 2nd Sherwood Foresters ... The part taken by the 2nd Sherwood Foresters, when they gained and held on to the ground captured, stood out alone. I regret very much the losses they sustained."

**Corporal James Jobling, aged 25**
**2nd Battalion Sherwood Foresters**
**Notts and Derby Regiment**
**Died 1 July 1917**

James was the second son of George Rennison and Mary Ann Jobling of Wood Row, Plashetts. He was a native of Plashetts and worked as an underground haulage man at Plashetts Colliery.

**James is commemorated on the Loos Memorial to the missing.**

On the night of 13 August, the 78th Battalion Canadian Infantry relieved their fellow Canadians (85th Battalion) on the Front Line in the Avion Mill sector. They were in the line until late August. The Battalion Diary reports that on 14 August the enemy was very quiet apart from the exception of a small amount of very accurate counter battery work [5].

**Private William Dodds, aged 38**
**78th Battalion (Winnipeg Grenadiers)**
**Canadian Infantry**
**Died 14 August 1917**

William was born in Chollerton, the eldest son of Ralph and Isabella Dodds of the Crescent, Gunnerton. Before he emigrated to Canada in the early 1900s he worked like his father at a local sandstone quarry.

He was unmarried and whilst in Canada worked as Machine Helper in Winnipeg. Before he enlisted in July 1915 his papers show he had previous military experience with the local militia, the Winnipeg Grenadiers. It appears that he lied about his age on his form when joining the Canadian Military, claiming to be only 31.

**William is commemorated on the Annapolis Cemetery Memorial La Chaudière Military Cemetery, Vimy.**

**Pioneer John William Ritson, aged 45**
**305th Road Construction Company**
**Royal Engineers**
**Died 25 September 1917**

John was born in Hexham, the son of William and Mary Ritson of Hexham. The 1891 census shows the Ritson family living in Durham and John working as railway engine cleaner. In the summer of 1898 John married Christina (née Tailford). The 1901 census shows that John worked as a platelayer on the North Eastern Railway and that the family lived at Stocksfield. Later he worked at Black Pastures Quarry in Wall. The 1911 shows Christina living at Dale Cottage, Humshaugh, with five children and working as a charwoman, whilst John was living with his parents in Durham and working as an engine driver.

John joined the forces in Middlesbrough and initially trained with the Scottish Rifles before going overseas with the Royal Engineers

The Hexham Courant records that Christina received information that her husband had been accidentally killed. The events of death were that he was run over by a train at No 3 level crossing between Poperinghe and Remy at 6.10 in the morning.

The president of the inquiry into the soldier's death concluded:

> "I am of the opinion that in this case no blame can be attached to any of the RoD staff. There is no evidence as to whether the deceased, Private Ritson, met his death either by accident or suicide."

His gravestone is inscribed with the following:

**REST IN PEACE**

**John is buried in Lijssenthoek Military Cemetery**

The 127th Company Machine Gun Corps (MGC) was attached to 127th Brigade 42nd Division. After being on the Ypres Salient during the Passchendaele battle, on 26/27 September 1917 the 42nd Division took over the coastal sector of the Nieuport Front. The 127th Brigade held, in turn with the 125th Brigade, the left flank of the Front, positioned to the north and northeast of Nieuport, across the wide and deep Yser canal. The Front Line consisted mainly of breastworks and island posts, since much of the area was below sea level as much of the land had been flooded by the Belgian army in 1914 to form a barrier against the advancing Germans [6].

The 42nd Division history records:

> "There was little activity on these fronts other than artillery duels and aircraft bombing. The line was often under fire from heavy mortars and the bridges, dams, roads and back areas were constantly shelled."

Flooded area around Nieuport

William Moscrop is commemorated on both the Falstone Cross and St Peter's Church War Memorials. Although there is evidence of a large Moscrop family in this part of the North Tyne Valley, my extensive research of census records and other documents cannot directly link William to this family. The Memorial to those who served in the Great War at Greystead Church (who by implication did not die) records only two Moscrops: Joseph (Border Regiment) and John (Northumberland Fusiliers); William's name is not found on the Greystead Memorial. Extensive searches cannot identify any particular connection between William Moscrop with Falstone and surrounding areas.

Based on circumstantial evidence I believe the commemorated William Moscrop was the son of James and Annie Moscrop (née Burn). William was born in Haltwhistle in 1893. James, his father, was a shepherd. Based on various censuses it can be seen that the family led a migratory existence, moving from farm to farm. It can be seen that William's parents lived for some of time within the bounds of the Bellingham registration area. They were married in Bellingham area and their eldest child, Annie, was also born here.

**Private William Moscrop, aged 23**
**127th Company, Machine Gun Corps**
**Died 6 November 1917**

William was born in Haltwhistle, the second son of James and Annie Moscrop. The 1911 census shows the family living north of Gilsland at Black Shaws, which is now a derelict farm within the confines of Wark Forest. William, his father James and his elder brother Robert were all employed as shepherds. William married Sarah Ellen Easton in the early months of 1915 and was the father of two girls. After the war, the widowed Sarah lived in Bewcastle.

**William is buried in Coxyde Military Cemetery.**

## REFERENCES

1. WO95/3115. *War Diary 11th Battalion King's Royal Rifle Corps.*

2. WO95/2182. *War Diary 10th Battalion Northumberland Fusiliers.*

3. Marquis of Ruvigny and Raineval. *De Ruvigny's Roll of Honour 1914-1924, Vol. 4, page 177*

4. Wylly, H.C. Col. *The 1st and 2nd Battalions, The Shertwood Foresters in the Great War.* Pub: 1925 reprinted Naval and Military Press 2003.

5. data4.collectionscanada.gc.ca *War Diary 78th Battalion Canadian Infantry.*

6. Gibbon, F. P. *42nd (East Lancashire) Division.* Reprinted Naval and Military Press 2003.

# CHAPTER ELEVEN

# BATTLE OF ARRAS

*We shall not forget them; though we be forgot,*
*We who blazed the trails of Hell from Souchez to the crest;*
*We who saw the gloaming creep that night across the ridge,*
*Who hollowed out the ancient chalk, and laid them to their rest.*

From Burnett A Ward's *Vimy, November 11*

## VIMY RIDGE

The *Battle of Vimy Ridge,* fought by the Canadian Corps, was part of the British led *Battle of Arras*, a diversionary action to coincide with the French Nivelle Offensive which would take place (disastrously) a few days later, 50 miles to the south. Vimy Ridge, a German held escarpment, formed the northern boundary for the battle; the battle for this ridge took place from 9 – 12 April 1917 and formed an integral part of the opening phase of the *Battle of Arras* (9 April-16 May). Without the capture of the ridge, British operations further south would be subjected to enfilade fire.

The French requested that the attack, initially planned for Easter Sunday (8 April) be postponed for 24 hours. Accordingly, at 5.30am on the Easter Monday, in a snow storm, the Canadians mounted their attack against the ridge's defenders. During the night, hours before the attack, light Canadian and British artillery bombardments continued to pound the ridge; they stopped a few minutes before the attack to allow the guns to be recalibrated in preparation for a synchronised barrage. At 5.30am every piece of artillery available to the Canadians began firing. Within 30 seconds, mines in No Man's Land and under German positions were detonated. Light field guns laid down a creeping barrage whilst medium and heavy howitzers established a series of standing curtain barrages further ahead.

> It was on 9 April 1917 that all four of the Canadian Divisions first fought together. Indeed, many Canadians believe that this date signifies the birth of their nation. However, it interesting to note that Newfoundland, one of Canada's provinces, fought with Great Britain as an independent nation.

The Canadians captured most of the ridge on the first day of the attack. The town of Thélus fell during the second day of fighting, as did the crest of the ridge, once a salient of considerable resistance had been eradicated. The final objective, a fortified knoll located outside Givenchy-en-Gohelle, fell on 12 April.

The 4th Battalion Canadian Infantry were part of the 1st Brigade, 1st Division. For the attack at Vimy Ridge all four Canadian Divisions were used. The 1st Division formed the southern boundary for the assault, with the 2nd, 3rd and 4th Divisions to the north. In the southern part of the 1st Division's sector, battalions from the 2nd Brigade were used in its initial

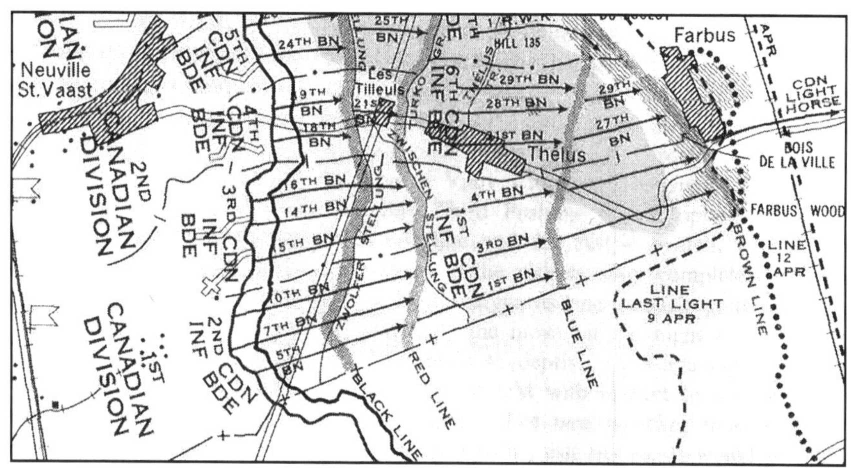


Attack of the 4th Battalion Canadian Infantry, 9 April 1917

attack. In this part of the battlefield the attacking troops had five objectives to capture: Black Line (Zwoller Stelung), Red Line (Zwischen Stelung), Blue Line, Brown Line and the artillery position in Farbus Wood. The 4th Battalion began its attack from the Red Line after its capture by troops from the 5th Battalion. When the barrage moved forward at 10.05am, the Battalion moved towards the Blue Line and reached it on time, although there were a number of casualties. At 12.26pm the battalion moved forward towards the Brown Line following the barrage, and by 2.00pm they had occupied and consolidated Farbus Wood. During the action of 9 May, Private Malcolm Mews was killed [1].

**Private Robert Malcolm Mews, aged 27**
**4th Battalion Canadian Infantry**
**(Central Ontario Regiment)**
**Died 9 April 1917**

Robert was born in Acomb. He was the son of District Councillor Watson and Elizabeth Mews who lived at Middle Farm, Acomb. Before emigrating to Canada in May 1913, he was employed for seven years as a cartman by Mr N C Fairlam, a grocer of Battle Hill, Hexham. Later he worked for his father, who was a farmer and carting contractor. In Canada, Malcolm worked as a teamster. On 9 August 1914 in York, Ontario, he married Ursula Ann Stobart of High Prudhoe, who had also emigrated to Canada. On his death, Ursula was left with a young child.

Malcolm enlisted in the Canadian Army on New Year's Day 1916, but after hearing that his mother was very ill he was granted leave to come back to the UK. Subsequently, he finished his basic training in England, arriving in France in late September 1916. The Hexham Herald, 23 September 1916, reported that Malcom attended his mother's funeral. At the time of his death his younger brother Watson, of the King's Own Yorkshire Light Infantry, was lying wounded in Fulham Military Hospital. Malcolm's gravestone is inscribed with the following:

**FOR HE SHALL GIVE HIS ANGELS**
**CHARGE OVER THEE**
**PSALMS 91:11**

**Malcom is buried in Bois-Carré British Cemetery, Thélus.**

On 7 April, in preparation for the forthcoming offensive, the three battalions who were in the Front Line (16th Royal Scots, 20th and 25th Northumberland Fusiliers) were each ordered to provide raiding parties; these consisted of three officers and one hundred men. The aim of these forays was to obtain identification information and to frighten the 'Boche'. At the 25th NF sector, the raiding party left the forward trenches and were easily able to penetrate as far as the enemy's second trench. However, no prisoners were taken but one officer and two men from the raiding party were killed, one of these being Private Robert Gibson [2,3,4].

**Private Robert Gibson, aged 26**
**25th (Service) Battalion (Tyneside Irish)**
**Northumberland Fusiliers**
**Died 7 April 1917**

Robert, the son of James and Isabel Gibson, was born in Blaydon. He lived with his aunt, Miss Richardson, of The Green, Acomb, who had brought him up. He was an esteemed member of the West Acomb Branch of the Independent Order of Rechabites. Before joining up he served his apprenticeship as a plumber with Mr Harrison of Hencotes and eventually found a job with Hexham Gas Company. Later, he was employed at the North Tyne Colliery, Wall.

Robert initially arrived in France in April 1915 with the local Territorial Battalion and was wounded on 22 May in the initial battles around Ypres (see page 50). After recovering from his wounds he returned to the 1/4th Northumberland Fusiliers with a new draft from Hexham in September 1915. He was wounded again during the attack of 15 September 1916 (see page 105). On returning to the Front in February 1917 he was drafted into the 25th Battalion Northumberland Fusiliers.

**Robert is buried in Roclincourt Military Cemetery.**

## THE FIRST BATTLE OF SCARPE: 9 – 14 APRIL 1917

Further south of Vimy Ridge the British Army were also able to make dramatic advances on 9 April. North of the River Scarpe, elements of the 4th Division penetrated the German lines and captured the village of Fampoux. South of the river the advances were less impressive. The ultimate objective for the 34th Battalion attack, which involved all three brigades (101st, 102nd and 103rd), was the capture of the ridge on which stood Le Point du Jour, a German strongpoint established around a farmhouse. Before this strongpoint could be tackled, the attacking troops had to capture three German Trench Systems designated Black, Blue and Brown. The 102nd Brigade (Tyneside Scottish) formed the centre of the attack with 103rd Brigade (Tyneside Irish) on its left (north).

Under the cover of darkness at 4.30am, men of 24th and 25th Battalions Northumberland Fusiliers (NF, Tyneside Irish) moved into No Man's Land, close to the German wire. As the artillery barrage finished they were able to rush the enemy trenches before the Germans knew what had hit them. On this dull and misty morning, both battalions were able to take their first objective, the Black Line, although by this time a lot of the officers had been targeted and killed by the Germans. As they struggled forward behind a barrage to capture the second objective, the Blue Line, they came under extremely heavy and accurate fire from their left flank and suffered a number of casualties, especially in 25th Battalion (NF). In spite on this, and through acts of extreme courage, the remnants of the 24th Battalion managed to take the Blue Line.

The Distinguished Conduct Medal (DCM) was an award for outstanding bravery. It was in the second tier of military decorations awarded to other [i.e. non-commissioned] ranks of the British Army and also to non-commissioned personnel of other Commonwealth countries. The medal was instituted in 1854, during the Crimean War, to recognise gallantry within the other ranks, for which it was equivalent of the Distinguished Service Order (DSO) awarded for bravery to commissioned officers. Although considered to be the army's second ranking gallantry award, the DCM was almost always seen as a "near miss for the Victoria Cross". Recipients are entitled to the post-nominal letters DCM.

The medal is made from silver and is 36mm in diameter. Originally the obverse of the medal depicted a trophy of arms as seen on early Army Long Service and Good Conduct Medals. In 1902 this was replaced by the effigy of the reigning monarch. The reverse on all issues bears the inscription 'FOR DISTINGUISHED CONDUCT IN THE FIELD'. The medal is suspended by an ornate scrolled bar. The medal ribbon was 32mm wide, divided into three equal parts: crimson, dark blue, crimson.

Private R Boyle was awarded the Distinguished Service Medal for handling his machine gun with great courage when all of his team were casualties; he went forward and captured an enemy machine gun. The commanding officer of 24th Battalion, Lieutenant Colonel Hermon, was killed as he crossed No Man's Land.

Further south, the attacking battalions of the Northumberland Fusiliers (NF) Tyneside Scottish met with less resistance [2,3,5].

**Private Richard Brown Glendinning, aged 38**
**24th (Service) Battalion Tyneside Irish**
**Northumberland Fusiliers**
**Died 9 April 1917**

Richard was the eldest son of Ninian and Hannah Robson Glendinning and was born in Cambo, Northumberland. The 1901 census shows he had left home, was single and working as a shepherd at Uswayford, above Alwinton in the Cheviots. In early 1905 he married Mary Jane Thompson in Bellingham. The 1911 census shows that Richard was working as a gardener in Hevingham, Norwich. He was the father of a son, also called Richard.

He volunteered to join the army in Norwich, days after the onset of hostilities. Richard was part of first contingent of Tyneside Irish to arrive in France in July 1915. His battalion was heavily involved during the *First Day of the Somme* (see page 91). It is reported that during his tours of duty he had been wounded on two occasions and had only been back in France for six weeks before his death. Following his death, his wife Mary returned to Bellingham and lived at Brookside Place. The Bellingham Parish section of the North Tyne Magazine contained this entry about Richard:

"He was an earnest Christian man, a good husband and father, a regular communicant, and a brave man. The world is better for such lives as his and while we feel his loss, we also still feel the power of his noble example."

**Richard is buried in Roclincourt Valley Cemetery.**

The leading waves of the Tyneside Scottish (102nd Brigade) for the attack, 21st and 22nd Battalions Northumberland Fusiliers (NF), moved silently into No Man's Land at 4.30am and crept as close as possible to the German line and the forthcoming British barrage, so that when it lifted they would be able to rush the German Front Line. By 6.30am, the 21st Battalion had taken its first objective, the Black Line. Similarly the 22nd Battalion met with success. Another advance of a further 1200 yards towards the Blue Line was made by both these battalions which they secured at 11am. Further progress was now the responsibility of the 20th and 23rd Battalions, Northumberland Fusiliers (NF). The 20th Battalion managed to capture the Brown Line, their first objective, but this was achieved at great cost, with one half of the battalion's strength becoming casualties. However, the men of the 20th NF reported that the German soldiers who were captured were demoralised. As night fell and the Brown Line was consolidated, snow began to fall [2,6,7].

**Corporal James Keaning, aged 29**
**20th (Service) Battalion Tyneside Scottish**
**Northumberland Fusiliers**
**Died 9 April 1917**

James was born in New Abbey, Kirkcudbrightshire and was the eldest son of Robert and Agnes Keaning. He married Annie (née Woodcock) in the spring of 1915, just before he was scheduled to go to France. After the war she lived at The Cottages in Scotswood. His brother John volunteered at the beginning of the war and served with the Gordon Highlanders and was awarded the Military Medal on 23 July 1916. James was a member of the Territorials based in Bellingham. He embarked for France on 20 April 1915 and fought at St Julien on the 26 April (see page 35). He was wounded in this action and after recuperation was transferred to the Tyneside Scottish.

**James is buried in Bailleul Road East Cemetery, St Laurent-Blangy.**

## THIRD BATTLE OF SCARPE: 3 - 4 MAY 1917

On 3 May the 6$^{th}$ Canadian Machine Company supported an attack by infantry as part of the Battle of Fresnoy. Two guns supported the Canadian 27$^{th}$ Battalion attack whist a further two guns supported the Canadian 31$^{st}$ Battalion attack. Further guns under Lieutenant Carter were held in reserve, but were called into action due to increasing casualties and gun damage. As he moved forward, Andrew Surtees was killed [8].

**Sergeant Andrew Surtees, aged 27**
**6th Brigade Canadian Machine Gun Company**
**Died 3 May 1917**

Andrew was the second son of Thomas and Isabella Surtees of Wheat Hill, Colwell, and was born in Chollerton. The 1911 census shows that he was living away from home, working on the Swinburne Estate. In 1912 he emigrated to Canada, sailing on the Virginian, which berthed in Quebec. He travelled west and settled in Calgary, following his profession as a mason. His attestation papers show that he had served with the Territorials in Hexham between 1909 and 1912. He was unmarried and joined the Canadian Army in August 1915. He saw action during the attack at Vimy Ridge in early April 1917. Andrew had three brothers, Thomas, Richard and Walter, who were serving with the forces; his brother Richard died in August 1918 (see page 222). It was apparent that Andrew was a natural leader and he rose rapidly to obtain the rank of sergeant. Major Eastham wrote to his parents from the Front on 6 May 1917:

> "I regret exceedingly to have to advise you that your son, Sergeant A Surtees, was killed in action two days ago. He was shot through the heart and died instantaneously without knowing what hit him … He had been with me for a long time and was one of the finest lads that I have ever known anywhere. Both officers and men had the highest opinion of him. Always willing and cheerful, he was one of the coolest and most reliable men under fire and never failed to inspire confidence in his section."

**Andrew is buried in Orchard Dump Cemetery, Arleux-en-Gohelle.**

## FLANKING OPERATION ACTIONS ON THE HINDENBURG LINE: 20 MAY -1 6 JUNE 1917

The 12th Northumberland Fusiliers (NF) were heavily involved in an attack scheduled for 16 June, east of Arras and the Sensée Valley. At 3.10am, under the cover of an artillery barrage, the NF attacked with the 13th Northumberland Fusiliers on their left and 2/2nd London Regiment on their right. The NF attacked on a single company front across three hundred yards of No Man's Land to capture a trench system called Tunnel Trench.

The Germans in this sector were determined not to give up their position cheaply and used a heavy artillery barrage and withering fire from rifles and machine guns against the attacking fusiliers. As they approached the trench they were heavily showered with stick grenades. Incredibly, despite this determined defence, some fusiliers from 'C' and 'D' Companies managed to penetrate the Tunnel Trench defences, but they were eventually overwhelmed and killed. The following two waves of 'A' and 'B' Companies realised that would be unable to get into the heavily defended position and instead consolidated in shell holes just in front of the German Line, withdrawing under the cover of darkness.

Of the 10 officers and 359 other ranks that went over the top, 3 officers and 54 men were killed that day, including James Craighill [9].

**Lance Corporal William James Craighill, aged 24**
**12th (Service) Battalion Northumberland Fusiliers**
**Died 16 June 1917**

James was born in Corsenside and was the son of William and Mary Craighill. The 1911 census reports that at 18 years old James was working at Elishaw Farm as a labourer. William was a serving Territorial when the war broke out.

**James is commemorated on the Arras Memorial to the missing.**

## REFERENCES

1. data4.collectionscanada.gc.ca *War Diary of 4th Battalion Canadian Infantry.*

2. Shakespear, Lt Col. J. *Thirty Fourth Division 1915-1919.*
Pub: 1921 reprinted Naval and Military Press 1998.

3. Sheen, J. A. *History of Tyneside Irish.* Pub: Pen and Sword, 1998.

4. WO95/2463. *25th Battalion Northumberland Fusiliers.*

5. WO95/2466. *24th Battalion Northumberland Fusiliers.*

6. Stewart, G. and Sheen, J. A. *History of Tyneside Scottish.*
Pub: Pen and Sword, 1999.

7. WO95/2462. *War Diary 20th Battalion Northumberland Fusiliers.*

8. data4.collectionscanada.gc.ca *War Diary of 6th Brigade Canadian Machine Gun Company.*

9. WO95/2155. *War Diary 12th Battalion Northumberland Fusiliers.*

# CHAPTER TWELVE

# THIRD BATTLE OF YPRES MESSINES RIDGE AND PASSCHENDAELE

*"I died in Hell – they called it Passchendaele"*
From Siegfried Sassoon's *Memorial Tablet,*

The plan was conceived for the Allies to make a major coastward offensive from Ypres during 1917; part of this plan demanded that the Messines-Wytschaete Ridge should be captured so as to protect the right flank of any future operations.

The Germans had occupied the Messines Ridge (the line running south of St Eloi through Wytschaete and Messines to Ploegsteert Wood) since 1914 and had consolidated their occupation by building strong defences. For any Allied attack to take place from the Ypres salient this stronghold to the south would need to be taken. The planned attack involved tunnelling companies digging and placing large quantities of explosives under the German Lines in twenty-one locations, although in the event only nineteen exploded as planned at precisely 3.10am on the morning of 7 June. After seventeen days of artillery barrage the guns became silent, encouraging the Germans to leave their dugouts in anticipation of an attack. The mines exploded a few minutes later and the resulting noise and shock wave were heard and felt in distant London. The Allied forces then rushed forward behind a creeping barrage, killing and capturing a great number of highly disorientated defenders [1].

The 11$^{th}$ Battalion Northumberland Fusiliers (NF) was in position on June 7 at Hill 60, at the extreme northern end of the attacking line. Their role in the day's attack was to capture Battle Wood and the Klein

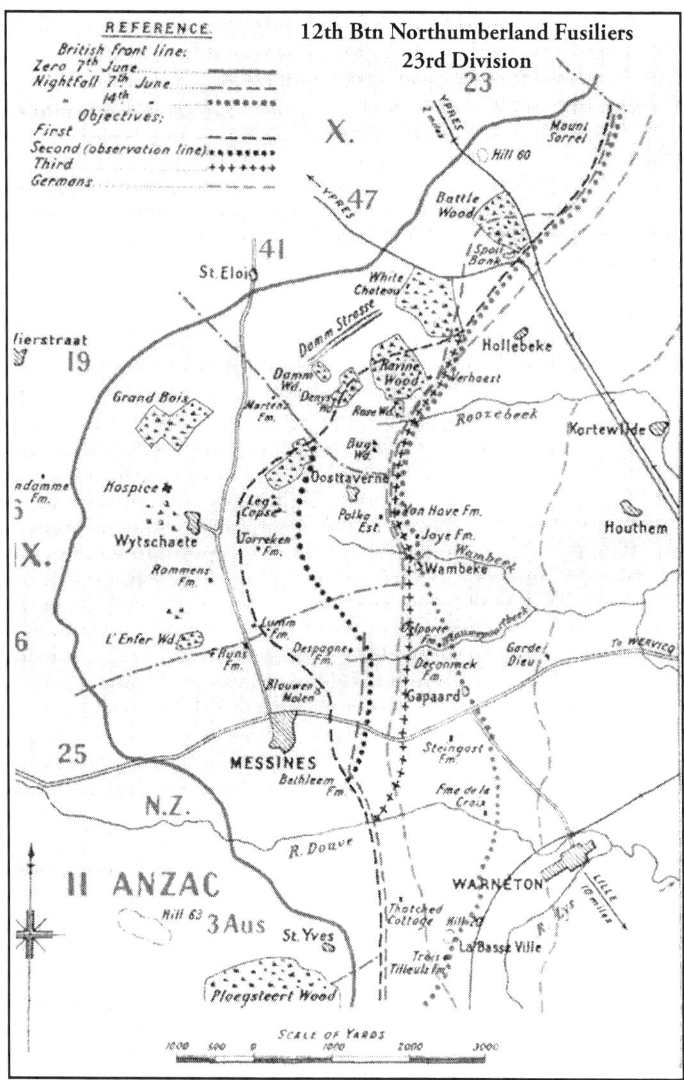


Battle of Messines Ridge, 1917

Zillebeke Spur as well as to cover the left flank of the attack by forming a defensive flank facing east. The Divisional attacking front stretched from Windy Corner to the Snout with initially the 11th NF as part of brigade reserve near Larch Wood Dugouts. When the mines exploded beneath Hill 60 the attacking battalions went over the top and the NF moved forward to occupy the original German Front Line. The enemy's retaliation was vigorous, especially around Lark Wood. Individual companies were moved in to reinforce the initial attacking battalions who had suffered rising casualties. 'E' company reinforced the 9th Yorks digging in on the right edge of Battle Wood. The next day, the 11th NF Battalion was reassembled and concentrated on supplying men for carrying parties. The War Diary for 9 June records that 2nd Lieutenant Bolton had been wounded during the previous day's operations [2].

**Second Lieutenant Robert Frederick Bolton, aged 24**
**11th (Service) Battalion Northumberland Fusiliers**
**Died 10 June 1917**

Robert was born at Rennington, near Alnwick, and was the eldest son of Sergeant Robert and Isabella Bolton of Tynedale Terrace, Wark. The 1911 census records that the family was living at Sanatorium Cottage and that Robert was working as a Stationary Fireman. His father, a Boer War veteran, was stationed at the Northumberland Fusiliers Depot in Newcastle. The Hexham Courant reports that before he volunteered to join the army he was living in Chollerton and was employed as a groom by the vicar of Chollerton.

Robert joined the Colours at a public meeting on Wark Green in June 1915. His initial training took place at Redcar and in April 1916, Robert was promoted to the rank of Sergeant. In September 1916 he underwent training for a commission, passing out with credit in January 1917. He embarked for France in March 1917.

Robert was wounded during the Battle of Messines, dying of his wounds. His gravestone is inscribed with the following:

**HIS NAME IS HALLOWED
IN THE HOME HE LOVED
LOVINGLY REMEMBERED**

**Robert is buried in Lijssenthoek Military Cemetery.**

On 18 July, a heavy preliminary artillery bombardment began which was intended to last for 10 days before the date scheduled for a forthcoming Allied offensive. However, for a number of reasons the date for the attack had to be rescheduled two days later, to 03:50 on 31 July, nearly seven weeks after the capture of Messines Ridge. The Allied bombardment used over 3,000 guns which fired over 4,250,000 shells. Given such an onslaught, the German Fourth Army expected an imminent offensive; any element of surprise was entirely absent. Facing this Front the German defences lay on a reverse slope and out of sight of ground observation, making it difficult to pinpoint targets. Air observation provided the solution. In response the Germans carried out extensive counter battery attacks.

**Gunner Thomas Isaac Normington, aged 34
210th Siege Battery, Royal Garrison Artillery
Died 20 July 1917**

Thomas was born in Lesingham Yorkshire, the son of Thomas and Alice Normington. He was married to Alice (née Wormold) and was the father of two children (Alice and Dorothy). He was employed as a gardener by Mr C H Hunting of Slaley Hall. Thomas was called up in July 1916 and went to France in March 1917, and was part of the ammunition column for the 210th Seige Battery.

Second Lieutenant M Wilkinson wrote, "I was only a short distance from him when he was killed, and his death was instantaneous so that he would suffer no pain".

**Thomas is buried in Duhallow ADS Cemetery, Ypres.**

## THIRD YPRES (PASSCHENDAELE) 31 JULY – 10 NOVEMBER 1917

This major British offensive was fought in extreme weather conditions. Official history for the campaign has divided the campaign into a number of major battles. Between these battles, local attempts were made to consolidate the land gained from the last thrust forward, during which men died repulsing German counterattacks. During the whole time, the opposing artillery were hurling shells at one another. This, coupled with the endless need to take supplies up to the men at the Front, resulted in countless deaths.

On the 31 July, the Allied troops faced a formidable German defensive system. Apart from the German Front Line, from early 1917 there were three further trench systems. The second line ran from Bixshoote in the north along the reverse slope of the Pilckem Ridge and then on to the Gheluvelt Plateau. Approximately 2,000 yards to the east, a third line began at Langemark and travelled south towards Gravenstafel, joining the second line on the Gheluvelt Plateau near Glencorse Wood. Between these lines ran the Steenbeek, a small river which by mid 1917 had become an extended bog. Further to the east lay the Flandern I line which ran in front of the Passchendaele Ridge and crossed the Gheluvelt Plateau behind Polygon Wood. The Germans had constructed hundreds of squat concrete pillboxes, low to the ground and camouflaged by a covering of mud and turf. These were manned by machine gun nests of up to forty men. To make matters worse, the numerous stone farmhouses of the area had been turned into highly fortified strong points. After the fall of the Messines Ridge the Germans added two further lines of defence: Flandern II running from Passchendaele village south to Menin and Flandern III on the reverse slope of the Passchendaele Ridge [3,4,5].

## PILCKEM RIDGE: 31 JULY – 2 AUGUST 1917

This attack was launched along an 11 mile front at 3.50am, following weeks of artillery bombardment. Under the cover of misty semi darkness, Allied troops advanced behind a precise creeping barrage. Across most of the battlefield they made early progress. To the north, troops managed to cross the Pilckem Ridge, whilst in the centre the attacking troops rapidly closed on the Steenbeek and captured St Julien. In the south, against the Gheluvelt Plateau, progress was slower or non existent. In the afternoon, under increasingly heavy rain, the Germans launched a series of determined counter attacks forcing a partial withdrawal, which were eventually checked and the line of advance consolidated. During the following two days, which were notable for their appalling weather, the line of advance was held against determined German counter attacks and shelling. To sum up, at some cost the battle saw considerable gains, but there was no sign of a breakthrough.

The **barrage** was developed during World War I. Trench warfare led to the necessity for firing at unseen targets by using observers and an increasingly scientific approach to gunnery. Gunners had to use increasingly complicated calculations to lay their guns. Individual guns were aimed so that their fall of shot was co-ordinated with others to form a pattern; in the case of a barrage, the pattern was a line. The term *barrage* was first used in English in the orders for the Battle of Neuve Chapelle in 1915. A *lifting barrage* was an artillery pattern in which the barrage lifted periodically to a target further back, such as a second line of trenches. This refinement was countered by the defenders infiltrating troops and machine guns into no-man's land or the areas between their own trench lines, so it was deemed necessary to comb the entire area of the advance with artillery fire. The answer was the *creeping barrage* (also called a *walking barrage*). This refinement was a barrage that lifted in small increments, perhaps 50 yards, so that it moved forward slowly, keeping pace with the infantry.

The 44th Company Machine Gun Corps was attached to 44th Brigade of the 15th Division, which on July 31 attacked the section of the Front immediately north of the Ypres-Roulers Railway, with the 55th Division further to their north and the 8th Division south of the railway. The 44th Brigade (9th Black Watch and to the south 8/10th Gordon Highlanders) attacked at 3.50am in dull weather, across ground left in a terrible state because of the relentless rain, forming the right portion of the 15th Division Front. Initially they met little opposition as the German Front Line had been wiped out. However, a number of concrete dugouts were still manned which required the help of supporting tanks. East of Frezenberg the troops in this sector were able to repel two intense counterattacks launched by the Germans. For the first day of the attack, the 44th Machine Gun Company was split up into sections, some of which formed the initial barrage under which these troops attacked. Furthermore, each battalion was allotted two machine guns to go forward in the attack. Some time during this day's action, David Jackson was killed [6].

At the beginning of the war, all infantry battalions were equipped with a machine gun section of two guns, increasing to four in February 1915. The sections were equipped with Maxim guns, served by a subaltern and 12 men. The obsolescent Maxim had a maximum rate of fire of 500 rounds per minute, so each was the equivalent of around 40 well-trained riflemen. The British Army had formally adopted the Vickers gun as its standard machine gun in 1912, using it alongside the Maxim. However, production of the Vickers gun could not keep up with the rapidly expanding army and the BEF was still 237 guns short of the full establishment in July 1915. Shortly after the formation of the MGC, Maxim guns were gradually replaced by the Vickers, which became the standard gun for the next five decades. The Vickers machine gun was fired from a tripod and was cooled by water held in a jacket around the barrel. The gun weighed 28.5 pounds, the water another 10 and the tripod weighed 20 pounds. Bullets were assembled into a canvas belt, which held 250 rounds and would last 30 seconds at the maximum rate of fire of 500 rounds per minute. Two men were required to carry the equipment and two the ammunition, with two extra men in case of casualties.

**Private David Jackson, aged 23**
**44th Company Machine Gun Corps**
**Died 31 July 1917**

David was born in Bewcastle, Cumberland, and was the eldest son of John and Mary Jackson of Bakethin, Plashetts. Before enlisting at Hexham in March 1916, he was employed as a shepherd. He was initially attached to the Northumberland Fusiliers. His cap badge clearly shows this. His medical records show that he was flat-footed. He was transferred to the Machine Gun Corps in November 1916.

After training at Grantham, he was sent to France in late April 1917, joining the 44th Company of the MGC. David was killed on the first day of the Passchendaele offensive.

**David is commemorated on the Menin Gate Memorial to the missing.**

The 2nd Lincolnshire Regiment (LR) formed part of the 25th Brigade 8th Division. Troops from the 8th Division were involved in the first thrust of an attempt to capture the Westhoek Ridge, south of the Ypres-Roulers railway. The 25th Brigade, including the 2nd Lincolns, was initially in support, and was given the dubious honour of being first to scale the ridge which had not been cleared of the enemy. As the Lincolns came over the crest, heavy German machine gun fire tore bloody gaps in the ranks of the forward companies. The enemy fire came mainly from the right flank which was exposed as the attack troops of the 30th Division had been held up earlier in the day. The LR consolidated their position on the reverse slope of the ridge and made a number of unsuccessful attempts to move forward. However, they did succeed in repulsing a number of determined counterattacks. Early next morning the depleted battalion was relieved [7,8].

**Private Henry Smith, aged 38**
**2nd Battalion Lincolnshire Regiment**
**Died 31 July 1917**

Henry was born in Simonburn and was the second son of Frank and Margaret Ann Smith of The Post Office, Simonburn. He was a tailor by trade, living in Gateshead and married to Jane Pearson Smith, becoming the father of four children, two boys and two girls, all of whom were under ten years of age when he was killed. Initially he worked as a tailor

with Mr Henry Hernman and later he became self employed. However, by the outbreak of war he was working as a cutter for Messrs Snowball in Gateshead. He embarked for France on 1 March 1917. While he was serving in France he was brought the shocking news that one of his children had been run over and killed. The Smith family had three other sons who fought during the Great War: Trooper Frank of the New Zealanders, who was badly wounded in Gallipoli, Staff Armourer Sergeant Smith of the RND and Trooper Douglas Smith of the South Irish Horse.

**Henry is commemorated on the Menin Gate Memorial to the missing.**

Remains of a German strongpoint taken on the 31 July 1917

*Photograph A Grint, 2011*

On 4 August the 2nd Battalion Royal Irish Rifles moved into dugouts under the ramparts of Ypres and the next day moved into the line in front of the Westhoek Ridge. The movement up to the Front resulted in some casualties through being caught by a heavy barrage as they were crossing through Chateau Wood. The Front was also taking a pounding. The attack scheduled for 9 August was to complete the capture of the Westhoek Ridge and thus straighten the line, which would allow further major operations to be undertaken. The 74th Brigade (Royal Irish Rifles) with the 18th Division to its right was to undertake the attack. The brigade was to attack along a 2,000 yard Front south of the Ypres-Roulers Railway. Along the Front, the distance to the objective varied from 250 yards on the left to 650 yards in the centre and 450 yards on the right. All four of the brigade's battalions were to be used. The Rifles in the centre were commanded to capture the heavily defended village of Westhoek. On the evening of 8 August very heavy rain fell, reportedly filling nearby shell holes to the brim; the conditions on the battleground were such that eight men were needed to trudge with a wounded man on a stretcher to the Advanced Dressing Station on the Menin Road. These conditions resulted in the postponement of the action by 24hrs until 10 August. Daniel's death is reported as 9 August; he must have been killed whilst waiting in the Front Line trenches after the postponement. On 10 August, 74th Brigade took part in the renewal of the attack. In a successful action, they captured Westhoek, although at a severe cost [9].

**Rifleman Daniel McKie, aged 19**
**2nd Battalion Royal Irish Rifles**
**Died 9 August 1917**

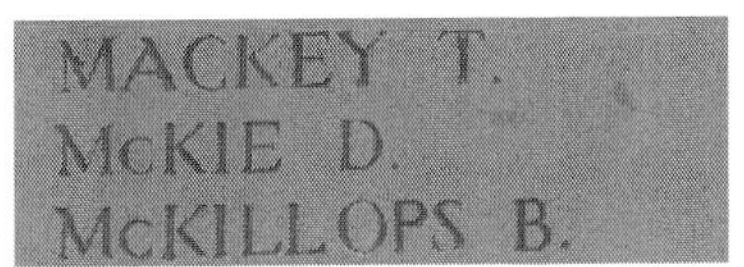


Daniel was born in Bellingham and was the eldest son of Thomas and Martha McKie. The 1911 census shows that the family of three sons and three daughters was living in Cruddas Terrace.

**Daniel is commemorated on the Menin Gate Memorial to the missing.**

At 4am on 13 August elements of the 6th Yorkshire Regiment were withdrawn from outposts west of the 'Steenbeek', a stream that had once flowed north-eastwards across the Ypres battlefield, but by 1917, because of continuous shelling, was now nothing more than an extended bog. The outposts would be no more than a series of unconnected shell holes, manned by up to ten soldiers. This planned evacuation allowed heavy Allied artillery bombardment of nearby enemy blockhouses without risk to their own men. By 3am on 14 August the outposts had returned to the 'Steenbeek', forming up in preparation for an advance. 'A' company

**The Lewis Gun** (or Lewis Automatic Machine Gun) is a World War I era light machine gun of American design that was perfected and widely used by the British Empire forces. It was first used during World War I, from July 1915. It is visually distinctive because of a wide tubular cooling shroud around the barrel and a top mounted drum-pan magazine containing 47 rounds. It was commonly used as an aircraft machine-gun. The gun's rate of fire was approximately 500–600 rounds per minute. It weighed 28lb (12.7kg), only about half as much as a typical medium machine gun of the era, such as the Vickers, and was chosen in part because, being more portable than a heavy machine gun, it could be carried and fired by a single soldier, although since the rate of fire used a magazine very quickly, he needed another to carry and load the magazines. The original official establishment was 4 per infantry battalion, initially to 6 selected Divisions, increasing as they were produced in greater numbers. By July 1918, infantry battalions possessed 36 each and even Pioneer battalions had 12. This very significant increase in battalion firepower enabled new and successful infantry tactics to be devised.

attacked on the right of the attack using 2½ platoons, the remainder with 'B' company in support. On the left 'C' company took up a similar formation with 1 platoon in support. At 4am the advance began supported by an artillery barrage. 'C' company easily gained its objectives. However, 'A' company met with hostile machine gun fire from dugouts untouched by the bombardment. On 'A' company front the Germans launched a number of localised attacks which were easily repulsed by rifle fire. That night the remnants of the battalion were relieved. Casualties for the attack were 2 officers wounded and other ranks 20 killed, 69 wounded and 26 missing [10].

**Private George Smith, aged 19**
**'A' Company 6th (Service) Battalion Yorkshire Regiment**
**Died 14 August 1917**

George was the only son of George William and Annie Smith of Ferry Road, Bridge End, Hexham. Before joining the forces he was employed in their seed department by Messers W Fell and Company who were nurserymen in Hexham, between Haugh Lane and the river. George joined the Colours on 6 October 1916 and proceeded to France on New Years Eve 1916. He was part of the battalion's Lewis Gun section.

**George is commemorated on the Menin Gate to the missing.**

Two of the three German bunkers which form the backdrop to the German cemetery at Langermarck.
*Photograph A Grint, 2011*

**Herbert Charles Onslow Plumer**

Plumer was educated at Eton and was commissioned into the York and Lancaster Regiment in 1876. From 1879 to 1886, he was adjutant of his battalion, and he went to the Sudan in 1884. Captain Plumer fought at the battles of El Teb and Tamai, and was mentioned in Despatches. In 1896 he served in operations in South Africa, where he organized and commanded a corps of Mounted Rifles, subsequently obtaining another mention in Despatches after which he was awarded the rank of brevet (or acting) Lieutenant-Colonel. He served with the Second Army in Flanders during World War I, during which he won an overwhelming victory over the German Army at the Battle of Messines in 1917, which started with what was described as the *loudest explosion in human history,* created by the simultaneous explosion of 19 mines. Plumer is generally regarded as one of the finest army commanders serving in France during World War I. Because of his infantry, as opposed to cavalry, background he deprecated the insistence on the value of the "breakthrough" and the effectiveness of cavalry to exploit the opening and reach the open country beyond the front line. As a career infantry officer it could be argued that he understood somewhat better what could reasonably be expected of his troops bearing in mind the terrain, the weather and morale. Plumer, a meticulous planner, would often express the plans of his superiors as being too ambitious and more often than not, as seen at the Third Battle of Ypres, he would be proved to be right. Plumer was very popular with the men gaining the affectionate nickname *Old Plum* and *Daddy Plumer.*

## LANGERMARK: 16 AUGUST – 18 AUGUST 1917

The *Battle of Langermark* was once again fought in appalling weather conditions. The battle began on 16 August when soldiers from eight British divisions attacked at 4.45am along a frontage of 12,000 yards following a creeping barrage. There was limited success in the north, where a 1500 yard gain was achieved, but, in the centre and to the south, failure was coupled with heavy casualties. Most of the failure can be explained by the fact that British artillery had not managed to destroy the German field batteries and their extensive fortifications. In the afternoon the Germans mounted determined counterattacks which forced Allied withdrawals from any gains they had made during the morning's fighting.

## MENIN ROAD RIDGE
## 20 SEPTEMBER – 25 SEPTEMBER 1917

Unhappy with the tactics of General Gough, who had been in charge of the Passchendaele offensive, Field Marshall Haig passed command to General Plumer (the architect of the Messines triumph). Plumer requested a delay so that he could establish his tactics of careful planning and overwhelming artillery superiority. Luckily, these preparations coincided with good weather; weeks of sunshine and wind dried up the saturated ground. There was intense training of the troops with the aim of securing the Gheluvelt Plateau. The preliminary artillery bombardment began on 31 August, increasing in intensity every day and helped by clear weather, thus observation conditions were good. At 5.40am on 20 September, 65,000 soldiers advanced along an eight mile Front screened by mist and protected by an immense creeping barrage; they quickly overran the German outposts and surviving strongpoints. By noon the British troops had gained all of their limited objectives. These were within the range of supporting artillery which, with the help of reconnaissance flights, was able to disperse any German threat of counterattack. Further consolidation of the newly acquired Front Line took place in the face of fierce German attempts to win back lost land.

## POLYGON WOOD: 26 SEPTEMBER – 3 OCTOBER 1917

Hard on the success of his attack along the Menin Road, Plumer prepared for another thrust forward of his line, by another 1200 yards. In this attack, Australian and New Zealand troops would be used to capture and secure the objective of Polygon Wood. The flanks of the attack would be protected on the left by 3rd and 59th Divisions and on the right by 33rd Division. The infantry attacked at 5.50am along a five mile Front following an immense protective barrage. By 9.45am all the objectives had been captured and secured. Clear weather during the afternoon assisted air observation of potential German threats which were readily disrupted and nullified by precise artillery barrages, causing heavy German casualties.

## BROODSEINDE: 4 OCTOBER 1917

This was the third of Plumer's limited-objective offensives. Australian troops were allotted the principle role in this attack, with British Divisions moving forward on both flanks. The attack, along an eight mile Front, was to begin at 6am following a surprise intense barrage on German positions. However, at 5.20am they were surprised by an intense German bombardment which fell on the assembled Anzac Troops, although this did not hinder the main attack. As the Australians surged forward they met advancing German infantry; following furious hand to hand combat, the attacking Germans were forced into submission. The German strongpoints just below the crest of the ridge were eventually taken, in a series of desperate struggles, and by 9am the ridge itself had fallen. Elsewhere, to the south of the battlefield, British forces reached the eastern edge of Gheluvelt Plateau, whilst to the north the advance towards Poelcappelle kept pace with the Anzac advance. However, during the evening of this costly victory, drenching rain once again set in, turning the battlefield into a quagmire once again.

The 21st Division was one of the formations that provided part of the southern flank of the attack. They forced eastwards from Polygon Wood towards Beclaere. It was the first time that men of the 1st Battalion East Yorkshire (64 Brigade 21st Division) (EY) had been engaged in this momentous conflict. On 4 October, after a number of logistical changes, 'B' company (EY) was allotted to the first wave of the attack alongside the 9th KOYLI and they helped capture the attack's first objective. The remaining three companies (EY) advanced in the rear of 10th KOYLI in order to capture the day's second objective. By 7.45am the attack had stalled and survivors of the attack began to dig in at the western end of Reutel Village. On a number of occasions during the afternoon, German troops were observed to be massing for a counter-attack, but were ably dispersed by the divisional artillery [11,12].

**Private William Hedley, aged 27**
**1st Battalion East Yorkshire Regiment**
**Died 4 October 1917**

William was born in South Dean, Roxburghshire, the eldest son of Alexander and Jemima Hedley. They lived at Lea Orchard, Bellingham. The 1911 census shows William, aged 20, working at Knoppingsholme farm as a horseman. He married Josephine Turnbull, (née Weatherson) in Weardale in June 1912 and became the father of two daughters. He attested for military service under the Derby Scheme in January 1916, in Morpeth. At this time, William and his family were living in Thornton Cottage, Hartburn; he was working as a farm horseman. He was mobilised in May 1917, and after basic training he went out to France in late August. Although reported as missing on 4 October 1917, it was not until July 1918 that William's family were officially notified of his death. After the death of her husband, Josephine Hedley and their daughters returned to live in Weardale.

**William is commemorated on the Tyne Cot Memorial to the missing.**

The $12^{th}$/$13^{th}$ Northumberland Fusiliers were part of the $62^{nd}$ Brigade $21^{st}$ Division. The division was positioned on the southern flank of the attack and in conjunction with the $5^{th}$ Division (right) and $7^{th}$ Division (left) were to form a defensive flank facing south south-east and east for the attacking Anzac troops to the north. They were also to achieve a position affording observation of the Reutel Beek valley and the spur running south east to Becelaere. The division attacked with the $62^{nd}$ Brigade on the left and its $64^{th}$ Brigade on the right. The $62^{nd}$ Brigade attack used the $3/4^{th}$ Queen's Royal West Surrey in its first thrust to secure its first objective, after which the $12^{th}$/$13^{th}$ would be used on the right of the attack to secure the final objective between the southern end of Judge Copse and Judge Cott on the left.

In moving up to their attack position the Fusiliers met with a hostile barrage but suffered only a few casualties. At 6am, the $12^{th}$/$13^{th}$ went over the top following the $3/4^{th}$ Queen's and after crossing Juniper Trench they came under fire on both flanks. On the right a German strong point, not destroyed by the first wave of Queen's troops, opened fire but was soon neutralised by 'A' company and 30 to 40 German prisoners were taken. In conjunction with the $1^{st}$ Lincolns, another strongpoint on the right was captured. All the time heavy German machine gun fire was being directed on the attacking Allied troops which resulted in a growing number of casualties, in spite of which the attackers began to consolidate their gains. At 7.40am the Allied barrage moved forward as planned allowing the capture of the final objective, although they still encountered heavy machine gun and artillery fire directed from the ridge opposite. Approximately 250 yards short of the final objective the attackers were forced to dig in. The total advance for the day was 1100 yards. The battalion faced no counterattacks during the rest of day. However, the War Diary records that heavy friendly fire constantly fell on the battalion in response to SOS signals sent up by neighbouring units [13].

**Lance Sergeant Wilfred Henry Charlton, aged 29**
**12th/13th (Service) Battalion Northumberland Fusiliers**
**Died 4 October 1917**

Wilfred was born in Acomb, the son of Stephen and Jane Charlton of 'Roselea', Humshaugh. He initially embarked for France with the first batch of the local Territorials in April 1915 and would see action during the desperate days of April/May 1915 (see page 35). He was later transferred to either the 12th or 13th Northumberland Fusiliers, which due to their casualties were amalgamated in August 1917 to become the 12th/13th. Although he was posted missing on 4 October 1917, it was actually October 1918 when his parents received official confirmation of his death. The Charltons were a patriotic family with six sons serving with the Allied forces. In October 1918, their youngest son, Arthur, who was serving with the Canadians, was in Addington Palace Hospital suffering from dysentery and recovering from a severe wound. The eldest son John, serving with the New Zealanders, was in hospital in Palestine with enteritis.

The King and Queen sent a message of sympathy to the Charlton family:

> "He whose loss you mourn died in the noblest of causes. His country will be ever grateful to him for the sacrifice he has made for Freedom and Justice."

**Wilfred is commemorated on the Tyne Cot Memorial to the missing.**

Broodseinde was viewed as an important victory. German losses had been high and along the Front a significant number of prisoners had been taken. Unfortunately, the advance had also been limited and had cost many Allied lives. That night, the rain began again in earnest and turned the churned up battlefield once more into a filthy, rat-infested swamp.

## POELCAPPELLE: 9 OCTOBER 1917

Haig sought to maintain the momentum of the assault and was encouraged by the scale of German casualties at Broodseinde and heartened by Army Intelligence's reports of the poor state of German morale. On the evening of 8 October the Allied troops moved forward through a sea of mud, hampered by a downpour of penetratingly cold rain. The main thrust of the attack would use elements of the 49th and 66th Divisions of II Anzac Corps, supported to the south by the 1st and 2nd Australian Divisions. In the north a number of British Divisions were employed, including the Guards Division at the northern extremity of the British attack. At 5.20am the exhausted and under-strength British and Australian troops attacked behind a ragged and inaccurate barrage. All along the Front they met ferocious machine gun fire from undamaged German pill boxes and machine gun nests located in shell holes.

The 1/4th York and Lancaster Battalion, as part of 148th Brigade 49th Division, attacked up the Wallemoen spur on which the village of Bellevue stood. After its capture the intention was for the battalion to attack the main ridge north of Passchendaele.

The men of the battalion had marched for eleven hours to their assembly point, arriving exhausted at 5.20am, only an hour before 'zero hour'. At the onset of their attack, they encountered the Ravenbeek, a stream, the bed of which was thirty to fifty yards wide, a watery morass, waist deep at its centre. Only a small number of men were able to cross this intimidating marsh. Throughout the day the attackers came under heavy machine-gun fire from pillboxes on the higher ground ahead. They also came under chillingly accurate sniper fire aimed at the battalion's stretcher-bearers. In the evening, the Germans attempted a counterattack, which was repulsed. Overall, the Allied attack lacked effective artillery support. In the evening the exhausted and severely reduced battalion was relieved by New Zealand troops.

Casualties for this attack were 4 officers and 42 other ranks killed, 5 officers and 191 other ranks wounded. Furthermore, 1 officer and 48 other ranks were reported missing, many of whom would be reported dead in the days ahead [14].

**Private Walton Bell, aged 33**
**1/4th Battalion (Hallam) York and Lancaster Regiment**
**Died 9 October 1917**

Walton was born in Hexham in 1885. The 1891 census shows him living with his grandparents, Robert and Rebecca Bell. He was a married man: at the time of his death; Annie (née Potts) lived with their three children (Nellie, Frances and Edward) in Elliott Terrace, Wark. Annie later remarried and eventually lived at Butts Bank, Fourstones, as Annie Smith.

Walton served his time as a butcher with John Dodd and was for some years employed by Haydon Bridge Cooperative Society. Just before the war, M J Miller of Wark employed him as a manager of his butcher's business. Walton signed up in November 1915 and was mobilised in March 1917. It was reported that when Walton left to join the forces, Mr Miller was forced to close his business. Walton was initially assigned to the 1/4th Northumberland Fusiliers, but was subsequently transferred to his final regiment. He had been in France for only six weeks before he was killed.

**Walton is commemorated on the Tyne Cot Memorial to the missing.**

The Australian 17th Battalion (2nd Australian Division) was part of the initial thrust on 9 October 1917. They attacked to the south of the Ypres-Roulers Railway and were ordered to provide protection for the right flank of the 66th Division. At 5.20am the attack opened with an artillery barrage and soon afterwards the troops moved forward, making good progress to their final objective: the north western part of the Keiberg spur. After fighting for twenty four hours the battalion was relieved and returned to the old Front Line [15,16].

**Private William Dodd, aged 33**
**17th Battalion, Australian Infantry**
**Died 9 October 1917**

William was born in Greystead, Bellingham, the second son of Matthew and Sarah Dodd. The 1881 census shows that the Dodds worked a 1500 acre farm employing 1 man and 1 woman. By 1891, however, the census shows the family, now with Sarah as the head, living in Kate's House, Wark. By the age of 16, William was working as a farm labourer and some time after 1901 he emigrated to Australia. His military papers show that he worked as a labourer in New South Wales. He was a single man and listed Kitty Dodd (his sister) in Greystead as his next of kin.

He enlisted in the Australian forces in April 1916 at the Cootamundra Base. After basic training he was attached to the 17th Battalion and arrived in Plymouth aboard the HMAT Ceramic late in November 1916. After a prolonged period of medical attention, William joined his battalion in France on 1 April 1917. He was wounded in action on 3 May when his battalion participated in an attack against the Hindenburg Line near Vaulx; the waiting troops were caught in a hostile barrage, ten minutes before their attack was due to begin at 3.45am. The battalion suffered over 290 casualties. William rejoined his battalion in early June and initially was reported as 'wounded' on 9 October 1917. This later changed to 'missing' and at a Court of Enquiry in late April 1918 William was confirmed as killed in action.

**William is commemorated on the Menin Gate to the missing.**

German Machine gun crew wearing gas masks

Poelcappelle was a costly disaster, with the British sustaining a considerable number of casualties and attaining practically none of the day's objectives.

## FIRST PASSCHENDAELE: 12 OCTOBER 1917

After the devastating results of the attack on 9 October, Haig sanctioned a continuation of the overall attack for Friday 12 October. Again, the Australians and New Zealanders were to shoulder the brunt of the attack, whilst to the north they were supported by five British divisions. In summary, the attack failed completely with severe British and Anzac casualties. Conspiring against the British were the continuous bad weather, the waterlogged terrain and – more importantly – inadequate artillery support. As the attack started the supporting barrage could only be described as 'desultory'. To cap it all, the onset of the attack coincided with the prevailing drizzle turning into torrential rain. Immediately, the attacking troops were severely mauled by German machine-gunners. Apart from in the north, where the Allies had some success, along most of the Front the attacking troops were forced back to the starting line.

The 48$^{th}$ Battalion was part of the Australian 4$^{th}$ Division which formed the right flank of the attack of 12 October, alongside the Ypres-Roulers Railway. Even during the move up to the line in preparation for an attack in the early hours of the morning, there were a number of casualties (1 officer and 12 other ranks killed). Following the creeping barrage as it moved forward, men of the 48$^{th}$ Battalion were saved from an accurate enemy barrage which pounded their jumping off position only four minutes later. However, soon they were faced with machine gun fire from across the railway from the left and also from their extreme right flank. The Battalion War Diary states, of their attempt to consolidate their position, "enemy sniping and machine gun fire became very persistently heavy and almost every man who showed himself became a casualty".

At 3.30pm a German counterattack was preceded by a barrage which fell on the battalion's position. This attack was initially stopped in its tracks, but a second wave was able to drive back the battalion's forward posts and many of the men were caught in the open by snipers. By the evening, under cover of fire from their own Lewis guns, the remnants of the battalion had retired to take up a defensive position in the very trenches in which they had begun the day [15,17].

**Lieutenant Henry Quentin Ridley, aged 34**
**48th Battalion Australian Infantry**
**Died 12 October 1917**

Henry was born in Wylam, Northumberland, the eldest son of Musgrave and Emily Kaye Ridley. He was educated at Harrow and was a member of Park House. The 1911 census shows that Henry, whose occupation was described as Timber Merchant, was living with Charles Noel Ridley at High Park End, near Simonburn, and whose occupation was also described as Timber Merchant. Henry's father had followed a similar profession. (Charles Noel died in 1915 of wounds received during the *Battle of Loos* (see page 305).

Some time between 1911 and early 1916, Henry emigrated to Australia. On enlisting with the Australian Imperial Force in Perth in February 1916, Henry stated that he was unmarried and gave his profession as 'farmer', near Broomehill southeast of Perth. He underwent his basic training at

Blackboy Hill Camp near Perth and within a month was promoted to Sergeant and by late 1916 he was commissioned Second Lieutenant. He left Australia aboard the troop carrier HMAT Argyllshire, arriving in Devonport in January 1917.

In May he was drafted into the 48th Battalion and in June he was promoted in the field, to Lieutenant. Between 13 and 22 September he was on leave in England. The battalion records report that Henry was killed by a shell during the engagement of 12 October.

**Henry is buried in Passchendaele New British Cemetery.**

The Guards attacked north of the Ypres-Staden railway, south of the Houthulst Forest. During the attack of 9 October the Guards Division successfully achieved its objective. However, on their left flank, the attacking formations had not been as successful, thus forming a dangerous salient, described "as more acute than a right angle" in the British Line. On the evening of 11 October, the 1st Grenadiers moved into the Front Line with two companies of Scots Guards, whose responsibility it was to get in touch with 51st Brigade. During the hand-over, the enemy put down a heavy gas shell barrage causing a large number of casualties. The attack made on 12 October was made with the help of an artillery barrage which was "irregular and ragged", as described in the Regimental History. However, the attack achieved its objective. Even so, contact with the left had still not been achieved, which left pockets of the enemy to cause significant irritation from artillery and sniper fire. The battalion was relieved during the evening of 13 October [18,19].

The War Diary reports that R Hall, of Wall, was killed during the day. Casualties within the ranks were 36 killed and 200 wounded or missing [20].

**Guardsman Robert Hall, aged 19**
**1st Battalion Grenadier Guards**
**Died 13 October 1917**

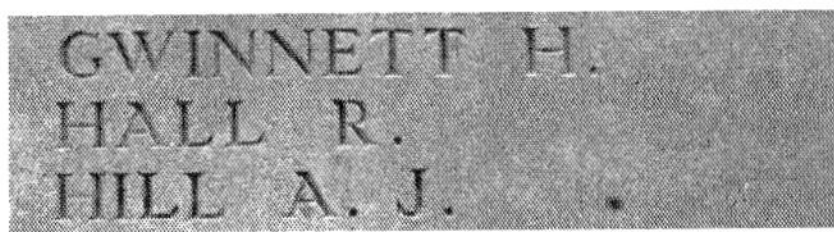


Robert was born in Wall, the son of Robert and Elizabeth Hall. He was the second youngest of seven children. Very soon after his birth the family moved to Bolam, near Belsay, where both Robert and his father worked as gamekeepers. Robert joined the Guards in May 1916.

**Robert is commemorated on the Tyne Cot Memorial to the missing.**

During the days leading up to the next major attack on the 26 October, the exhausted soldiers who had been involved in the attacks of the last few days were relieved from the Front Line.

The 12th Battalion Durham Light Infantry (DLI) moved into the Front Line to the east of Polygon Wood on 13 October. They remained at the Front for three days and during this time were subjected to very intense enemy shelling. They were also attacked by a group of low flying German aircraft which repeatedly machine-gunned their position. By the time the DLI left the trenches on the evening of 16 October over thirty men (including Paxton Dodd) had been killed [21,22].

**Private Paxton Dodd, aged 28**
**12th (Service) Battalion Durham Light Infantry**
**Died 14 October 1917**

Paxton was born in Hexham, the second son of Paxton and Mary Ann Dodd of Haugh Lane, Hexham. Paxton had four brothers and five sisters.

He married Annie J Clark in the autumn of 1915 and they lived at Bridge End, Bellingham. She died in April 1918. As a boy, Paxton had joined the Post Office in Hexham; following this he worked for two years in Humshaugh as a postman. Subsequently, he moved with his job to Bellingham, from where he delivered the post on horseback. He offered his services under Lord Derby's Scheme in the winter of 1915. He had only been in France a few weeks (September 1917), before he was killed in action.

**Paxton is commemorated on the Tyne Cot Memorial to the missing.**

"... a shell burst slick upon the duck-boards;
so I fell into the bottomless mud, and lost the light."

*Memorial Tablet, Siegfried Sassoon*

On the night of 12th/13th October, the 26th Battalion Northumberland Fusiliers moved into the Line, north-west of Poelcappelle. The Battalion War Diary records that the conditions were very bad: half the countryside was flooded and the whole area was a sea of mud. The battalion was relieved on the night of 16th/17th and marched initially to Stray Farm and next morning to Bridge Camp. On 14 October, 13 Fusiliers were killed including Richard Harrison and Robert Hedley [23,24,25].

**Private Richard Edward Harrison, aged 23**
**26th (Service) Battalion Northumberland Fusiliers**
**Tyneside Irish**
**Died 14 October 1917**

Richard was born in Dalston, Cumberland, the eldest son of Thomas and Sarah Ann Harrison of Tile Row, Plashetts. Like his father, Richard worked underground in the local colliery. He went to France with the initial draft of the Territorials in April 1915 and was involved in the fighting of 26 April 1915, (see page 35). The St George's Gazette (31 August 1915) lists him among the wounded and after a short time in a hospital in France, he quickly returned to the firing line. The North Tyne Magazine for November 1916 reports that he was wounded again during the action of 15 September on the Somme, (see page 105). Subsequently, Richard was posted to the Tyneside Irish, to die a year later.

**Richard is commemorated on the Tyne Cot Memorial to the missing.**

**Lance Corporal Robert Hedley, aged 29**
**26th (Service) Battalion Northumberland Fusiliers**
**Tyneside Irish**
**Died 14 October 1917**

Robert was born in Thorneyburn, Northumberland, the only son of Elizabeth and Robert Hedley. He was a married man; his wife Jessie McKie Hedley lived in Aberdeen after the war. At the onset of hostilities Robert volunteered to join the forces and arrived in France in September 1915 with the 12th Battalion Northumberland Fusiliers (NF).

This battalion was involved in the disastrous advance on Hill 70 during the *Battle of Loos* (see page 67). At some stage he was allocated to the 23rd NF and then transferred to the 26th NF.

**Robert is commemorated on Tyne Cot Memorial to the missing.**

At this time, because of the high casualties suffered by both the 24th and 27th Northumberland Fusiliers (NF), the two battalions were amalgamated. On 20 October this amalgamated battalion was attached to the 102nd Brigade and moved to the Front Line near Poelcappelle. On 22 October the battalion was involved in a local attack having been allocated the task of covering the left flank of 18th Division.

The 20th NF would provide covering fire. The attack, under the cover of a barrage, made a good start and the battalion was employed to rout out the defenders of Requette Farm which had been bypassed by the 18th Division. Two German machine guns and twenty five prisoners were taken.

The battalion stayed in the Line until midday of 24 October. The War Diary describes the casualties for this action as 'light'. However, among the dead was Robert Rutter [24,26].

**Private Robert Rutter, aged 32**
**27th (Service) Battalion Northumberland Fusiliers**
**Tyneside Irish**
**Died 23 October 1917**

Robert, the son of Robert and Rosanna Rutter of the Crags, Barrasford, was born at Newton by the Sea, Northumberland. He married, Margaret ('Maggie', née Crisp) in early 1917 whilst on leave from the Front. Maggie had already lost two brothers to the horrors of the war. (see pages 130 and 311).

Before enlisting as a volunteer shortly after the outbreak of hostilities, Robert was employed at Barrasford Whinstone Quarry as a stone breaker. He was also a very active member of Barrasford Football Club.

Initially he enlisted with the local Territorials, but did not see service in France until after November 1915. The newspapers reported that he had been wounded twice.

The Hexham Herald reported that he had been wounded on 15 September 1916 (see page xx), whilst serving with the Territorials. Subsequently he was transferred to the Tyneside Irish and was killed in action. A letter to his wife from Captain James McIntyre reports

> "…he was killed in action in performance of his duty. He was killed instantaneously, suffering no pain."

**Robert is commemorated on Tyne Cot Memorial to the missing.**

# SECOND PASSCHENDAELE
# 26 OCTOBER – 10 NOVEMBER 1917

Houthulst Forest from the south

Although *Second Passchendaele* was primarily a Canadian affair, British and Australian Divisions were involved in attacks on the flanks in support of the Canadian thrust. The initial assault on 26 October, yet again in soaking rain, saw the Canadians cross the flooded Ravenbeek and advance a further 500 yards towards the village of Passchendaele. The attacks on the flanks proved to be costly failures. On 30 October the Canadians renewed their attack and gained the outskirts of the village of Passchendaele, which was finally taken by the Canadians on the morning of 6 November during intense hand to hand fighting

On the northern flank, troops from the 63$^{rd}$, 58$^{th}$ , 57$^{th}$ and 50$^{th}$ (Northumbrian) Divisions were used in costly operations. The evening of

24 October was the first experience for the 50th Division of the four month struggle known as Passchendaele. The 149th Brigade relieved elements of the 34th Division just south of Houthulst Forest and astride the Ypres to Staden Railway line. The 1/4th Northumberland Fusiliers (NF) moved into the trenches in the right subsector whilst the 1/7th took up position on the left sub sector [27,28,29,30].

Orders outlined that on 26 October, the 149th Brigade would attack (with the 1/4th NF on the right, 1/5th NF in the centre and 1/7th on the left) across the lowland swamps with the grim Houthulst Forest to the north. To the south, elements of the 57th Division would also be mounting an attack. Because the right hand side of the Front was now effectively a swamp, it was decided to reduce the width of the attack from three companies to two companies in each battalion.

As the troops waited on 25 October for the forthcoming attack, the War Diary reports that the Front Line companies were constantly shelled by its own howitzers which resulted in some casualties. The attack began at 5.40am on 26 October, following behind a creeping barrage. If the going had been better the advancing troops would have had no problem with keeping up with the barrage. Wyrell wrote of the attack:

> "The rain had however done its deadly work, for all the gallant fellows could do was to drag themselves along through the thick clinging mud and water at a much slower pace than the barrage, which soon got ahead. Then from the "pill boxes" and shell holes murderous fire was poured upon them. Many fell dead; some of the wounded fell into the gaping holes of water and were drowned; fortunate were those who escaped, but on went the survivors."

Private Joseph Pickard (1/5th Northumberland Fusiliers) recalls:

> "When the whistle went and you went forward it was a toss up whether your legs would come or not! The ground was yellowy green soft quicksand. I got one leg in there and two fellows got hold of my rifle and pulled me out … you couldn't walk … there was hardly anyone left when we got to the wire."

That evening, the attack was suspended and the brigade withdrawn. By nightfall 18 officers and 367 men from 149th Brigade had been killed. Countless more would die of their wounds in the following days.

**Private Frank Armstrong, aged 30**
**1/4th Battalion Northumberland Fusiliers**
**Died 25 October 1917**

Frank was born in Canonbie, the son of George and Mary Armstrong.

NORTHUMBERLAND FUSILIERS

| LANCE CORPORAL | PRIVATE | PRIVATE |
|---|---|---|
| DOBSON T. | ARKLE J. | BUCKLEY J.J. |
| EASTWOOD A.S. | ARMES L.V. | BULMAN J. |
| ELDRET J.W. | ARMSTRONG F. | BURN C.H. |
| ELLIS G. | ARMSTRONG J.T. | BURN T.E. |

**Frank is commemorated on the Tyne Cot Memorial to the Missing.**

From 1 to 8 November, the 1/4th Battalion Northumberland Fusiliers (NF) were in Caribou Camp, near Hazebrock. They provided working and carrying parties, including those erecting shelters in the support line or carrying duckboards towards the Front Line. The War Diary states that a Lewis Gun Guard was provided at Caribou Camp against enemy aircraft. During the battalion's time at Caribou Camp, Thomas Saint died and his body was lost during the course of the war.

**Private Thomas Pearson Saint, aged 25**
**1/4th Battalion Northumberland Fusiliers**
**Died 5 November 1917**

Thomas was born in Humshaugh, the son of Joseph and Jane Saint. The 1911 census shows a family of four sons and two daughters and Thomas working as a cowman. Thomas' name appears on the Hexham Territorals' Roll of Honour and states that he had joined the 1/4th Northumberland Fusiliers (NF) following Lord Kitchener's appeal for recruits, although he does not appear to have gone with the first batch of Territorials in April 1915. Some time before 1917 he was posted to the 1/5th Battalion NF, and after a further posing to the 1/6th NF he was finally transfered to his orginal battalion.

**Thomas is commemorated on the Tyne Cot Memorial to the missing.**

Royal Field Artillery Battery

The 82nd Brigade, Royal Field Artillery, was attached to the18th Division, whose troops were involved in both the First and Second Battles of Passchendaele. The Divisional Front was south of the village of Poelcappelle and north of the 9th Divisional Front. The thrust for their infantry attacks was northeast towards Westroosebeke [31,32].

**Gunner James Rae Anderson Wylie, aged 33**
**'A' Battery 82nd Brigade Royal Field Artillery**
**Died 31 October 1917**

James, the son of John and Isabella Wylie of Plashetts, was born in Canonbie, Dumfriesshire. He was married to Margaret (née Hymers) in the winter of 1913. During the conflict Margaret would suffer the loss two brothers, George (see page 32) and John (see page 99) as well as her husband. The 1911 census shows that James was a reservist and was presumably called up at the beginning of hostilities in 1914. He was the father of two children, Frances and Joan. He disembarked in France with his artillery brigade in July 1915. His gravestone is inscribed with the following:

**UNTIL THE DAY BREAK (sic)**

**James is buried in Minty Farm Cemetery.**

The 250th Brigade (1st Northumbrian Brigade) was a pre-war Territorial Brigade. They moved into the Passchendaele battlefield on 23 October 1917 and formed part of the Centre Artillery XIV Corps, Left Brigade, and were positioned around the cross roads in what had once been Langemark. 'B' Battery was positioned on the left [33,34].

The Brigade History describes the landscape into which the brigade found itself:

> "No green thing remained, no vestige of house or village church, of chateau or farmstead upon what had been a fair countryside. All was sunk beneath a sea of black stinking mud, the roads or tracks across which were discernible only in that they appeared smoother and more like rivers than the rest."

**Mustard Gas**

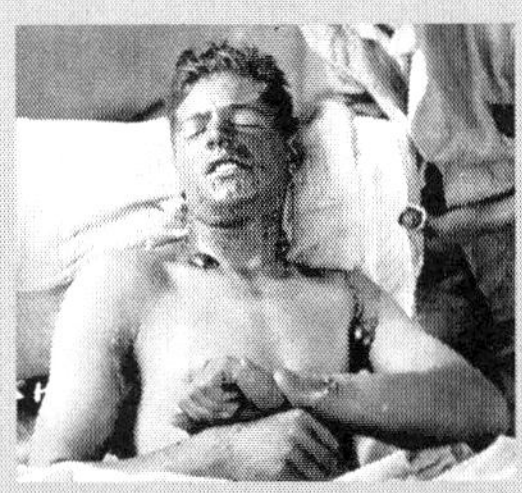

The most widely reported and, perhaps, the most effective gas of the First World War was mustard gas, a vesicant, which was introduced by Germany in July 1917 before the Third Battle of Ypres. A blister agent, or vesicant, is a chemical compound that causes severe skin, eye and mucosal pain and irritation. These gases are named for their ability to cause severe chemical burns, resulting in painful water blisters. The Germans marked their shells yellow for mustard gas and green for chlorine and phosgene, so they called the new gas *Yellow Cross*. It was known to the British as *HS* (*Hun Stuff*), while the French called it *Yperite* (named after Ypres). Mustard gas is not a particularly effective killing agent (though in high enough doses it is fatal), but it was used to harass and disable the enemy and pollute the battlefield. Delivered in artillery shells, mustard gas was heavier than air, and it settled to the ground as an oily liquid resembling sherry, from which vapour would rise. Once in the soil, mustard gas remained active for several days, weeks, or even months, depending on the weather conditions. The skin of victims of mustard gas blistered, their eyes became very sore and they began to vomit; it caused internal and external bleeding and attacked the bronchial tubes, stripping off the mucous membrane, which was extremely painful. Fatally injured victims sometimes took four or five weeks to die from exposure. One nurse, Vera Brittain (read *Testament of Youth* for a full account), wrote: "I wish those people who talk about going on with this war whatever it costs could see the soldiers suffering from mustard gas poisoning. Great mustard-coloured blisters, blind eyes, all sticky and stuck together, always fighting for breath, with voices a mere whisper, saying that their throats are closing and they know they will choke."

All batteries were continually subjected to counter action from the enemy, including drenching the area with mustard gas. On 24 October, the brigade started a 48hr bombardment coinciding with the renewal of the attack by the 149th Brigade (see page 192). As the infantry advanced at 5.40am on 26 October, the Germans turned all their counter-batteries on to 259th Brigade's positions. Every night the enemy drenched the positions with mustard gas: "So intense was this gas that everything once touched was infected with it. Two men died horribly from eating bread which had been splashed by this stuff". The brigade lost men to both the gas and to the shelling, casualties of which lay horribly mutilated in the mud.

On 1 November the Brigade reduced its firing to the smallest possible quantity and withdrew men so as to reduce the ever mounting casualties.

The Brigade History records:

> "Enemy Artillery concentrates on Battery area with gas shell each night, usually firing about a thousand shells in four or five hours. Casualties from this have been heavy; apparently most cases occur from men getting gassed while filling sand bags in ground that had been gas shelled … Gas of mustard type was almost exclusively used … Casualties from shell fire have not been very heavy, but unfortunately a large proportion has been fatal."

**Gunner Thomas Lauderdale, aged 37**
**'B' Battery 250th Brigade Royal Field Artillery**
**Died 1 November 1917**

Thomas was born in Reedsmouth, the son of Thomas and Jane Lauderdale. His mother died in 1887 when Thomas was eight. In early 1913 he married Kate Eleanor Reed of Haltwhistle, who worked as a lady's maid at Reedsmouth Hall. In the early months of 1914 he became the father of a son, John. Before he was conscripted into the army he was working as a gamekeeper for Mr Ulric Charlton of Reedsmouth Hall. The Hexham Herald reported that Thomas was killed during the evening of 1 November 1917 having been in France since late 1916. After he was killed the grieving family moved to Bellingham. Sadly, Kate died in 1925. His gravestone is inscribed with the following:

**BELOVED HUSBAND OF KATE E. LAUDERDALE**

**Thomas is buried in Artillery Wood Cemetery.**

The *Battle of Passchendaele* finally ground to a halt without achieving a momentous victory. After 113 days of fighting the British and Dominion troops managed to advance around five miles at the expense of 250,000 casualties. One of the consequences of the fighting was the creation of another vulnerable salient, which would readily be relinquished during the German advances of April 1918.

## REFERENCES

1. Oldham, P. *Messines Ridge*. Pub: Pen and Sword 1998.

2. WO95/2182. *War Diary 11th Battalion Northumberland Fusiliers.*

3. MacDonald, L. *They called it Passchendaele.* Pub: Penguin 1978.

4. Prior, R. and Wilson, T. *Passchendaele, The Untold Story.*
Pub: Yale University Press 1996.

5. Barton, P. *Passchendaele. Unseen Panoramas of the Third Battle of Ypres.*
Pub: Constable and Robinson, 2007.

6. Stewart, J. Lieut-Col. DSO. and Buchan J. *The fifteenth (Scottish) Division.* Pub: 1926 reprinted Naval and Military Press 2002.

7. Simpson, C.R. Maj-Gen. *The History of the Lincolnshire Regiment 1914-1918.* Pub: 1931, reprinted Military and Naval Press 2002.

8. WO95/1730. *War Diary 2nd Battalion Lincolnshire Regiment.*

9. WO95/2247. *War Diary 2nd Battalion Royal Irish Rifles.*

10. WO95/1804. *War Diary 6th Battalion Yorkshire Regiment.*

11. Wyrall, E. *East Yorkshire Regiment in the Great War 1914-1918.*
Pub: 1928, reprinted Naval and Military Press.

12. WO95/2161. *War Diary 1st Battalion East Yorkshire Regiment.*

13. WO95/2155. *War Diary 12th/13th Battalion Northumberland Fusiliers.*

14. WO95/2805. *War Diary 1/4th Battalion (Hallam) York and Lancaster Regiment.*

15. Bean C. E. W. *Official History of Australia in the War of 1914-1918, Vol. 4.*

16. AWM4 23/34/27. *War Diary 17th Battalion Australian Infantry October 1917.*

17. AWM4 23/65/21. *War Diary 48th Battalion Australian Infantry October 1917.*

18. Ponsonby F.. Lieut-Col. *The Grenadier Guards in the Great War of 1914-1919.* Pub: 1920 reprinted Naval and military Press 2003.

19. Headlam, C. DSO. *History of the Guards Division in the Great War 1915-1918.* Pub; 1924. reprinted Naval and Military Press 2002.

20. WO95/1223. *War Diary 1st Battalion Grenadier Guards.*

21. Miles, Capt. W. *Durham Forces in the Field.*
Pub: 1920 reprinted Naval and Military Press 2004.

22. WO95/1223. *War Diary 12th Battalion Durham Light Infantry.*

23. Shakespear, Lt Col. J. *Thirty Fourth Division 1915-1919.*
Pub: 1921 reprinted Naval and Military Press 1998.

24. Sheen, J. A. *History of Tyneside Irish.* Pub: Pen and Sword, 1998.

25. WO95/2467. *War Diary 26th Battalion Northumberland Fusiliers.*

26. WO95/2467. *War Diary 27th Battalion Northumberland Fusiliers.*

27. Wyrall, E. *The Fiftieth Division, 1914-1919.*
Pub: 1939, reprinted Naval and Military Press 2002.

28. WO95/2828. *War Diary, 1/4th Battalion Northumberland Fusiliers.*

29. Buckley, F. Capt. *War History of the Seventh Northumberland Fusiliers.*
Pub: T. M. Greirson.

30. Buckley, F. Capt. *Q. 6. A. and Other Places.*
Pub: Spottiswoode and Ballentyne 1920.

31. Farndale, M. Gen. KSO. *History of the Royal Regiment of Artillery, Western Front 1914-18.* Pub: the Royal Artillery Institution, 1986.

32. WO95/2024. *War Diary, 82nd Brigade Royal Field Artillery.*

33. Ommanney, C. H. *The War History of the 1st Northumbrian Brigade R.F.A (T.F.) August 1914-July 1919.* Pub: J.W. Hindson 1927.

34. WO95/2817. *War Diary, 250th Brigade Royal Field Artillery.*

# CHAPTER THIRTEEN

# BATTLE OF CAMBRAI

*Sombre the night is.*
*And though we have our lives, we know*
*What sinister threat lurks there.*
From – Isaac Rosenberg's *Returning, we hear the larks*

The *Battle of Cambrai* was launched by General Byng at 6am on the morning of 20 November 1917 along a six mile Front from Hermies in the north to Gonnelieu in the south. Over 476 tanks, six infantry and two cavalry brigades in conjunction with 1,000 artillery pieces were used. Within hours of this surprise attack the German defenders had been forced to retreat nearly four miles towards Cambrai and for the first time in the war, British forces had taken the three trench systems of the Hindenburg line. Buoyed on by these exceptional gains, Field Marshall Haig ordered a full scale continuation of the Allied thrust. However, by the second day the progress was slowing down, although Flesquières was captured. From this date the Allied momentum was showing signs of stalling owing to the lack of reserves available to persevere with what had appeared to be a momentous breakthrough. On 28 November the offensive ground to a halt and British troops were ordered to prepare defensive positions.

After the initial shock the German commander Marwitz initiated a number of counterattacks. With troops coming back from the Russian Front he was eventually able to deploy 20 divisions. The major attack began at 7am on 30 November with rapid advances. On the Bourlon Ridge the Germans met intense resistance and suffered heavy casualties, although during the day's fighting the Allies did hold on to the ridge, but elsewhere the Germans made gains. On 3 December they captured La Vacquerie,

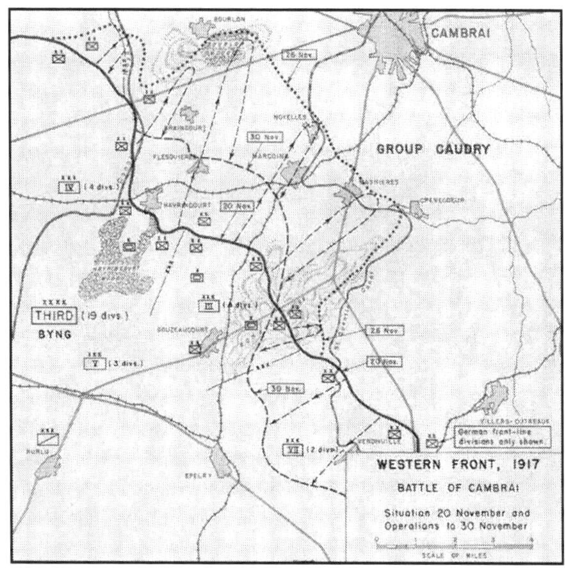


forcing the British to withdraw from positions east of the St Quentin Canal. Following the German recapture of the Bonvais Ridge, the British gradually lost their grip on the gains of 20 November; Field Marshal Haig ordered a retreat from the salient. By 7 December all of the hard won territory had been abandoned apart from a portion of the Hindenburg Line around Havrincourt, Ribécourt and Flesquières. Furthermore, the Germans gained some land south of Welsh Ridge. Casualties were around 45,000 for each side, with 11,000 Germans and 9,000 British captured [1,2,3].

German soldiers recovering a British Mark IV tank.

On 26 November, the 3rd Battalion Grenadier Guards took over a section of the Front Line on the south-east edge of Bourlon Wood opposite the village of Fontaine-Notre-Dame. The Guards Brigade attack on 27 November was along a Front extending from the village of Fontaine to a point 1000 yards east of the centre of Bourlon village. The objectives for the attack were the capture of the German Front Line, and subsequently the railway station and the eastern outskirts of Fontaine. The 3rd Grenadier was on the right; the 1st Coldstream in the centre; the 2nd Irish on the left.

After a bitterly cold night of snow and sleet the attack got underway at 6.20am, following a light artillery bombardment. In a steady drizzle, the attack went on without promised tank support, which was late in arriving. As soon as the Guards left their trenches they were met by heavy machine gun fire and as they approached German wire they realised that it was unbroken by the bombardment. Nonetheless, Nos 1 and 3 companies of the Grenadier Guards managed to force through this obstacle and to capture the German line, although their casualties were heavy.

To take their second objective, the station, the Grenadiers were involved in a series of costly house-to-house fights. After very fierce fighting the Germans were eventually driven eastwards. However, with mounting casualties and a number of precarious defensive positions, the Guards ran the risk of being encircled by the enemy. It was decided that, with no chance of any reinforcements, it was necessary to retire to the day's starting line.

*The History of the Grenadier Guards* states that this was one of the only failures in which the Guards division took part, resulting in the near annihilation of one of its brigades. Casualties for the Grenadiers were three officers killed and six wounded, whilst among other ranks the total casualties were 270 [4,5,6].

**Guardsman William Cuthbert Robson, aged 20**
**3rd Battalion Grenadier Guards**
**Died 27 November 1917**

William was born in Wall and was the youngest son of William Cuthbert and Mary Robson of Front Street, Wall. He was one of six brothers serving with the forces. Before he enlisted he had been employed for over five years as a butcher by Mr R Hedley of Humshaugh. William attested in December 1915 in Hexham and was posted to the Guards in October 1916.

**William is commemorated on the Cambrai Memorial to the missing.**

On 5 November, orders were given for the Northumberland Hussars to move up into the Third Army Area, as part of the build up for the Battle of Cambrai. On 22 November sections of 'B' squadron were allocated to the various divisions holding the Front Line. Troops under Second Lieutenant Robson were allocated to the 29th Division. During the German counterattack on the 30 November it was reported that Robson and a number of his troopers were last seen going towards Quentin Ridge, in order to stem the enemy attack. The next day, when the front was stabilised and as the Germans were pushed back, William's body was found. His records show that his body was initially found 2000 yards east of the village of Villers Guiglain and was subsequently interred at Gouzeaucourt. Twelve deaths were recorded from this action [7]. The history of the regiment states:

> "... and there is no doubt that they fought to the end in a manner worthy of the tradition of the regiment ..."

**Second Lieutenant William John Robson, aged 36**
**No 3 Troop, 'B' Squadron, 1/1 Northumberland Hussars**
**Died 30 November 1917**

William was the eldest son of Matthew and Elizabeth Robson of Snabdough, Bellingham. The Robsons were described as a typical North Tyne farming family. He was privately educated by the Reverend V Nevis in Bellingham. William played rugby for Tynedale and for a number of seasons was described as one of their best forwards. At the start of the war William was serving as a Private with the Newton Hall Section of the Northumberland Hussars (NH), arriving at Zeebrugge on 5 November 1914. On New Year's Eve 1915 William dislocated his shoulder falling from his horse and returned to England for treatment, returning to his regiment in June 1916. Soon afterwards he was accepted for Officer Training College and was commissioned in November 1916, returning to the regiment in early February 1917. William died intestate; it is reported that his estate was valued at £645 9s 1d. Later, the Robson family was faced with further horror: William's younger brother Graham (Royal Inniskilling Fusiliers) was lying dangerously ill in Rouen; his wounds would require the amputation of one of his legs. A further brother, Anthony, serving with the New Zealanders in Palestine, had already had his leg amputated below the knee.

The Hussars played an instrumental part in containing the Germans on the 24 October 1914 at *Polygon Wood,* when they won distinction as the first Territorial unit to go into action. On his death, a friend of William's wrote:

"Whether heading the scrum, digging a trench, or leading his men, he was always in action doing two men's work." His Colonel wrote:

"He was a splendid fellow overall, and is a great loss in the regiment as an officer and as a man. His sort cannot be replaced. The opinion I had of him was what Mark Anthony said of Brutus. 'This was a man.' And indeed his friends will agree that he could have no better epitaph".

His gravestone is inscribed with the following:

**DIED FOR KING AND COUNTRY**

**William is buried in Gouzeaucourt New British Cemetery.**

The 2nd Grenadier Guards were stationed in the Cambrai Salient from 23 November when two of its companies relieved the 9th Royal Scots near Cantaing until 26 November. During this time no casualties were recorded. At daybreak on 30 November the Germans attempted a counterattack against the recent Allied gains. The 1st Guards Brigade, including the 2nd Grenadiers, was ordered to advance towards Gouzeaucourt which was reported to be in German hands. As they advanced, the roads became blocked by retreating soldiers. At Metz the battalion assumed artillery formation and advanced to Gouzeaucourt Wood, where a few casualties resulted from shelling. Being in reserve they watched as the other battalions of the brigade re-captured Gouzeaucourt. Orders were subsequently received for the Grenadiers to be involved in an attack on Gauche Wood. Although tanks had been promised as part of the attack, none materialised and the attack was launched without them. The enemy retaliated with a heavy barrage that fortunately landed behind the advancing troops but the Guards were nonetheless faced with heavy machine-gun fire.

The Battalion History reports, "it is difficult to understand with the machine guns posted at the edge of the wood, the enemy did not wipe out the whole battalion".

In essence, the battalion crossed the ground to the edge of the wood with few casualties, but here the machine guns took a heavy toll. Soon it came to hand to hand fighting and the Germans found that they were no match for the Grenadiers with the bayonet, and were slowly forced eastwards from the wood. Later counterattacks were seen off by steady fire and determined bayonet attacks. Later in the day some dismounted cavalry moved up to cover the right flank. By the night of 2 December, when the Grenadiers were relieved, the casualties for the battalion were 153 killed, wounded and missing [5,6,8]. In a letter describing the attack, an officer of 18th Bengal Lancers wrote:

> "We occupied the captured trench in between the Grenadiers and Coldstream … I have now seen His Majesty's Guards in action and fought alongside of them, and I take off my hat to them. They can die like a gentleman, without a groan. Four of our men were carrying a Guardsman who appeared to be suffering considerably. I asked him who he was, and he instinctively straightened himself as best he could and said, 'A Grenadier', his tone implying how proud he was to be one, and what I also thought, how magnificent they were."

**Guardsman George Spraggon, aged 37**
**2nd Battalion Grenadier Guards**
**Died 2 December 1917**

George was born in Barmoor, Northumberland, and was the youngest son of William and Alice Spraggon. He was educated at Ford Village School and in Haltwhistle. He married Elizabeth Jane Violet (née Browell) at Haltwhistle Parish Church in July 1903 and was the father of three daughters and a son. The youngest, Alister Charles, would never see his father. Before the war the family lived at Laverick Cottage, High Warden, and George worked as a Gamekeeper. George attested in December 1915 and joined the guards in October 1916, arriving in France in early April 1917. He died of wounds received at Cambrai, at No 5 Casualty Clearing Station.

**He is buried at Tincourt New British Cemetery.**

REFERENCES

1. Horsfall, J. and Cave, N. *Flesquières.* Pub: Pen and Sword 2002.

2. Horsfall, J. and Cave, N. *Bourlon Wood.* Pub: Pen and Sword 2002.

3. Horsfall, J. and Cave, N. *Right Hook.* Pub: Pen and Sword 2002.

4. Ponsonby, F. Lieut-Col. *The Grenadier Guards in the Great War of 1914-1919.* Pub: 1920 reprinted Naval and military Press 2003.

5. Headlam, C. DSO. *History of the Guards Division in the Great War 1915-1918.* Pub: 1924 reprinted Naval and Military Press 2002.

6. WO95/1219. *War Diary 3rd Battalion Grenadier Guards.*

7. Pease, H. *The History of the Northumberland (Hussars) Yeomanry.* Pub: Constable and Company Limited, 1924.

8. WO95/1215. *War Diary 2nd Battalion Grenadier Guards.*

# CHAPTER FOURTEEN

# WESTERN FRONT 1918

*They went with songs to battle, they were young,*
*Straight of limb, true of eye, steady and aglow.*
*They were staunch to the end against odds uncounted;*
*They fell with their faces to the foe.*

From Laurence Binyon's *For the Fallen*

## OVERVIEW

The winter of 1917/1918 was atrocious. After its efforts at *Arras, Messines, Passchendaele* and *Cambrai* the British Army was exhausted and severely undermanned; a number of battalions could muster fewer than 300 men. To compound the problem, on 3 November 1917 the War Office informed Field Marshall Haig that they would not be able to replace expected losses. In fact, by 31 October 1917 the manpower shortfall was close to 256,000 men, and Haig and his GHQ staff privately believed that by the end of the year the gap could be as high as 460,000.

In response to this devastating news, on 24 November 1917 Haig advised the War Office that unless more troops were forthcoming he would have to break up 15 of his 57 divisions to bring the remaining formations back up to strength. In late 1917, Prime Minister Lloyd George had moved six of Haig's divisions to Italy in order to shore up the Italian Army which was perilously in disarray. The Cabinet Committee on Manpower disagreed with Haig and proposed an alternative: a reduction from 12 infantry battalions to 9 in every division. The military members of the Army Council protested against this move – which affected every regiment of infantry and cut through an organisational structure for which every officer and man had been trained – but to no avail. The army moved to the 9-battalion structure in early 1918 and was still coming to terms with its effects well into 1918.

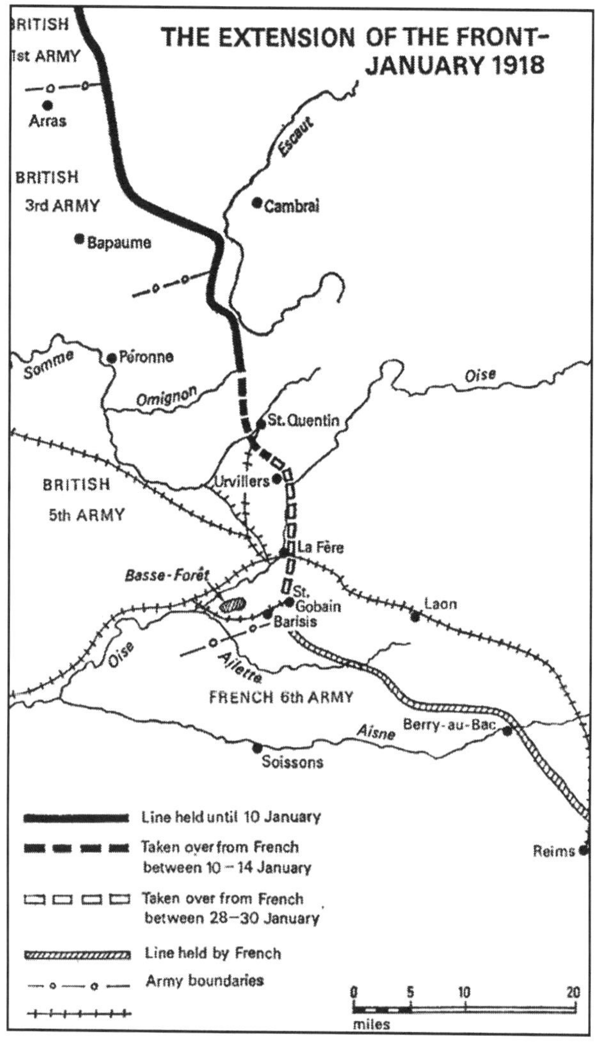


Courtesy of the Long Long Trail
www.1914-1918.net

On top of this, even though his available military strength was dwindling, Haig was ordered to extend the line occupied by the British. At an Anglo-French conference between Lloyd George and Ferdinand Foch on 9 October 1917, it was recommended that the British should take over more of the line. Commander-in-Chief Philippe Pétain asked the British to relieve his Sixth Army down as far as Barisis, which required six more divisions in the Front Line. Haig said that he would do his best, but knew that this move was the end of Allied aspirations for continuation of the offensive. On 3 December 1917, Haig ordered all of his Army Commanders to organise their zones for defensive purposes. For this the British adopted a two zone system along its Front:

*The Forward Zone*, which would contain a number of highly defended redoubts which were not physically connected but would allow lines of interconnected killing zones between them if the weather were clear.

*The Battle Zone*, which would be more stringently defended and where the main fighting would take place if the Front were threatened

Even in March 1918, many of the tired and confused soldiers, as well as many of their commanders, did not fully understand the workings of this new system.

From 10 to 14 January the line was extended southwards from the Omignon River to south of St Quentin and later from 28 to 30 January further southwards to Barisis, an extension to the Front of forty two miles. The under-strength Fifth Army under Herbert Gough would take on this responsibility. Gough reported on his new posting:

> "The trench system was in a very neglected state. On some parts of the front there was no continuous line, no dugouts or observation

> posts, and communication trenches were few and provided inadequate cover ... it had naturally been organised to receive from and deliver towards Paris. It now had to face towards the British centres of activity ... I saw to my surprise parties of French civilians busy filling in trenches and removing wire along a line ... east of Villers-Bretonneux. Almost my first act ... was to stop all further demolition ... and commence its reconstruction. Nothing existed in the rear beyond a good line of wire. By 17 December: Telephone lines on this front had not been buried and it was estimated that it would now require 500 men working continuously, two or three months, to carry out this important work properly."

This was carried out at a time when enemy strength was growing daily as a result of the collapse of the Eastern Front. The USA was moving troops to France at last, but it would be many months before they represented a large-scale effective fighting force.

From the German perspective, at the end of 1917 the German high command found itself in a particularly favourable situation. The October Revolution and the subsequent disintegration of the Russian Army would allow the Germans to concentrate their fighting forces on the Western Front. On 3 March the former Russian Allies concluded a separate peace with the signing of the Brest-Litovsk Treaty. It was in this context that Ludendorff began to prepare a massive and, what he hoped would be, decisive attack to be launched the following spring, before the American Army could fulfil its fighting potential on European soil. The offensive would bear on the British Army which the German strategists considered to be exhausted after fighting four bloody and fruitless offensives in the course of 1917. They also had the temporary advantage in numbers afforded by nearly 50 divisions freed by the Russian surrender. Four separate German attacks, codenamed *Michael*, *Georgette*, *Gneisenau*, and

*Blücher-Yorck* were planned. *Michael* was the main attack, which was intended to break through the Allied lines, outflank the British forces which held the Front from the River Somme to the English Channel and defeat the British Army. Once this was achieved, it was hoped that the French would seek armistice terms. The other offensives were subordinate to *Michael*, and were designed to divert British Troops from the main theatre of action, the Somme

Tactically, for these advances the German army concentrated many of its best troops into stormtrooper (sturmtruppen) units, trained to infiltrate and bypass enemy front line units, leaving these strong points to be 'mopped-up' by follow-up troops. The stormtroopers' tactics were to attack and disrupt enemy headquarters, artillery units and supply depots in the rear areas, as well as to occupy territory rapidly. This process gave the German army an initial advantage in the attack, but meant that the best formations would suffer disproportionately heavy casualties, while the quality of the remaining formations declined as they were stripped of their best personnel to provide the stormtroops.

New artillery tactics were also developed. There were three phases: a brief attack on the enemy's command and communications (headquarters, telephone exchanges, etc), destruction of their artillery and lastly an attack upon the enemy Front Line infantry defences. Bombardment would always be brief so as to retain the element of surprise. These new tactics were made possible by the vast numbers of heavy guns (with correspondingly plentiful amounts of ammunition for them) that Germany possessed by 1918. The scene was being set for disaster, which eventually happened when the enemy struck in March 1918. It was Gough's under-manned Fifth Army that bore the brunt of the German *Operation Michael* offensive on 21 March 1918; the inability of his army to hold the line and stem the German advance led to his dismissal.

Andrew Robert offers a more favourable assessment of Gough's contribution:

> "... the offensive saw a great wrong perpetrated on a distinguished British commander that was not righted for many years. Gough's Fifth Army had been spread thin on a forty-two-mile front lately taken over from the exhausted and demoralised French. The reason why the Germans did not break through to Paris, as by all the laws of strategy they ought to have done, was the heroism of the Fifth Army and its utter refusal to break. They fought a thirty-eight-mile rearguard action, contesting every village, field *and, on occasion, yard* ... With no reserves and no strongly defended line to its rear, and with eighty German divisions against fifteen British, the Fifth Army fought the Somme offensive to a standstill on the Ancre, not retreating beyond Villers-Bretonneux."

However, by withstanding everything the Germans could throw at them during March, April, May and June the British Army was able eventually to frustrate all of these attacks and by August it was able to mount a momentous counterattack which would lead to eventual victory in November.

## ALONG THE WESTERN FRONT

Lijssenthoek Cemetery is a large cemetery situated to the west of Ypres. Lijssenthoek was out of the range of most of the German Field Artillery and as a result a large number of casualty clearing stations were set up around the village and there was need for a large cemetery. Today this cemetery contains over 10,700 identified casualties. Christopher Elliott is identified as "Died" which usually implies that he died as result of illness, e.g. pneumonia, rather than of wounds sustained in action.

**Private Christopher Elliott**
**1/4th Battalion King's Own Yorkshire Light Infantry**
**Died 10 February 1918**

Christopher was born in Newcastle. He initially joined the reserve battalion of the Hexham Territorials, the 3/4th Northumberland Fusiliers, in August 1915. In January 1916 he was billeted at Hallstile Bank undergoing specialist training as a machine gunner. Some time later he was transferred to the Kings Own Yorkshire Light Infantry.

**Christopher is buried in Lijssenthoek Military Cemetery.**

Corporal W Moore's Squad, Coldstream Guards, March 1917

During the night of 26 February the wire was cut in front of the German line near Arras in preparation for a major raid by the Coldstream Guards on the night of 27 February. The War Diary notes that the raiding party came up from Arras by train. The raid was scheduled for 12.25am and the area for attack came under an intense barrage from artillery, trench mortars, machine guns and Lewis guns. As the barrage faded, the raiding party moved quickly forward before the Germans realised what was happening. Twelve prisoners were quickly taken and a number who refused to surrender were bombed into submission. This was a very successful raid, netting twelve prisoners with no British losses. However, as the raiding party was making their way back along Chili Avenue (a communication trench) it received a direct hit from a 5.9 inch shell killing four men, including John Bullock [1,2].

**Private John Harle Bullock, aged 26**
**1st Battalion Coldstream Guards**
**28 February 1918**

John was the son of William and Annie Jane Bullock of Camp Hill, Barrasford; he was the second son of four children. The 1911 census shows that John was working on his father's farm. John enlisted with the Coldstream Guards in October 1916.

Nine days after John's death, his older brother William (East Yorkshire Regiment) died at home and was buried with full military honours (see page 376). The youngest son, Thomas, was also serving with the forces.

The news of John's death was reported to his parents in a letter from the Captain of his company:

"My company had just carried out a successful raid on the enemy's line in which all concerned had behaved in a most gallant manner well worthy of the best traditions of the regiment and had regained our trench without a single casualty. Whilst proceeding down the communication trench the raiding party received a direct hit from the enemy's artillery."

His gravestone is inscribed with the following:

**HE LIVES FOR EVER**
**IN OUR LOVE ENSHRINED**
**FROM FATHER, MOTHER**
**SISTER AND BROTHER**

**John is buried at Brown's Cross Cemetery, Roeux.**

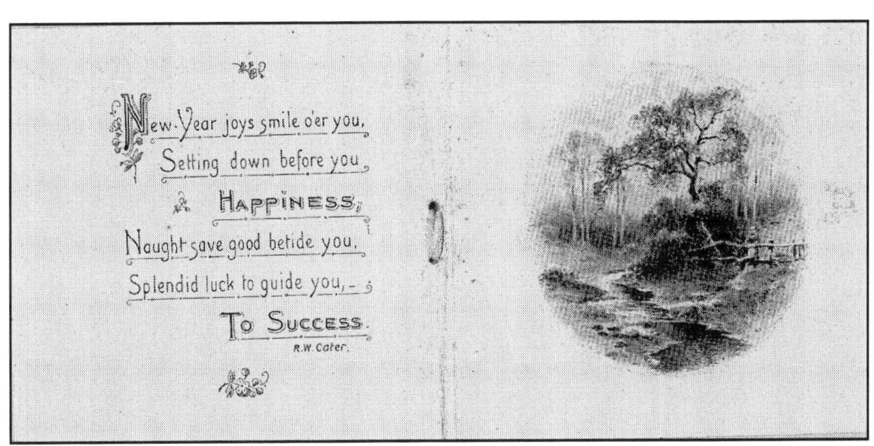


A New Year's message from John's uncle, Robert Harle

Robert Blain appears to have been one of about 115 men from Northern England who were with the 81st Training Reserve Brigade, which embarked for France late in June 1917, spending a few weeks at the No. 34 Infantry Base Depot at Étaples and subsequently transferring to the 1st Northampton Regiment on 14 July 1917 as replacements for the battalion's severe losses at Nieuport on 10 July [3].

**Private Robert Blain, aged 26**
**Attached 2nd Trench Mortar Battery**
**1st Battalion Northamptonshire Regiment**
**Died 13 June 1918**

Robert was born in Harraby, Cumberland, the son of David and Alice Blain. The 1911 census records that he was living at West Mill Hills Farm and working as a horseman for Richard Davison. By the time he joined the Colours, it was recorded that Robert was working at New Drift Farm in Acomb. His gravestone is inscribed with the following:

**TO MEMORY EVER DEAR**

**Robert is buried in Cambrin Military Cemetery.**

In late July, the 11th Battalion East Yorkshire relieved the 15th West Yorks in the Front Line near Vieux Berquin, east of Hazebrouck. On the evening of 28 July a platoon from 'A' company attempted a raid on the enemy's line [4,5].

**Private John William Welton, aged 18**
**11th (Service) Battalion East Yorkshire Regiment**
**Died 28 July 1918**

John was the fourth son of John and Margaret Welton of The Craggs, Barrasford. William joined up on 8 October 1917, when he had reached eighteen. Before going into the Army he worked at the quarries in Barrasford. He embarked for France at the beginning of July. John had been with his battalion for scarcely three weeks before he was killed. Lieutenant Colonel Gurney (Battalion Commander) noted that at this time the average age for the battalion was 19, due to terrible losses it had sustained during the fighting of March and April 1918.

Second lieutenant R Prindle wrote to John's parents:

> "Your son John William was killed yesterday … It will no doubt be a little consolation to you to know his death was instantaneous, and therefore painless … "

**John is buried at Le Grand Hasard Military Cemetery, Morbecque.**

The 1st West Yorkshire Regiment was based in the Dickebusch sector, south west of Ypres. On the night of 8/9 August the battalion was involved in a local action against the German Front Line. The attack was timed to coincide with an attack by the 2nd Durham Light Infantry and other elements of the 41st Division on the right (west). These attacks began at midnight on what was an exceptionally dark night. The aim was to drive the Germans from the crest of the Viestraat Ridge, which the enemy was using as an observation platform to direct accurate shelling of the communication channels. The Yorks attack failed, because the defenders from the German 8th Division offered stubborn resistance, but the Durham attack was much more successful. Casualties for the West

Yorkshires included 3 officers wounded, 1 taken prisoner; other ranks 3 killed (of whom Arthur Lowes was one), 41 wounded, 6 missing and 2 taken prisoner [6,7].

**Private Arthur Lee Lowes, aged 20**
**1st Battalion West Yorkshire Regiment**
**(Prince of Wales's Own)**
**Died 9 August 1918**

Arthur was born in Acomb, the youngest son of Robert Parker and Alice Lowes of Meadow Terrace, Hexham. Having offered his services before the permitted age, he finally enlisted on his eighteenth birthday and embarked for France in October 1917. Before the hostilities, he worked as a clerk for Messrs Fell & Co Ltd at their Wentworth Nurseries.

**Arthur is buried in Kemmel No 1 Cemetery, south of Ypres.**

On 21 August the 9th Northumberland were ordered forward to take over half of the Front Line from the 11th Suffolk and were in position by 2am on 22 August. Later in the day the battalion was ordered forward, but met with considerable opposition near Merillon. 'D' company suffered many casualties during the advance [8,9].

**Private Richard Gibson Surtees, aged 26**
**'D' Company 9th (Service) Battalion**
**Northumberland Fusiliers**
**Died 22 August 1918**

Richard was born in Chollerton, the third son of Thomas and Isabella Surtees of Colwell Fell House. His brother Andrew was killed serving with the Canadians in May 1917, (see page 158). Another brother was serving in France, whilst a fourth brother was serving in Egypt. Before enlisting, Richard was employed in agricultural work and for several years had worked for Messers Urwin of Cocklaw. The 1911 census shows that at that time he was working as a quarry labourer. Richard initially joined the Northumberland Hussars in 1914 and was stationed at Gosforth Park and Scarborough. He embarked for France with the Hussars in March 1917 and was subsequently transferred to the Northumberland Fusiliers. During the heavy fighting of March and April 1918 he was wounded. He returned to the Fusiliers after convalescence.

Captain H Ansell of Richard's Company wrote:

> "It was during an advance that the battalion were engaged in, and our flank was being subjected to heavy machine gun and rifle fire, your son was hit by a sniper in the head, death was almost instantaneous. I do trust that the consolation of knowing how well your son was liked by all and that he died the very highest and noblest form of death in the service of his King and Country, will in some measure help to atone for this heavy blow you have been called to bear."

Private J C Tweedy ('D' Company) wrote to Miss Surtees:

> "By the death of your dear brother, Dick ... the platoon and battalion loses one of the best lads it ever had. I am pleased to say we buried him in a nice place and we erected a cross both at his head and feet. The inscription ... Pte R C Surtees ... Killed in action Aug 22 1918, Sleep on, dear Dick and take your rest; They miss your most who loved you best. Ever remembered by his platoon."

**Robert is buried in Merville Communal Cemetery Extension.**

After the Canadians' triumph at the *Battle of Amiens* in early August 1918, the 13th Battalion Canadian Infantry, (1st Division, 3rd Brigade), were withdrawn from the fray. However, by late August men of the Canadian Corps were required to take up positions in front of Arras. The perceived plan was for these troops to attack eastwards astride the Arras-Cambrai road and force their way through the Drocourt-Quéant Line south of the Scarpe. The attack was planned for 1 September but was eventually delayed to the following day.

During the night of 27 August, the 13th Battalion relieved elements of the 5th and 6th Brigades in the Neuville Vitasse sector. Up to the time of the major attack, the role of the Front Line troops was to carry out minor, localised forays to straighten the Front and to provide satisfactory 'jumping off' positions. On 29 August all four companies of the 13th Battalion were involved in these aggressive actions; the Battalion History reports that 4 other ranks were killed and 7 other ranks wounded by shell fire during the day. On 30 August, parties from the 13th Battalion were sent forward to reconnoitre the area attacked earlier in the day by other elements of the 1st Division. Later, 'A' and 'D' Companies moved up into the captured area, with 'B' and 'C' advancing in support. No mention is made of any soldiers being killed, although it mentions that Capt Donald was wounded [10].

**Private Charlton Richley**
**13th Battalion Canadian Infantry**
**Royal Highlanders**
**Died 30 August 1918**

Charlton, the son of William and Mary Richley, was born in Corsenside (British Census) or Wark (Canadian and USA data) in 1882. He appears to have been one of twelve children. The 1891 census shows that the family lived at Long Crag, Little Swinburne, and that William was working as a waterworks attendant. By 1901 Charlton had left the family home and was boarding with the Hunters of Long Crag, working as a labourer.

In 1909 Charlton, aged 27, sailed from Liverpool aboard the SS Cedric, arriving at Ellis Island on 3 July. The ship's manifest shows him as a single man; he was going to visit Mr John Marshall of Bachelors Hall, Danville, Virginia. (Danville at this time had a thriving textile industry). His next of kin was reported as his brother William of Wark. In 1910, the United States Federal Census shows Charlton lodging at Newark Ward 10 Essex, New Jersey. When Charlton volunteered to join the Canadian Army in late August 1917 he was still single, living at 901 Duckland Avenue, Baltimore, Maryland, and working as labourer. His next of kin was reported as John Richley.

The CEF Burial Register records that Charlton was killed by an enemy shell whilst on sentry duty.

**Charlton is commemorated on the Vimy Memorial to the missing.**

## REFERENCES

1. Headlam, C. *History of the Guards Division in the Great War 1915 - 1918.* Pub: 1924, reprinted Naval and military Press 2001.

2. WO/1219. *War Diary 1st Battalion Coldstream Guards.*

3. Private Communication *Great War Forum, 1914-1918 invisionzone.com/forum*

4. Wyrall, E. *East Yorkshire Regiment in the Great War 1914-1918.* Pub: 1928, reprinted Naval and Military Press 2002.

5. *WO95/2357 .War Diary 11th Battalion East Yorkshire Regiment.*

6. Wyrall, E. *The West Yorkshire Regiment in the war 1914 - 1918.* Pub: 1924 - 1927, reprinted Naval and Military Press 2002.

7. WO95/1618 *War Diary 1st Battalion West Yorkshire Regiment.*

8. Cooke, C. H. Capt. *Historical Records of the 9th Battalion Northumberland Fusiliers.* Pub: 1928.

9. WO95/2466. *War Diary 9th Battalion Northumberland Fusiliers.*

10. data.collectionscanada.gc.ca *War Diary 13th Battalion Canadian Infantry, August 1918.*

# CHAPTER FIFTEEN

# GERMAN ADVANCES 1918

*For all we have and are,*
*For all our children's fate,*
*Stand up and take the war,*
*The Hun is at the gate!*

From Rudyard Kipling's *For All We Have and Are*

## OVERVIEW

During 1917 the British Army had continually been on the offensive at *Arras, Messines, Passchendaele* and *Cambrai,* with an ever increasing level of casualties. In early 1918, the British Army was committed to extending the length of its Front Line, assuming duties hitherto undertaken by the French; this was an extra responsibility of twenty eight miles, from St Quentin to Barisis. To say the least, the French defensive positions had been seriously ill-maintained and in places were non-existent. Also, the British High Command had instigated a new doctrine called 'Defence in Depth' which required all levels of command to learn and instigate fresh training systems. At home, the War Cabinet imposed two further constraints on the British forces. First, they decided to limit the level of reinforcements to the army, which compromised the BEF operational effectiveness. Secondly, they required the reorganisation of divisions by a reduction of their battalions: 115 infantry battalions were disbanded as the fighting strength of each division was reduced from 12 to 9 battalions. This task was completed by March 4 and it affected both the morale and the fighting efficiency of each division. All this time, British Army Intelligence was gathering lots of information on the build up of German forces facing them and they foretold that a big attack was in the offing.

## GERMAN ADVANCES

As early as November 1917, the German High Command decided that they must *attack* rather than simply *resist*, the British Army; in 1917 the British had inflicted major, although not terminal, damage on the German Army. They perceived that after the rigours of 1917 the British Army would be exhausted, and therefore vulnerable. Furthermore, the window for an attack in the spring of 1918 would be well before the Americans could enter the fray with any force. In the Germans' favour was that the war on the Eastern Front was all but over and was formally ended by the Russians by the Treaty of Brest-Litovsk, releasing a large number of troops to fight on the Western Front. The Germans spent a long time in assessing where the attack should be made: Flanders, around Arras, Verdun or either side of St Quentin; they drew up plans for each of these locations. In January 1918 the area north and south of St Quentin was selected for the attack. The Germans concluded, rightly, that the British-held positions stood on ground favourable for attacking infantry, that defences were weak or non-existent and the defenders were spread too thinly to give any effective resistance. The date of the battle, known as the Kaiserschlacht (Kaiser's Battle), was set for 21 March 1918. The Germans had developed infiltration techniques where highly mobile units penetrated gaps in the newly commissioned and unfinished British defence system, whilst stronger points were mopped up later. At many points along the Front the Germans outnumbered the British by four to one [1,2].

## MICHAEL OFFENSIVE

At 4.40am on 21 March, on a very misty morning along a 50 mile Front, the calmness was shattered by an immense artillery barrage from over a thousand artillery pieces of various sizes. For the next five hours, the Germans systematically destroyed, using high explosive and gas shells, the British command, communication and heavy gun positions far behind

Lightly armed German Stormtroopers moving rapidly through the Allied Lines under the cover of a dense fog.

the British Front. Later, the onslaught concentrated on the garrisons of the British outpost line and their forward defences. At 9.40am, following a shorter barrage of the British forward lines, a mass of German infantry surged forward led by an élite core of stormtroops. Hidden by the dense fog, they quickly overran many of the forward positions of the British outpost line and strove to press forward, picking their way around points of resistance. In the afternoon it became clear that to the south of St Quentin the British had suffered severe losses; that night, orders were issued for a limited withdrawal, which within days could only be called a major retreat.

On 12 March the 1st Battalion Royal Fusiliers (RF) were in the Line in front of Vendelles, (east of Peronne and north west of St Quentin). During this time in the Line patrols found that a number of gaps had been created by the Germans in their own wire. On the 19 March the RF were relieved by the 8th Battalion The Queens (Royal West Surrey). The Regimental History states (on 17 March): "... and five days later they could easily see German officers examining the British positions with field glasses", persumably studying the ground over which they would make their attack on 21 March. At the time of the German attack, the Royal Fusiliers were out of the Line, but were quickly moved forward into battle positions. Companies 'A' and 'B' were moved into the Front Line, whilst 'C' and 'D' took up a position nearer to Vendelles. Although compelled to wear gas helmets and under artillery and air bombardment, casualties were comparatively light. On 22 March the battalion was forced to retire through the 50th Division positions to a defensive position near Bernes. During this operation the battalion suffered heavy casualties [3,4].

**Lance Corporal John Peter Waugh, aged 21**
**1st Battalion Royal Fusiliers**
**Died 22 March 1918**

John was born in Bellingham and was the eldest son of William John and Margaret Waugh of St Cuthbert's Terrace, Bellingham. The family owned a Tailor and Drapers business in Bellingham. John was educated at the Reed Charity School and later at the North Eastern County School (now Barnard Castle School). It is highly likely that John would have been employed in his father's business before he was conscripted into the army under Lord Derby's scheme in late November 1915. The North Tyne Magazine for May 1918 reports that John was killed by a shell. The news of his death was passed to his father from a comrade who was wounded at the same time.

**John is commemorated on Pozières Memorial to the missing.**

Some time during 21 March 1918, when the serious extent of the German Advance was becoming clearer, the 11th Durham Light Infantry were ordered forward to assist in covering the retreat of the British Army south of the Somme. That evening, a number of men were attached to Divisional Reserve, whilst 'D' company was attached to 61st Brigade. On 23 March the remnants of the battalion were positioned near Offoy, defending the canal, where their line extended to the outskirts of Canizy. As dusk approached, German snipers were active and the position was raked by machine-gun and trench mortar fire [5,6].

**Company Sergeant Major David Sinclair Robson, aged 34**
**11th (Service) Battalion Durham Light Infantry**
**Died 23 March 1918**

David was born in Wark, the eldest son of James and Annie Robson. At 17 he was working as a railway porter at Wark Station. Later, he joined the army and the 1911 census shows that he was, at 28, serving as a corporal with the 1st Battalion Durham Light Infantry (DLI) garrisoned at Nasirabad, Rajputana in India. When hostilities broke out, David was in England either on leave or as a serving reservist. As a result he went out to France with the 2nd Battalion Durham Light Infantry on 8 September 1914. He was awarded the 'Mons Star'. In 1914 the 2nd Battalion DLI saw action at the Battle of Aisne Heights. Later, David was transferred to the 11th Battalion which was raised in Newcastle and which embarked for France as a pioneer battalion in late July 1915 [3,4].

**David is commemorated on the Pozières Memorial to the missing.**

On 21 March both of the Auckland Regiments were billeted near to St Omer. When the severity of the situation eventually unfurled, the two Auckland Battalions left Cassel Station on the evening of 24 March, on their journey towards the Somme. During the morning of 25 March the train reached its destination of Hangest-sur-Somme and by chance motor transport was available to take the 1st Battalion eastwards towards the ongoing battle. On the west side of Amiens the troops set out to march and by the evening the 1st Auckland were in bivouacs near Dernancourt. Towards midnight the Aucklanders were assembled and they marched eastwards, arriving on 26 March at an assembly point between Hedauville and Mailly-Maillet. The New Zealanders found themselves in a gap that had developed between the 4th and 5th Corps and ahead was the enemy who were desperate to pass through the gap and capture Amiens and Doullens. Thus, the 1st Auckland advanced astride the Mailly-Maillet to Pusieux Road in the direction of Serre. Just to the east of the village, near a windmill, the New Zealanders were checked by machine-gun fire and as they advanced in artillery formation they began to take casualties, but managed to make it to the foot of the Serre Ridge. 15th Company managed to move forward and capture a number of machine guns, allowing other comrades to advance. A dusk attack by the Aucklanders against the German line was made with cold steel and in panic the Germans broke; a few were taken prisoner, many were killed and the remainder ran. As night fell, the new position was secured. All night the newly won position was attacked by the Germans. All next day (27 March) the enemy bombarded it heavily with minenwerfer and artillery fire. Many casualties occurred [7].

**Minenwerfer** ("mine launcher") is the German name for a class of short range mortars used extensively during the First World War by the German Army. The weapons were intended to be used by engineers to clear obstacles, including bunkers and barbed wire, that longer range artillery would not be able to target accurately.

**Private John Ellison, aged 35**
**1st Battalion Auckland Regiment**
**New Zealand Expeditionary Force**
**Died between 26 March and 27 March 1918**

John was born in Angerton, near Morpeth, and was the eldest son of William and Elizabeth Ellison. UK census records can be found for John in 1881 and 1891. Before John volunteered to join the New Zealand Army he worked as a bushman. He was part of the 22nd draft of reinforcements for 'A' Company of the Auckland Infantry Regiment which set sail from Wellington on 16 February 1917 on the HMNZT Aparima. Days before his departure he married Florence Jane Elizabeth Lilley of Tauranga, North Island. His next of kin, however, is recorded as his mother, Elizabeth, of Whitstone House, Woodburn.

**John is commemorated on**
**Grevilliers (New Zealand) Memorial to the missing.**

**Lance Corporal James Dobson Davidson, aged 34**
**Army Service Corps**
**886th Motor Transport Company,**
**attached XVIII Corps Heavy Artillery**
**Died 27 March 1918**

James was born in 1883 in Warden. He was the son of James and Margaret Davidson. Father James worked on the railways as a signalman. The 1901 census shows young James, aged 17, working as a groom. James married Mary Hannah, (née Scott) in the summer of 1909 and in the summer of 1911, they became parents of a son, William. At the time of his enlistment in 1914, James was employed by Mr A M Allgood of Walwick Grange as a chauffeur. The Davidson family lived at Humshaugh Fell. James arrived in France in May 1915. The Hexham Herald reported that James died in a French Ambulance, from gunshot wounds to both legs.

**James is buried in Dompierre French National Cemetery**
***although originally he had been buried in***
***Tricot Communal Cemetery French Extension.***

From 23 March, as the 1/4th East Yorkshire Regiment (ER) moved into the Line from their reserve position at Harbonièrres, they were committed to stemming the German advance. From this point the ER was involved in the *Actions at Somme Crossing* (24-25 March) and the *Battle of Rosières* (25-27 March). By nightfall of 27 March the ER held a position astride the Rosières to Vrély road which they had managed to hold throughout that day, withstanding an enemy attack which they had repulsed. At dawn on 28 March they withdrew under orders to a reserve position south of Rosières, but after a prolonged attack, which forced the units on either flank to withdraw, the ER withdrew to a line south-east of Caix. On 29 March the ER were again on the march to secure a position in a wood along the Domart sur la Luce to Roye road immediately south of Démuin. The ER had not been occupying this position for very long before they faced a heavy German attack which forced them south-westwards. By 7pm the ER were defending the Line running south east from Thennes to the eastern corner of a large wood on the Moreuil to Démuin road. During these desperate rear guard actions on 29 March, Andrew Cowans was killed [8,9,10].

**Serjeant Andrew Cowan, aged 37**
**1/4th Battalion East Yorkshire Regiment**
**Died 29 March 1918**

Andrew was born in Bellingham, the son of William and Violet Cowan. He volunteered for the Northumberland Yeomanry as did his older brother William, and both served in South Africa during the Second Boer War. The press reported that Andrew was taken prisoner by the Boers; he related that his captors searched him for money but they found none as he had hidden his money in his boot. On returning home he became a game keeper on the Chesters Estate. The 1911 census shows that he was single and working as a farm labourer at Eals Farm, Bellingham. On the outbreak of hostilities he volunteered and joined the local Territorial battalion of the Northumberland Fusiliers and proceeded to France in April 1915. His previous military experience would have been important to the Territorial Battalion and helped him with his promotion. He saw action at the *Battle of St Julien* (see page 37). Some time later he transferred to the East Yorkshire Regiment.

**Andrew is commemorated on the Pozières Memorial to the missing.**

The 8th Machine Gun Battalion, recently reorganised, was part of the 8th Division which was rushed to the Somme on 22 March 1918. 'C' company were attached to 25th Infantry Brigade and by 6pm that evening were marching to Harbonièrres. During 23 March the battalion took up positions along the Somme Canal, some near Bethencourt whist others

were positioned near Brie. On 24 March the Germans attacked the Line of the Canal de la Somme and at dawn were crossing the canal near Fontaine-les-Pargny and Bethéncourt. During the next two days the Allied Front Line was progressively forced westwards. In the afternoon of 26 March the battalion was withdrawn to a line between Vrély and Rosières which was held until the early hours of 28 March when they were forced to withdraw still further, to a line between Vrély and Caix. All day the enemy attacked persistently; by midday the battalion had received orders to retire across the river near Moreuil as the enemy applied more and more pressure on the crumbling defences. On 29 March, after frantic defensive actions, it appeared that by that night the German offensive had been held to the east of Moreuil. Some time during 22 to 29 March, Thomas Moore was wounded and subsequently died on 29 March. The Hexham Herald reported information received from the Enquiry Branch of the Red Cross which reported that Private T S Moore of the Machine Gun Corps died of his wounds on 29 March and was interred at Le Cateau. The Red Cross report was in fact unfounded; our Thomas Moore is rightly commemorated on the Arras Memorial to the missing. My further research revealed that it was a *J C* Moore from Yorkshire who died on the 29 March and is buried at Le Cateau. A question of mistaken identity [11].

**Private Thomas Snowball Moore, aged 33**
**8th Machine Gun Battalion**
**Died 29 March 1918**

Thomas was the eldest son of William and Mary A Moore of Garden House, Nunwick, Northumberland. The 1901 census reports Thomas, aged 15, living with his aunt, Amy Hutchinson, in Acomb. No record of Thomas is found on the 1911 census for England and Wales, and it seems that he had moved to Scotland: the London Gazette for 2 August 1912 recorded that 'Warder Thomas Snowball Moore' of the Scottish Prisons

Service had been awarded a certificate as an assistant clerk of the Abstractor Class. Thomas' limited war record shows that he enlisted in Glasgow. His brothers, George, William and Henry, also served in the forces.

**Thomas is commemorated on the Arras Memorial to the missing.**

The 154th Field Company Royal Engineers was attached to 37th Division. Battalions from the 37th Division held the part of the Front Line along the Ancre Valley. On Friday 5 April the Germans renewed their attack north and south of the River Somme in a desperate attempt to renew the momentum of their offensive. The heaviest attack took place along the River Ancre. Even though by nightfall it was apparent that the Germans had not effectively gained any ground and that their drive towards Amiens was over, they continued to bombard British held territory [12].

Field Companies of the Royal Engineers were armed, unlike members of the Labour Corps who also were involved in construction projects. They provided engineering assistance in the construction of roads, defences and bridges, the provision of water supplies as well as the demolition of obstacles and bridges, but could be called upon to fight as infantrymen, if needed.

**Sapper John Thomas Harding, aged 21**
**154th Field Company, Royal Engineers**
**Died 8 April 1918**

Thomas was born in Humshaugh, the youngest son of Archibald and Hannah Harding of Storey Terrace, Wark. The 1911 census reports that the Harding family were living in Wark and that John, aged 14, was working as an apprenticed joiner, following in the footsteps of his father. He attested in July 1916 and joined the Royal Engineers Reserve

in the November. From the reserve he spent time at Deganway, North Wales, where he was based in July 1917 when he was awarded two days' punishment for smoking in the cookhouse. He arrived in France in September 1917, initially serving with the Duke of Cornwall's Light Infantry, before being transferred back to the Engineers.

Thomas was mortally wounded on the night of 8 April whilst digging trenches. Apparently, two shells landed amongst the sappers and wounded six men, including Thomas. He was carried to the nearest dressing station, but an artery in the leg had been severed. He lost a lot of blood, and eventually died of his wounds. His gravestone is inscribed with the following:

**REMEMBERED BY FATHER, MOTHER,**
**SISTERS AND BROTHERS**
**WARK ON TYNE**
**TO MEMORY EVER DEAR**

**Thomas is buried in St Amand British Cemetery.**

On 19 April the 19th Battalion Durham Light Infantry (DLI) came into the Line south of Martinsart Wood, which extended across the valley to the south. A British counterattack was planned for 7.30pm on 22 April, but a quarter of an hour before zero hour the German artillery opened up with shrapnel shells on the British trenches, and their heavy artillery pounded Martinsart Wood. Helped by a British bombardment, the DLI attacked on a two company Front into the face of intense machine gun fire. 'W' company on the right made 250 yards whilst 'Y' company on the left managed to advance 400 yards. By 9pm it was clear that a gap existed between these two companies, in the new Front, so the companies in reserve sent forward platoons to plug the gap. Orders were later received for the attackers to dig in where they lay. 'Y' company found itself in an untenable position and at 4am withdrew to their original Front Line. During this action Robert Robson was killed [5,12].

**Corporal Robert Ramsay Robson, aged, 24**
**19th (Service) Battalion Durham Light Infantry**
**Died 22 or 23 April 1918**

Robert was born in Acomb, the second son of Robert and Rebecca Robson. He was educated at Queen Elizabeth Grammar School in Hexham. He trained as a 'pupil teacher' and passed second in the King's Examination. Those around him in Acomb felt that a lad with such brilliant gifts should go to college and it was arranged that friends of the parish would provide the fees for him to attend Bede College in Durham. However, Robert preferred to go into employment and he became an assistant master at Barnard Castle Church School.

He was a keen Territorial Soldier and embarked for France in April 1915, where he would be involved in the desperate defence of Ypres during April and May. Some time later he was transferred to the 19th Durham Light Infantry. The local press reported that he held the rank of Sergeant. A memorial service was held in St John Lee Church.

One of his officers wrote:

> "It was just after an attack by our battalion that poor Bob was killed. The attack had finished and we had just got dug in nicely and things had quietening [*sic*] down. In his duty he was looking over the top to see if any enemy infantry movement was a foot when he was shot through the head by machine gun bullets and died instantaneously and without pain ... He is now lying in peace, his earthly struggles finished in a grave behind the Lines ... I found him out to be the most willing lad I ever came across out here, and always a soldier, and a man."

**Robert is buried in Martinsart British Cemetery.**

On 24 April the 42nd Battalion Australian (11th Australian Brigade) held part of the brigade's Line in the Sailly-le-Sec sector between Bouzencourt in the north, and east of Vaux le Somme and Corbie. The Battalion Diary records that at 4am on 24 April the Germans carried out a concentrated bombardment of their position. About 1000 shells were fired by the Germans; these were mainly gas shells interspersed with some high explosive shells. The majority of the gas used was marked as Green Cross Mark 11 which contained phosgene, but some Blue Cross shells were also used. The diary also reports that only one casualty resulted from the bombardment, namely John Hutchinson [14,15].

**Private John Thomas Hutchinson, aged 28**
**42nd Battalion Australian Infantry**
**Died 24 April 1918**

John was born in Birtley, Northumberland, the third son of Ralph and Adamenia Hutchinson of Birtley Shields, Wark. The 1901 census shows

John was working as a farmer on his late father's farm. John emigrated to Australia in 1912 and before joining the Australian Army in November 1916 was living in Queensland and working as overseer.

John travelled to England to complete his training on board the troopship Wiltshire, which berthed in Devonport in early April 1917. He proceeded to France in the July and joined his battalion in August.

During late 1917 his battalion was involved in a number of actions during *Third Ypres* (*Passchendaele*). When Germany launched its offensive across the Somme, his battalion was rushed to the area to play its part in stopping the German drive towards Amiens.

John was killed in action by an enemy shell during a heavy enemy bombardment, whilst his battalion was in the Sailly-le-Sec sector.

At the end of John's obituary in The North Tyne Magazine of June 1918, the vicar wrote:

> "Let not sorrow dim your eye,
> Soon shall every tear be dry."

The following is found on his headstone:

**FAITHFUL UNTO DEATH**

**John is buried in Bonnay Communal Cemetery Extension.**

# GEORGETTE OFFENSIVE: 9 – 29 APRIL 1918

Following close upon the Michael Offensive on the Somme, on 9 April the Germans launched a second offensive along a front from Armentières and Béthune. The Germans called this offensive the code name 'Georgette'. The Allied Line was ruptured near Laventie, where a weak Portuguese division was unable to withstand the German onslaught and fled from their positions; this compelled the Allies to retire to Estaires. South of the evolving gap the 55th Division held firm, thus forcing the main thrust of the German attack northwards. By 11 April, Armentières had been abandoned and Field Marshall Douglas Haig issued the following appeal to his army:

> "…to fight it out! Every position must be held to the last man: there must be no retirement. With our backs to the wall ... each one of us must fight on to the end."

By close of play on 12 April the Germans had captured Ploegsteert Wood, Messines Village, Wytschaete and St Eloi. As they approached Hazebrouck, an important rail head for the Allies, their advance was beginning to falter and the Allies were able to hold their ground. Next day the 34th and 59th Divisions near Bailleul were able to frustrate the German advance and on Messines Ridge, which had been captured in 1917, the Australian and New Zealand troops defended their positions with great élan.

On April 15 the Allies withdrew from the bloodied ground gained during the Passchendaele campaign, (see page 161) and defended a line around Ypres (as in 1915). Many attacks were conducted by the Germans to re-establish themselves on the high ground around Ypres and make the Anglo-French defence untenable. They launched their final attack on 29 April where they used as many as thirteen divisions to break the Allied resistance. This epic failure brought to an end the German hopes for the Georgette Offensive [16].

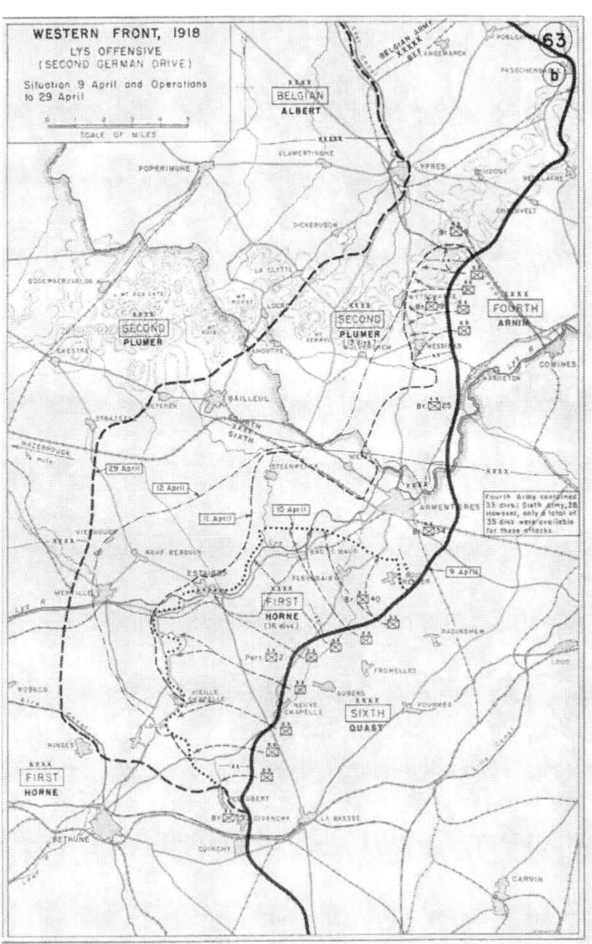

The 9th Battalion Northumberland Fusiliers (NF) were manning the brigade's Front (103rd Brigade, 34th Division) in the Rue de Bois salient to the south of Armentières. At 3pm on 10 April, after heavy fighting and continual German incursion, the 9th NF were ordered to retire westwards across the River Lys. This withdrawal was covered by the 11th Suffolk Regiment and was in the nick of time. To the north, Ploegsteert and Messines villages had fallen. At the end of this arduous day, the 9th NF were allocated to Brigade Reserve, positioned north of Nieppe (the rest of the brigade was to be found lining the railway east of Les Trois Tilleuls). On 11 April the 103rd Brigade reported that their defensive Line had been broken and the 9th NF was ordered forward to mount a counterattack, which successfully forced the enemy backwards. During the afternoon the Germans managed to capture Steenwerck station rendering the brigade's position around Nieppe untenable. As the battalion retreated to the west of La Crêche, their headquarters came under artillery fire. A hit from a 5.9 shell, killed Major John Allen, Sergeant Stafford and six other soldiers [17,18].

**Major John Stanley Allen MC, aged 26**
**9th (Service) Battalion Northumberland Fusiliers**
**Died 11 April 1918**

John was the youngest son of John and Caroline Allen of Castle Hill, Bellingham. He attended the Reed School, Bellingham, the North Eastern County School (now Barnard Castle School) and was a graduate of Christ College Cambridge. He was an all-round athlete. In March 1915 he married Grizel Crichton, daughter of Mr Crichton of Lanarkshire, and became the father of a son.

**The Military Cross (MC)** is a military decoration awarded to officers and (since 1993) other ranks of the British Armed Forces, and formerly also to officers of other Commonwealth countries. The MC is granted in recognition of "an act or acts of exemplary gallantry during active operations against the enemy on land to all members, of any rank in our Armed Forces". The award was created in 1914 for commissioned officers of the substantive rank of Captain or below and for Warrant Officers. In 1979, the Queen approved a proposal that a number of awards, including the Military Cross, could in future be awarded posthumously. The cross is 46mm in height and 44mm wide and made from ornamental silver, with straight arms terminating in broad finials decorated with imperial crowns, suspended from a plain suspension bar. The obverse has a Royal Cypher in the centre. The ribbon width is 32mm and consists of three equal vertical stripes: white, purple, white.

He enlisted as a Private in the local Territorial battalion at the start of the war. In the following months he was awarded a commission with 9th Battalion Northumberland Fusiliers. He was awarded the Military Cross in July 1916 and finally gazetted Major.

John was award his Military Cross for actions at midnight (6/7 July) when the 9th NF attacked Quadrangle Support, the village of Contalmaison on the left and Mametz Wood on the right. The Battalion History described this as a 'difficult proposition'. Newspaper reports describe the action in which Captain Allen achieved his award:

> "During 7 July [1916] although he was wounded three times, Captain Allen refused to report himself as a casualty. His courage and resource were instrumental in reforming the line and he affected a withdrawal at a critical juncture with coolness and judgement."

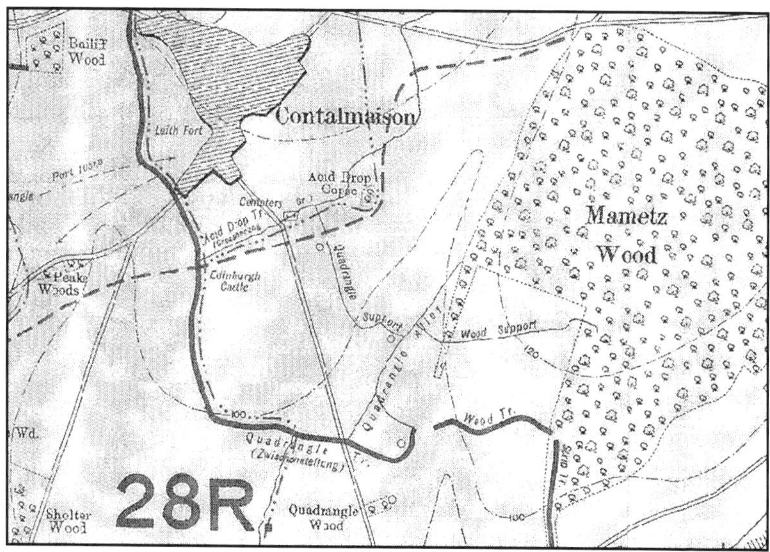


Attack of 9th Northumberland Fusiliers, 7 July 1916

Major Allen was at home during March 1918 and left for the Front on Easter Sunday. The National Probate Calendar shows that John left an estate of £982 10s 4d.

**John is commemorated on the Ploegsteert Memorial to the missing.**

By 2pm on 10 April the 22nd Northumberland Fusiliers (NF), under increasingly intense enemy fire, were ordered to retire, company by company, from the Front Line near Bois-Grenier. However, a thick mist prevented air observation by the enemy, limiting their observation of this manoeuvre. A similar withdrawal was followed by their sister battalion, the 23rd NF; all trench stores and anything of use to the enemy were destroyed as they moved out. The two battalions took up defensive positions when they reached the Estaires to Lys line. As the 22nd Northumberland moved towards their positions, 'D' company came under heavy machine fire and was unable to take up its allotted position and they were forced to withdraw their left flank. As a result, 'B' company, which was in reserve, came forward to extend the flank to form a switch line facing north, from the Nieppe Trench System to the River Lys. As dawn broke on 11 April the Germans attacked from the south and forced their way into the Pont de Neippe area. This allowed them to open fire into the rear of the two Northumberland Battalions. 'C' Company of the 22nd Northumberland was detailed to cover the withdrawal of the battalion. Although 'A', 'B' and 'D' Companies got away to safety, virtually all of 'C' Company became casualties, although they managed to hold up the enemy for some time [19,20].

**Private William Ninian Robson, age 32**
**22nd (Service) Battalion Tyneside Scottish**
**Northumberland Fusiliers**
**Died 11 April 1918**

William was born in Falstone, the eldest son of William and Margaret Robson. His father died in 1897 leaving William to be the family's breadwinner. He was educated at the Reed Charity School. Before he was conscripted he worked on the land as a labourer and lived with his widowed mother in Charlton village. After her son's death Margaret, his mother, went to in live at Leaplish, near Falstone.

**William is commemorated on the Ploegsteert Memorial to the missing.**

During the middle of the afternoon of 9 April the 1/5th Northumberland Fusiliers (NF) (149th Brigade) moved up to support the 150th Brigade, with orders to counterattack any section of the line which was overrun by the Germans. The Line of the Rivers Lys and Lawe was to be held at all costs.

Of the new recruits, an officer wrote:

> "The youths from home, conquering inexperience and the first fight of battle, vied with our veterans in tenacity, resolution and faithfulness."

By the night of 9 April the Germans had forged a ten mile 'dint' in the British Line between Givenchy and Bois-Grenier, creating dangerous salients to the north and south. On 10 April the Germans committed heavy artillery fire about the river crossings at Lestrem and Estaires, but this attack was held by elements of the 50$^{th}$ Division. The 1/5$^{th}$ Northumberland Fusiliers, who were holding Pont Levis, were attacked under the cover of a violent artillery bombardment. Behind this bombardment the Germans were able to force their way over the bridge by sheer weight of numbers, but in doing so many of them were killed or injured. On 11 April the 149$^{th}$ Brigade was forced back towards Melville and formed a Line between Estaires and the Neuf Berguin road. The 1/5$^{th}$ NF held the right sector with the 1/4$^{th}$ NF on the left. In the afternoon the Line was forced further west but its new situation was precarious, with the right flank open. This required a further withdrawal, which began at 2.30am on 12 April, to a line between Vierhoek and the Neuf Berguin crossroad, where the 1/5$^{th}$ NF held a position. After prolonged fighting during the day, the remnants of the 149$^{th}$ Brigade were relieved during the night of 12/13 April by the 4$^{th}$ Guards Brigade [21].

**Private Joseph Turnbull, aged 20**
**1/5$^{th}$ Battalion Northumberland Fusiliers**
**Died 12 April 1918**

Joseph was born in Bellingham, the son of John Joseph and Margaret Turnbull of Fountains Terrace, Bellingham. Joseph senior was head teacher at the National Elementary School. The 1911 census shows Joseph, aged 13, attending school. He also attended the Reed Charity School.

**Joseph is commemorated on the Ploegstreet Memorial to the missing.**

The 1st Leicestershire Regiment (LR) were part of 71st Brigade of 6th Division. On 13 April the 71st Brigade was in Divisional Reserve. Later in the day it was attached to 49th Division who were stationed on the Neuve Église Front. The men spent the night of 13 April in trenches south-east of Dranoutre. At 4pm on 14 April a heavy bombardment pounded the 71st Brigade position. During this bombardment the Germans launched an attack, which was contained. During darkness the brigade's forward rifle pits were evacuated and by 11pm the 71st Brigade Front had become the Front Line which was occupied by one company of 9th Norfolk, the 1st Leicestershire and the 2nd Sherwood Foresters. Two further companies of the 9th Norfolk were in reserve.

At about 1.30pm on 15 April, the Germans began heavy shelling of the brigade area. Subsequently it was learnt that the Norfolk company on the right had been driven back, which made the position of 'A' company of the LR very precarious. Initially the LR was able to hold their exposed position, although a number of trenches were evacuated. Later that afternoon, under continuing enemy pressure, the LR was compelled to fall back under heavy artillery fire to conform to the line held by the Norfolks on the right. The overall position worsened when the Germans managed to bring up a field gun to within a few hundred yards of the British Front Line, which was able to fire point blank at the trenches. As night fell the Germans increased their pressure on the Front, especially in the area held by 'A' company. All available men, including servants and orderlies, were sent forward and eventually a continuous line was formed. With help of British Artillery the enemy's attack eventually petered out. At 2am on 16 April the 71st Brigade were relieved, withdrawing to the west of Mount Kemmel [22]. On the return of the brigade to its original division the following message was sent by the 49th Divisional Commander:

> "Wish to record my very warm appreciation of the services of the 71st Infantry Brigade whilst under my command. All ranks did splendidly."

**Corporal Joseph Teasdale Eddy, aged 23**
**'A' Company 1st Battalion Leicestershire Regiment**
**Died 17 April 1918**

Joseph was born in Acomb, the son of John and Mary Ann Eddy. He married Alice (née Speiro), in the summer of 1917. At the time of his death, Alice lived at Tynevale View, Hexham, but subsequently moved to Osborne Terrace, Newcastle. Joseph was a member of the Hexham Territorials, and arrived in France on 18 April 1915 as a Private. He was involved in the fighting of 26 April 1915 (see page 35). Subsequently he was transferred to the Leicestershire Regiment. Joseph was admitted to a casualty clearing station on 15 April 1918 with serious wounds to the abdomen and from these he died two days later. His gravestone is inscribed with the following:

**HE GAVE HIS LIFE**
**A RANSOM FOR MANY**

**Joseph is buried in Haringhe, (Bandaghem) Military Cemetery.**

# BLÜCHER-YORCK OFFENSIVE 27 MAY – 6 JUNE 1918

On 27 May the Germans launched their third offensive, code named Blücher-Yorck, through the Chemin des Dames Ridge in the Champagne Region of France. The subsequent battle is known as the *Third Battle of the Aisne.* At the time of the offensive, four divisions of the British IX Corps, of which the 50th Northumbrian Division was part, formed the Front Line.

In early morning of 25 May the 1/4th and 1/5th Battalions Northumberland Fusiliers (NF) took up positions in the 149th Brigade's forward defence zone (nearest to No Man's Land). Two companies from each battalion manned the forward outposts, one company was positioned in the first line trenches and one company positioned in the Battle Line trench system.

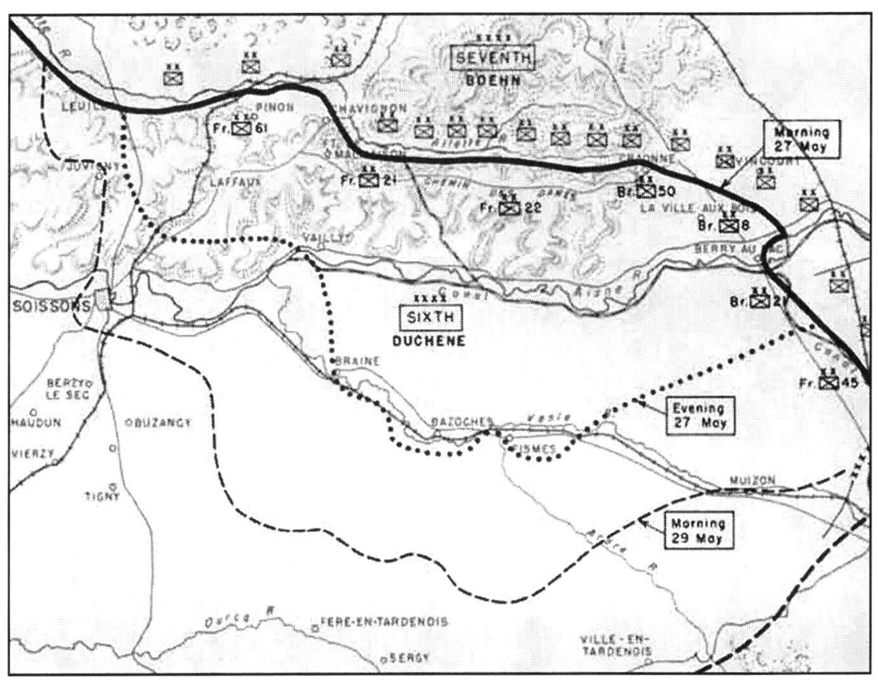

The 1/6th Battalion NF was held further back in reserve [23,24].

At 1am on Monday 27 May, the forward defence zone suffered an intense artillery barrage consisting of a mixture of high explosive and gas shells, which resulted in many casualties.

Colonel Johnston of the 250th Royal Field Artillery wrote [25]:

> "... the German barrage was very accurate against both the highly vulnerable infantry position and his own artillery positions flooding them with a mixture of high explosive and gas."

Chemin Des Dames, (Ladies' Way)
The Californie Plateau
*Private collection Alan Grint*

The Reverend Callin wrote [26]:

"But on the stroke of 1 o'clock the whole front from Soissons to

> Reims [*sic*] broke into flame, and we knew that for the third time in ten weeks we were up against the real thing. Within fifteen minutes it was obvious that the Hun had an extraordinary concentration of guns of every calibre, and that his bombardment had been organised beforehand in most thorough and accurate fashion. A big proportion of gas was used; about four varieties were recognised in later French and British reports. The whole line was deluged with shells, and the front trenches especially must have been reduced to a pulverised mass."

At 3.45am the German infantry attacked along the whole Front. Survivors from the two companies of fusiliers which had manned the forward outposts withdrew to the forward trench Line, which they defended using Lewis gun and rifle fire. The Germans' initial attack was broken up and the enemy retired. However, by 4am the Germans had reformed and using four tanks they broke through the 1/4th NF's right flank near Butte de Margrave; the Germans were able to advance towards the Battle Line. This was held by one company of the 1/4th NF and by companies of the 1/6th Northumberland Fusiliers, which had by this time been brought up from reserve. Although the fusiliers offered stiff resistance, the enemy tanks soon broke through the right flank of this defence. Behind this Line, in the Battle Zone, were four small French-built redoubts. At one of these, Centre Morceau, remnants of the 1/4th and 1/6th Battalions NF collected under the leadership of Lieutenant-Colonel Gibson and were able to hold it for some time. By 5.30am, Centre Morceau was under attack from the front, the right and the rear. Survivors finally withdrew to the Butte de l'Edmond, another one of the French built redoubts, which had already suffered the effects of the enemy bombardment: all four of its machine guns had been damaged. Together with elements of the Divisional Machine Gun Corps the dwindling force offered further resistance. At this point Lieutenant-Colonel Gibson was killed whilst organising the defences.

The battle of 27th May is described in Conan Doyle [27]:

> The bombardment began early in the morning of May 27th, and was said by the British veterans to be the heaviest of the war. Such an opinion meant something, coming from such men. The whole area from Soissons to Rheims was soaked with gas and shattered with high explosives, so that masks had to be worn 10 kilometres behind the lines. A German officer declared that 6000 guns were employed. Life was absolutely impossible in large areas. The wire was blown to shreds and the trenches levelled. The men stuck it, however, with great fortitude, and the counter barrage was good enough to hold up the early attempts at an infantry advance. The experiences of the 149th Infantry Bde may be taken as typical. The front line battalion was the 4th Northumberland Fusiliers under Colonel Gibson. Twice the enemy was driven back in his attempt to cross the shattered wire. At 4am he won his way into the line of outposts, and by 4.30 was heavily pressing the battle line. His tactics were good, his courage high and his numbers great.
>
> Colonel Gibson meanwhile had held on most tenaciously with a nucleus of his Fusiliers at a post called Centre Marceau. The telephone was still intact, and he notified at 5.45 that he was surrounded. He beat off a succession of attacks with heavy loss to the stormers, while Temperley (6th NF) was also putting up a hopeless but desperate fight. Every man available was pushed up to their help, and they were ordered to hold on. A senior officer reporting from Brigade Headquarters says: "I could hear Gibson's brave, firm voice say in reply to my injunctions to fight it out, 'Very good, sir. Good-bye!'" Shortly afterwards this gallant man was shot through the head while cheering his men to a final effort.

It is reported that some of the Germans committed acts of barbarity towards captured British soldiers.

Private Joseph Hodgson, 1/4th Northumberland Fusiliers, a miner from Alston reported [28]:

> "At the same time as I was taken, one of our lads was buried in the trench with his head and shoulders sticking out. Ten minutes or a quarter of an hour after the men in the trench had surrendered one of the Germans threw a hand grenade at this man and killed him. I do not know what unit this German belonged."

Sergeant Harold Betts, 8th (Service) Battalion Lincolnshire Regiment, of Raunds, Northamptonshire reported [29]:

> "On the day of my capture [27 May 1918] I saw some of our wounded, about five of them, who had been caught by a shell, killed by the Germans, who bayoneted them ... I also saw a platoon of Northumberland Fusiliers lined upon a parapet before a German Flammenwerfer -15 of them were killed. There was no German officer there it was done by the German soldiers on their own. When my party came up in charge of a German officer, a Lieutenant, he stopped it."

Conan Doyle also reported on how the germans treated British prisoners:

> "So rapid had been the hostile advance that the dressing stations were captured, and many of our doctors and wounded fell into the hands of the Germans to endure the hard fate which these savages so often reserved for the brave but helpless men who fell into their power."

**Lieutenant Colonel Bertrand Dees Gibson, aged 42**
**DSO and Croix de Guerre avec Palms**
**1/4th Battalion Northumberland Fusiliers**
**Died 27 May 1918**

Bertrand was the only son of Colonel Wilfred and Ann Gibson of Ruradean, Hexham, and the grandson of the late Charles Gibson, town clerk of Salford, Lancashire. He was born in January 1876 at Maidens Cross and was educated at Ushaw College, Durham. He qualified as a solicitor and went into partnership with his father in 1899. He practised in the Hexham and Haltwhistle Courts and acted as solicitor to Hexham Farmers' Protection Association. Bertrand married Margaret Elizabeth (née Jackson, of Stainton, Yorkshire) in the summer of 1907. He was very athletic and was reputed to have been one of the finest lawn tennis players that Tynedale had produced. A sporting polymath, he also captained Northumberland at Hockey. He played cricket and was a playing member of Tynedale Rugby Football Club.

Bertrand joined the pre-territorial, 1st Volunteer Battalion of the Northumberland Fusiliers in 1900. He spent time at the School of Musketry at Hythe and was appointed instructor of musketry for the battalion. At the onset of hostilities he was promoted to the rank of Major. He proceeded to France with his battalion in April 1915 and saw action within days of arriving in France (see page 35). During this battle the battalion commander Lieutenant Colonel Forster was killed and Bertrand assumed command. In the summer of 1915 he was gazetted to Lieutenant Colonel. Bertrand earned his DSO in January 1917 for his courageous fighting on the Somme in September 1916 (see page 105). The Hexham Herald of 28 July 1917 reported that Bertrand was in the Third General Hospital, Wandsworth, suffering with nervous exhaustion, but on reporting fit for duty he was not content with a desk job and insisted that he rejoin his battalion at the Front, which he did in April 1918.

**Croix de Guerre**

Soon after the outbreak of World War I, French military officials felt the need for a new military award. Already at that time, the *Citation du Jour* (Daily Service Citation) existed to acknowledge soldiers, but it was just a sheet of paper. At the end of 1914, General Boëlle, Commandant in Chief of the French 4th Army Corps, tried to convince the French administration to create a formal military award; he was supported by Maurice Barrès, the noted writer and deputy of Paris. On 23 December 1914, the French deputy Georges Bonnefous proposed a legislative bill to create the *Croix de la Valeur Militaire* (Cross of Military Valour) signed by 66 other deputies. On 18 January 1915, Émile Driant submitted this bill but the proposed military award was renamed the *Croix de Guerre* (*Cross of War*). The bill was adopted on 2 April 1915. The *Croix de Guerre* recognizes gallantry by any member of the French military or its allies; degrees indicate the importance of the former soldier's role during World War I. The lowest degree is represented by a bronze star and the highest degree is represented by a silver palm. The medal was designed by the sculptor Paul-Albert Bartholomé. It is 37mm in diameter showing four arms and two crossed swords. The center of the front side shows the symbolic profile of the French Republic: a young woman wearing a Phrygian cap. The words *République Française* (French Republic) encircle the portrait. The back of the medal shows the dates of the conflict: first, it was 1914–1915 then 1914–1916, 1914–1917 and finally 1914–1918. The ribbon was green with seven narrow vertical red stripes

Bertrand was awarded the Croix de Guerre avec Palms, posthumously, in recognition of his leadership on 27 May 1918, the day he died. A wife, a son and a daughter survived him. The citation for French *Croix de Guerre avec Palms* stated:

> "This officer was in command of his Battalion, which was holding the front line trenches on May 27, 1918 in the Aisne sector. He continued to send information of the enemy's advance until his Headquarters were completely surrounded. He then collected all available men of his Headquarters' party, and although attacked on three sides it was due to this officer's personal example and total disregard of danger that the enemy were delayed in their advance for a considerable time. He was shot through the head and killed whilst standing on the parapet to get a better view of the enemy, when at the time they were advancing up a communication trench."

The Hexham Herald initially reported that Bertrand had been killed by a shell. This information was received in a letter from Captain Gregory (Adjutant), who at the time was in hospital in England recovering from wounds received on the day that Bertrand was killed. However, the Reverend Callin reported that he was killed by a sniper's bullet. The Divisional History recorded that "Lieutenant-Colonel Gibson was a Territorial Officer of great experience and reputation, a fine soldier and was greatly beloved by his Battalion".

The Reverend Callin wrote of Lieutenant- Colonel Gibson:

> "Thus the Battalion lost its Commanding Officer, a man revered and loved by all. All nerve and will, he died fighting to the last, the very incarnation of courage. A born leader and a superb soldier, he had joined the Fusiliers in the early Volunteer days, finally becoming Commanding Officer in the summer of 1915. His name will be ever remembered by those who knew him as one of the straightest, strongest men we have known."

His wife had the following inscribed on his gravestone:

**IN GLORIOUSLY PROUD MEMORY**
**OF MY BELOVED HUSBAND**
**"UNTIL"**
**QUO FATA VOCANT**

**Bertrand is buried in La Ville-aux-Bois British Cemetery, (Aisne).**

An attempt was made by two companies of the 1/5th Northumberland Fusiliers to reinforce the Battle Zone which was unsuccessful. Just after 6am, the last of the redoubts were captured and from this moment the Northumberland Fusiliers ceased to exist as fighting units.

**Second Lieutenant Edward Phillips, aged 34**
**1/5th Northumberland Fusiliers**
**Died 27 May 1918**

Edward was the second son of John and Jane Phillips of Crag House, Falstone. He was a well known North Tyne farmer. In April 1918 he was involved with his battalion during the struggles at Messines and Melville. His battalion, as part of 50th Division, was mentioned by Field Marshall Haig in his Despatch of 28 May for their determined resistance. A further three brothers were all serving with the forces. He appears to have died of wounds received on 27 May.

**Edward is commemorated on the Soissons Memorial to the missing.**

Later in the day, remnants of these units formed a defensive position at the canal bridge south of Chaudardes. By 9am they realised that their position was untenable and they were forced to cross the Aisne where further small parties of men gathered together, forming an *ad hoc* battalion, which held this position until 3.30pm until they were ordered to retire and concentrate on the high ground above Concevreux. The new, temporary line was defended until 4pm when the enemy drove them out.

**Private George Hutchinson, aged 22**
**1/4th Northumberland Fusiliers**
**Died 27 May 1918**

George was the son of Henry and Alice Hutchinson of Acomb. Before the hostilities, he was employed at Black Pastures Quarry and he enlisted voluntarily in 1915, when he became eighteen.

**George is commemorated on the Soissons Memorial to the missing.**

In support of the 149th Brigade was the 1st Northumbrian Brigade of the Royal Field Artillery, a pre war Territorial Force. Rumours were rife; there were warnings that 'something big' was going to take place and they received orders to inspect their gas curtains and to be ready to meet and overthrow a Bosch attack. At 1am on 27 May all hell broke loose. Colonel Shiel wrote:

> "With a flash that lit the whole sky and a crash a second later that madc us dive for cover, the War began. The Germans advanced rapidly getting in behind the infantry along its flanks before they had time to defend themselves."

Letters written by Colonel Johnstone described how batteries received direct hits, whilst men, working in respirators because of high levels of gas, became increasingly weary as they tried vainly to man their guns. Batteries were soon surrounded by German troops and they were forced to surrender. Up to 6am, 'A' Battery had been in operation under extreme conditions and had one gun knocked out; they had suffered a number of casualties. When it became apparent that the battery was threatened with encirclement by German troops, the men removed the breech blocks and sights from each artillery piece and retreated southwards. Colonel Johnstone wrote that, following this withdrawal, both Shiel and Richardson reported to him; he noted that Richardson appeared to be "dead beat". The War History of the Brigade records that a party of officers and men, including Richardson, made a bid to get back to their own lines and set off through a wood. They had to pass through a German barrage and Francis was hit. His fellow officers, Dickinson, Graham, Meek and Willis, carried him for two to three hundred yards, after which he was carried further, on a mattress, to Chaudardes, where the men decided that he was dead and his body was left by the wayside [25].

Later Johnstone wrote of Richardson:

> "He was a gallant fellow, and did not know what fear was".

**Lieutenant Francis Alymer Richardson, aged 35**
**'A' Battery Northumbrian Brigade**
**Royal Field Artillery**
**Died 27 May 1918**

Francis was born in Carlisle, the son of the late Reverend Francis and Mrs Frances Richardson. The Reverend Richardson had been the vicar of Corbridge. Francis was educated at Seascale Preparatory School and at Richmond School. He was gazetted Second Lieutenant in September 1915 (Royal Field Artillery, TF) and promoted Lieutenant in 1916. He served in France from January 1916 and during this time was twice mentioned in Despatches by Douglas Haig for gallant and distinguished services in the field [30]. The Hexham Courant reported that Francis' sister, Christina Richardson of West Park, Corbridge, received the tragic news that her brother had died of wounds received in action on 27 May [30].

**Francis is commemorated on the Soissons Memorial to the missing.**

Victory seemed near for the Germans, who by 30 May 1918 had captured just over 50,000 Allied soldiers and well over 800 guns. However, having advanced by 3 June to within 35 miles of Paris, the German army was beset by numerous problems, including supply shortages, fatigue, lack of reserves and many casualties, together with counter-attacks by (and stiff resistance from) newly arrived American divisions, who engaged them in the Battles of *Chateau-Thierry* and *Belleau Wood.* On 6 June 1918, following many successful Allied counter-attacks, the German advance halted on the Marne, short of its major objective, as had the 'Michael' and 'Georgette' offensives in March and April of that year.

## REFERENCES

1. MacDonald, L. *To the Last Man, Spring 1918*. Pub: Penguin 1999.

2. Stevenson, D. *With our Backs to the Wall.* Pub: Allen Lane 2011.

3. O'Neill, H. C. OBE. *The Royal Fusiliers in the Great War.*
Pub: 1922 reprinted Naval and Military Press 2002.

4. WO95/1613. *War Diary 1st Battalion Royal Fusiliers.*

5. Miles, Capt. W. *Durham Forces in the Field,*
Pub: 1920 reprinted Naval and Military Press 2004.

6. WO95/2108. *War Diary 11th Battalion Durham Light Infantry.*

7. Burton , O. E. MM. 2nd Lieut. *The Auckland Regiment 1914-1918.* Pub: 1922 reprinted Naval and Military Press 2003.

8. Wyrall, E. *The Fiftieth Division, 1914-1919.* Pub: 1939, reprinted Naval and Military Press 2002.

9. Wyrall, E. *East Yorkshire Regiment in the Great War 1914-1918.* Pub: 1928, reprinted Naval and Military Press2002.

10. WO95/2835. *War Diary 1/4th Battalion East Yorkshire Regiment.*

11. WO95/1702 *War Diary 8th Machine Gun Battalion.*

12. WO95/2523 *War Diary 154th Field Company, Royal Engineers.*

13. WO95/2484. *War Diary 19th Battalion Durham Light Infantry.*

14. Bean C. E. W. *Official history of Australia in the War of 1914-1918.*

15. AWM4 23/59/18. *War Diary 42nd Battalion Australian Infantry April 1918.*

16. Tomaselli, P. *The Battle of the Lys 1918.* Pub: Pen and Sword 2011.

17. Cooke, C. H. Capt. *Historical Records of the 9th Battalion Northumberland Fusiliers.* Pub: 1928.

18. WO95/2466. *War Diary 9th Battalion Northumberland Fusiliers.*

19. Stewart, G. and Sheen, J. A. *History of Tyneside Scottish.* Pub: Pen and Sword, 1999.

20. WO95/2463. *War Diary, 22nd Battalion Northumberland Fusiliers.*

21. WO95/2828. *War Diary, 1/5th Battalion Northumberland Fusiliers.*

22. WO95/1622. *War Diary, 1st Battalion Leicestershire Regiment.*

23. Wyrall, E. *The Fiftieth Division, 1914-1919.* Pub: 1939, reprinted Naval and Military Press 2002.

24. WO95/2828. *War Diary, 1/4th Battalion Northumberland Fusiliers.*

25. Ommanney, C. H. *The War History of the 1st Northumbrian Brigade R.F.A (T.F.) August 1914-July 1919.* Pub: J.W. Hindson 1927.

26. Callin, R. W. Rev. *When the Lantern of Hope Burned Low.* Pub: J Catherall 1919.

27. Conan Doyle, A. *The British Campaign in France and Flanders, January to July 1918.* Pub: Hodder and Stoughton 1919.

28. WO/161/100/412. *Private Joseph Hodgson, 1/4th Northumberland Fusiliers, returning Prisoner of War Interview.*

29. WO/161/100/392. *Sergeant Harold Betts, 8th (Service) Battalion Lincolnshire Regiment, returning Prisoner of War Interview.*

30. Marquis of Ruvigny and Raineval. *De Ruvigny's Roll of Honour 1914-1924*, Vol. 4, page 168,

# CHAPTER SIXTEEN

# ADVANCE TO VICTORY

*Shall they return to beating of great bells*
*In wild train loads?*
*A few, a few, too few for drums and yells,*
*May creep back, silent, to village wells,*
*Up half-known roads.*
From: Wilfred Owen's *The Send-Off*

## THE BRITISH OFFENSIVE IN PICARDY (8 AUGUST – 3 SEPTEMBER)

## BATTLE OF AMIENS 8 – 11 AUGUST 1918

The Battle of Amiens marked the start of the British advance that culminated in the signing of the Armistice of 11 November 1918. Canadian troops were secretly moved on to the Somme and took over the southern part of the Australian Front Line. The Canadian and Australians manned the line for the advance south of the River Somme. A French force was positioned at the southern end of the attack. To the north of the River Somme, British divisions formed up for the advance. The extent of the Front was from Albert in the north and, for the Canadians, Villers Bretonneux in the south [1].

On 8 August at 4.20am, just before first light and in dense fog, nearly 100,000 British Australian and Canadian soldiers opened the offensive using a crushing bombardment, 400 tanks and wave after wave of infantrymen. The noise of the tanks had been concealed by unseen aircraft droning in the sky above. This momentous attack completely

**Erich Friedrich Wilhelm Ludendorff**

At the outbreak of war, Ludendorff was appointed as Deputy Chief of Staff to the German Second Army under General Karl von Bülow; the German assault in the first few days of August 1914, according to the Schlieffen Plan for invading France, gained him national recognition. The Germans experienced their first major setback at Liège, when Belgian forces killed thousands of attacking German troops. On 5 August Ludendorff took command of the 14th Brigade; he cut off Liège and called for siege guns. By 16 August Liège had fallen, allowing the German First Army to advance. As victor, Ludendorff was awarded Germany's highest military decoration for gallantry, presented in person by Emperor Wilhelm II. Elsewhere, Russia was waging war more effectively than the Schlieffen Plan anticipated, forcing German forces to withdraw as the Russians advanced into East Prussia. Only a week after Liège's fall, Ludendorff was called by the Kaiser to serve as Chief of Staff on the Eastern Front. Ludendorff, with Paul von Hindenburg, replaced General von Prittwitz, who had proposed abandoning East Prussia. After the Battle of Łódź in November 1914, Ludendorff was promoted to Lieutenant-General.

In August 1916, Erich von Falkenhayn resigned as Chief of the General Staff. Paul von Hindenburg took his place; Ludendorff assumed the title *First Generalquartiermeister* and insisted that all orders were to be sent out jointly; thus he became the chief manager of the German war effort, with the popular General von Hindenburg his pliant front man.

It was Ludendorff who in 1917 advocated unrestricted submarine warfare to break the British blockade. In the winter and spring of 1917/18, Ludendorff planned and directed Germany's final Western Front offensives; although not formally a commander-in-chief, Ludendorff directed operations by issuing orders to the staffs of the armies at the Front. This final push to win the war fell short, and on 8 August 1918, Ludendorff realised that the war was lost and ordered his men to hold their positions while a ceasefire was negotiated. At this point, Ludendorff was close to a mental breakdown, sometimes in tears, and his worried staff called in a psychiatrist. After the war, he went into exile in Sweden until 1920, when he returned to Germany.

overwhelmed the enemy's defences: 13,000 prisoners were taken and between 300 and 400 guns captured. By nightfall, the Allies had made an advance of between six and seven miles.

Charles Bean, the official Australian Historian, wrote:

> "A little later the mist suddenly cleared, and for a moment all eyes on the battlefield took in the astonishing scene: infantry in lines of hundreds of little section-columns all moving forward – with tanks guns, battery after battery, the teams tossing their manes."

General Erich Ludendorff, the German Commander, wrote of 8 August:

> "... was the Black Day of the German Army in this war. The 8 August put the decline of that [German] fighting power beyond all doubt. The war must be ended."

The 14th Brigade Royal Field Artillery was part of 16th Army Brigade which was used to support the Australian assault. The Australians were assembled to the north of Villiers Bretonneux. On 8 August the 16th Army Brigade produced a barrage so thick and accurate that all the phases of the first objective of the day were achieved by 7am. As the attack progressed rapidly forward, brigades of 16th Army Brigade pushed well forward clearing a valley which was holding up the infantry advance [2].

**Gunner John Fletcher, aged 28**
**'A' Battery 14th Brigade Royal Field Artillery**
**Died 9 August 1918**

John was born in Elsdon, the eldest son of Edward and Margaret Baty Fletcher of Lane Head, Bellingham. The 1911 census shows that John was working as a horseman on a farm at High Green, Greenhaugh. He was a married man, marrying Marion (née Graham) in Gateshead in the spring of 1914. He was the father of at least three children. When conscripted into the army, John and his family were living in Bellingham. After John's death, Marion moved back to Gateshead where she had been born. John died of wounds received on the day of the initial advance.

**John is buried in Adelaide Cemetery, Villiers-Bretonneux.**

The 1st Battalion Australian Machine Gun Corps was attached to the Australian 1st Infantry Division. The 3rd Machine Gun Company was attached to the 3rd Infantry Brigade. These units were not involved on the first day of the Allied advance, but began their campaign at 8am on 10 August. They advanced over open, flat land towards higher ground above Lihons and Bois Crépy. Because the 2nd Infantry Brigade troops had not taken their objectives, the advancing troops came under terrific machine gun fire and a moderate hostile barrage before they crossed their own front. Progress was slow, although on the right of the attack, Bois Crépy was captured. The 3rd Infantry Brigade Diary states that "their own barrage was wretched, skimpy and without sting" [3,4,5].

**Private Albert Edward Dodd, aged 29**
**3rd Machine Gun Company**
**1st Battalion Australian Machine Gun Corps**
**Died 10 August 1918**

Albert was the third son of Robert and Dorothy Dodd of Swinburne Wood, Barrasford. This family had already received the news of the death of Albert's brother Alfred on the Somme in September 1916, (see page 119). A further two sons were also serving in France.

After basic schooling, Albert was initially employed by the Swinburne Estate, but later joined the Newcastle City Police Force. He emigrated to Western Australia and was employed as a policeman in the Kalgoorlie Gold Fields. He was a married man, his wife Alice, (née Forster of Rowlands Gill) lived at 44 Hare Street, Kalgoorlie. By 1919, Alice had moved back to England and was living at Railway Cottages, in Rowlands Gill.

Albert enlisted with the Australian forces in November 1916 at Blackboy Hill and sailed on board HMAT Berrima, arriving in England in February 1917. After further training, including a spell at Grantham, he transferred to the Australian Machine Gun Corps. Exactly a year after his departure from Australia he arrived in France. On 19 March 1918 he was gassed and spent the next few weeks in hospital in Boulogne, missing the onslaught of the German advances of March, April and May. He rejoined his unit at the end of May. On August 10, Albert was wounded and died that night in the 53rd Casualty Clearing Station, of gun shot wounds to the abdomen. He was buried by the Rev F R Thurlow at Daours Cemetery.

**Albert is buried at Daours Communal Cemetery Extension.**

On 14 August, intelligence was obtained that the enemy was withdrawing from the front held by the 1st Battalion East Yorkshire, (EY). Probing patrols found that not only the German Front Line but also their Support Lines and Beaumont Hamel were deserted. The 9th Battalion Kings Own Yorkshire Light Infantry (KOYLI), occupied the enemy's deserted trenches with the EY in support. On 15 August both of these battalions were ordered to move forward with the East Yorks passing through the positions held by the 9th KOYLI to occupy a bridgehead over the Ancre. However, the enemy held a ridge in front of the battalion and the advance stalled soon afterwards [6,7].

**Private Francis Fowler, aged 18**
**1st Battalion East Yorkshire Regiment**
**Died 15 August 1918**

Frank (Francis) was born in Great Swinburne and was the eldest son of Thomas and Margaret Fowler. He was conscripted into the forces in November 1917, presumably on his eighteenth birthday.

**Frank is buried in Knightsbridge Cemetery, Mensil-Martinsart.**

## THE SECOND BATTLE OF THE SOMME
## BATTLE OF ALBERT 21 - 23 AUGUST 1918

The Battle of Albert was the start of a northward extension of the British Advance of 8 August. On 21 August, the Allies made a large scale attack along a Front from Albert to Arras. In the north (Arras) the Third Army commanded by General Sir Julian Byng was used, whilst in the south the attack was undertaken by elements of Fourth Army under General Sir Henry Rawlinson. This advance across the 1916 Somme Battlefield would involve troops from three divisions: the 17th, 21st and 38th.

The 2nd Lincolnshire Regiment transferred to the 21st Battalion in February 1918 and was involved in the battle to recapture Albert; their Front for the attack was centred on the area around Grandcourt. By 5.45am the Lincolns had captured Beaucourt-sur-Ancre. Suffering very few casualties they continued their advance, enveloped in a dense mist, towards the railway line on the north bank of the Ancre.

Later that afternoon 'A' and 'D' companies were relieved by Northumberland Fusiliers as a large number of men in these companies were suffering from the effects of gas. The other two companies 'B' and 'C', which were holding the outpost line, were ordered forward with 'C' company on the right flank of this advance. After passing through the front held by the 1st Battalion Lincolnshire Regiment, they consolidated their position in a sunken road. Unfortunately, this position came under enfiladed machine gun and rifle fire and from trench mortar fire from the direction of Grandcourt. Enemy soldiers were also able to get around the left flank of 'B' company. During one of the incursions by the Germans, Lieutenant Walton was killed. The War Diary reports the date of Walton's death as the 21 August, but databases report it as 22 August [8,9].

**Lieutenant George Pears Walton, aged 29**
**1/4th Northumberland Fusiliers**
**Attached 'C' Company**
**2nd Battalion Lincolnshire Regiment**
**Died 22 August 1918**

George was the youngest son of John Pears and Frances Mary Walton of Acomb High House and Green Ends, Alston. He was educated at Sedburgh School, where he was Head of House and a prominent member of the rugby team. Subsequently he attended Durham College of Science. George spent a few years in Canada and on his return in 1912 helped in the management of the family's interests in Messrs Walton and Cowper's lead and coal mines. He played as a forward for Tynedale Rugby Club and was a key player when the team won the Northumberland Senior Cup in 1914.

He enlisted in December 1914, in Morpeth, as a private in the 19th Battalion (Service) Northumberland Fusiliers (NF). As George had spent three years with the Officer Training Corps whilst at Sedburgh School, he was quickly gazetted Second Lieutenant in April 1915. He arrived in France on 11 June 1915, to serve with the 1/4th Battalion NF. In early August 1916 George was admitted to 7th Stationary Hospital in Boulogne with a wound caused by tripping over a strand of wire causing him to fall into a trench and pierce his right hand on a piece of galvanised iron. George was also seriously wounded on 16 September 1916 (see page 105) at High Wood, when a bullet caused a series of compound fractures to his right humerus, a wound that would leave him with a permanent deformity. A Medical Board certified him fit for light duties in May 1917. After a further long period of convalescence, George's dogged determination assured his return to active service in June 1918 when he was attached to the Lincolnshire Regiment. A letter from his commanding officer to his brother Mr J C P Walton of Greens End, Alston, described how George was killed:

> "Your brother was killed in action during the present British Advance. He was hit on the 22 August after his battalion had been through some very hard fighting and whilst his company was advancing to take a most important enemy position."

A plaque in St John Lee Church records that Lieutenant Walton was killed at Beaucourt-sur-Ancre whilst attached to the Lincolnshire Regiment. His gravestone is inscribed with the following:

**TO LIVE IN HEARTS**
**WE LEAVE BEHIND**
**IS NOT TO DIE**

**George is buried in Queens Cemetery, Bucquoy.**

On 23 August, 13th Royal Fusiliers (RF) moved up for an attack on the German Front Line which now lay to the west of the town of Bapaume. The attack followed a creeping barrage. The left flank met considerable opposition from a German strongpoint in the brickworks and for a time it was feared that the attack would fail due to the heavy opposition they encountered. Groups of Fusiliers managed to work their way around the flanks of the brickworks and they eventually quenched resistance from this German position, taking sixty prisoners. The two companies on the right flank initially encountered little resistance and a large number of German prisoners were returned to the rear.

As the attacking troops clambered up the sides of the railway embankment they ran into fierce rifle and machine gun fire; an intense struggle followed during which the attackers used trench mortars. They managed to scale the eastern bank of the embankment and intensify their fire causing the Germans to lose heart and to begin to surrender in large numbers. The Battalion Diary records that the attack appears to have been a surprise to the Germans as when they cleared out the dugouts in the walls of the cutting:

> "there was ample evidence of a meal that had just been prepared and hot coffee was steaming on the tables".

Nearly three hours after the start of the attack, troops from the 1/1st Hertfordshire Regiment took up the attack allowing the Fusiliers to regroup. Later in the afternoon the RF pushed forward for a second time meeting heavy fire from the enemy and it became clear that no further progress would be made without the support of artillery or tanks.

During the day the RF took over 500 prisoners for a total cost of 1 officer and 33 other ranks killed, (this does not include figures for wounded or missing in action) [10,11].

**Private Robert Sidney Plant, aged 19**
**1st Company, 13th (Service) Battalion Royal Fusiliers**
**Died 23 August 1918**

Sidney was born at Sandhoe, the second son of Mr and Mrs Plant of the Hermitage Cottage, Hexham. He was a chorister at Stagshaw Church. After leaving school he was employed as under-chauffeur by Mr Noble of Sandhoe House. He also spent a year at the Motor Department at Elswick.

Sidney enlisted in the Services on Easter Monday 1917, his eighteenth birthday. He had been rejected earlier because he was under age. Initially he was attached to Motor Transport at Grove Park where he passed his examinations as a qualified driver. Subsequently he was transferred to the Royal Fusiliers crossing to France in February 1918.

**Sidney is buried in**
**Aichiet-Le-Grand Communal Cemetery**
**Extension.**

During the early hours of 24 August, the 1/2nd Battalion London Regiment, made their way forward towards the Front Line from their position near Basseux. Their destination was the Boiry Reserve Trench and Boiry Works, a German strongpoint which had been captured the previous day by elements of 168th Brigade. This manoeuvre was to strengthen the position in expectation of a German counterattack. During the night of the 24 August the Germans fired a large number of gas shells into the area held by the battalion [10,12].

Apart from being commemorated in the Catholic Church at Bellingham, John Kirkland is also commemorated on a private memorial on the west wall of the church hall of the West End Methodist Church in Hexham. This building opened in 1905 and was used as the United Methodist Church until the present church was opened in 1936. When the new church was ready the family requested that the plaque be left in place as this was the building that John knew during his time living in the town.

**Private John Kirkland, aged 19**
**1/2nd Battalion City of London Regiment**
**Royal Fusiliers**
**Died 24 August 1918**

John was born in Bellingham, the eldest son of George and Edith Kirkland. When the family lived in Bellingham the children attended St Oswald's Roman Catholic Church and John was also educated at the Reed Charity School. However, the 1911 census reports the Kirkland family living in Scotswood, Newcastle, with John, now aged 12, still attending school. His father worked on the railways as an engine driver, and at some point the family moved to

Hexham, where they lived in Kingsgate Terrace. Before he was conscripted into the army John had moved to Wylam where he was employed at the local station as a goods clerk. He was initially attached to the 2nd Reserve Cavalry Regiment and arrived in France at the end of March 1918. The following is found on his headstone:

**UNTIL THE DAY BREAKS**

**John is buried in Summit Trench Cemetery, Croiselles.**

The 2nd King's Own Yorkshire Light Infantry were part of the advance taking place to the south of the River Somme and east of Péronne. After being part of the attack that captured Herleville, they were relieved from the Front on 24 August. However, they were back in the vanguard of the offensive by the 27 August, taking up a section of the outpost line east of Deniécourt on 29 August. The battalion headquarters were based near Misery. During the night of 29/30 August the Battalion Headquarters came under an intense artillery bombardment and a number of officers and men were killed [13,14].

**Lance Corporal James Douglas Robertson, aged 19**
**2nd Battalion King's Own Yorkshire Light Infantry**
**Died 30 August 1918**

James was born in Reedsmouth, the eldest son of Charles and Kate Robertson of West Woodburn. The 1911 census reports that the Robertson family was living at Whitsun House Cottage, East Woodburn, and that James, aged 12, was still at school. James was conscripted into the army and would not have been in France for many weeks before his death.

**James is buried in Brie Cemetery.**

# SECOND BATTLE OF BAPAUME
# 31 AUGUST – 3 SEPTEMBER

During the last week in August, unrelenting eastward attacks by the British had forced the Germans into perpetual retreat. By 29 August the Germans were back to the line from where they had started their offensive in late March. However, near Péronne the pursuit was halted by the watery barrier of the River Somme and some immensely strong German defences sited on Mont St Quentin.

British Royal Field Artillery battery in action
(probably a posed picture)

The 168th Brigade Royal Field Artillery was attached to 32nd Division. In the final days of August, infantry from the 32nd Division, positioned south of Péronne and due east of Barleux, were ordered to advance and gain observation positions monitoring crossing of the Somme Canal; the high ground east of Misery was highlighted as being of strategic importance for this purpose. On 29 August, although the forward infantry patrols met very little opposition, the British artillery came under severe attack from German counter battery artillery [2,15].

**Gunner George Gray, aged 28**
**168th Brigade, Royal Field Artillery**
**Died 1 September 1918**

George was born at Milbourne, Northumberland, the youngest son of William and Margaret Jane Gray of Wall. He was educated at Higham Dykes, Langley and Wall Church of England schools. Before joining the army he was employed at Messrs William Weir and Co at Hexham Saw Mill. In May 1917 he enlisted in the Royal Scots Greys (a cavalry regiment) and was subsequently transferred to the Royal Field Artillery. He had served in France from April 1918 when he was killed. In a letter to Mrs Gray, an officer explained that her son had been wounded in action on 29 August and that he had died at a casualty clearing station two days later. The letter went on to say, "His willingness and devotion to duty made him a gallant soldier". His gravestone is inscribed with the following:

**AT REST**

**George is buried in Daours Communal Cemetery Extension.**

## BREAKING THE HINDENBURG LINE

During the last week of August and first weeks of September 1918, Britain's First, Third and Fourth Armies attempted a series of operations to move their formations into contact with a formidable collection of German defences called the 'Siegfried Stellung' (Siegfried Line) but better known to the British as the Hindenburg Line. Between 26 and 30 August, battle raged as the British forces moved up towards the Drocourt-Quéant

Line in preparation for the assault on this vital German position, which was breached during 2-3 September. On 9 September 1918, the 15th Battalion Durham Light Infantry (64th Brigade) moved up in preparation for the attack and capture of Chapel Hill which lay east and slightly north of the village of Heudicourt. Chapel Hill was defended by a redoubt and by the Cavalry and Cavalry Support trench systems – still known by their old British names although now in German hands. As the DLI formed up they came under heavy machine gun fire, but Cavalry Support trench was captured after heavy fighting. At 5.30pm the battalion once again formed up and continued the attack on Cavalry Trench and was able to capture a part of the system, again after heavy fighting. In response, the Germans launched a strong counter-attack but failed to recapture the trench. However, later in the day, a second counterattack drove the DLI back to Cavalry Support. During the next day, 10 September, the Germans launched a determined attack against Cavalry Support Trench but were driven back. On 11 September the battalion was relieved [16,17].

**Private Ray Morris Evelyn Proudlock, aged 19**
**15th Battalion Durham Light Infantry**
**Died 10 September 1918**

Ray was born in Bury St Edmonds, Suffolk and was the son of John and Mary Ellen (born in the USA) eventually of Fourlaws Hill Top, Bellingham. John, Roy's father, worked on a number of estates in Northumberland, Suffolk and Yorkshire as head gamekeeper; for example, the 1911 census reports the Proudlock family living at Hipswell Lodge near Richmond, Yorkshire.

Ray was conscripted in September 1917 and his records show that he trained as a motor mechanic. On attesting he tried to join the RFC but was not accepted, even though he appeared to have the relevant skills. He initially served with the 51st (Graduated) Battalion, a training battalion based in Chelmsford. In April 1918 he travelled to France and was transferred to the 15th Battalion Durham Light Infantry (DLI).

**Ray is buried in Gouzeaucourt New British Cemetery.**

On 5 September the 1st East Yorkshires (EY) moved up to Sailly-Saillisel and on 6 September took up a position north of Fins, then moving to Sorel-le-Grand where they formed the 64th Brigade Reserve. At 4am on 9 September other elements of 64th Brigade (15th DLI and 9th KOYLI) attacked Chapel Hill and Lowland Ridge. The attack was successful: Chapel Hill and Lowland Trench were captured.

After two German counterattacks, what remained of the morning attack was forced to withdraw to the line of the Lowland Support Trench, (see above). At 9pm the EY received orders to attack Chapel Hill in the early hours of 10 September. Owing to the intense darkness they were unable to get into position and were thus late in following the barrage which fell at 5.15am. Furthermore, in the confusion the attack moved in a northerly rather than a north-easterly direction and as a result was a complete failure. The bill for this farcical affair was 1 officer and 5 other ranks killed, 2 officers and 36 other ranks wounded and 4 officers and 138 other ranks missing, (presumably killed) [6,7].

**Private Roger Robson Potts, aged 19**
**1st Battalion East Yorkshire Regiment**
**Died 10 September 1918**

Roger was born in Falstone, the son of Thomas and Mary Potts; he was one of eight children. His father Thomas worked as a tailor. His older brothers worked at the local coal mine and it's highly likely that Roger

would have worked at the local mine before he was conscripted into the army on his eighteenth birthday. He would not have been in France for any time at all before he met his death. He was wounded in action, dying of his wounds at either the 3rd Canadian or the 59th Casualty Clearing Stations. His gravestone is inscribed with the following:

**NOTHING IN MY HAND I BRING**
**SIMPLY TO THY CROSS I CLING**

**Roger is buried in Varennes Military Cemetery.**

## BATTLE OF HAVRINCOURT: 12 SEPTEMBER 1918

In this action, formations of the Third Army were allocated to capture the high ground of the Trescault and Havrincourt spurs and advance the line to within assault distance of the Hindenburg Position. However, it was only at Havrincourt that the British managed to enter the Hindenburg Line system.

## BATTLE OF EPÉHY: 18 SEPTEMBER 1918

The Allies made further progress in breaking this immense defensive structure by the capture of a series of strong, outlying German posts on the ridges between Le Verguier and Epéhy. Australian troops managed to penetrate into the Advanced Hindenburg System. During the last week of September a number of major Allied offensives were launched on the Western Front; two of the offensives were against the Hindenburg Line whilst the third was in Flanders.

## BATTLE OF THE CANAL DU NORD, 27 SEPTEMBER – 1 OCTOBER 1918

Divisions from Britain's First and Third Armies were required to attack across the northern extension of the Hindenburg Line towards Cambrai. In order to succeed in this, they needed to cross the formidable defensive obstacle of the Canal du Nord

Canadian Combat Engineers constructing bridges across the Canal du Nord, September 1918

On 25 September 1918, the 2/4th King's Own Yorkshire Light Infantry, (KOYLI) moved up from Behanies to Frémicourt and by the evening of 26 September were in positions east of Hermies ready to start their attack. The initial attack against the Hindenburg Support line between Flesquières and east of Ribécourt on the 27 September was undertaken by battalions from the 3rd Division. After these had taken their first objective, the 2/4th KOYLI were required to take up the attack. At 4.30am on 28 September the attack was continued and initially was successful: the Hindenburg Support Line was taken and a large number of prisoners were sent back to the British Lines. Forward movement was the name of the game that day, although Robert Cowens would pay with his life for the day's advances. For the rest of the KOYLI, fighting would continue till the end of the month [13,18].

**Private Robert Cowens, aged 18**
**2/4th Battalion King's Own Yorkshire Light Infantry**
**Died 28 September 1918**

Robert was born in Corsenside, the only surviving son of Henry and Elizabeth Cowens. Before being conscripted into the army Robert was preparing to follow a career in teaching; he had been educated at Morpeth Grammar School for three years and was a student teacher at Kirkwhelpington School. Robert's younger sister Hannah, aged fourteen at the time, received a poignant letter from a Private James Hamilton of the Scottish Rifles, telling her that he had found a soldier dead on the battlefield and from a letter of hers lying by his side he had inferred he was her brother.

**Robert is buried in Grand Ravine British Cemetery, Havrincourt.**

On the night of 25/26 September the 1st Battalion Northumberland Fusiliers (NF) occupied a series of trenches to the east and north-east of Havrincourt. At about 5.10am, ten minutes before the attack by the NF on the morning of 27 September was due to begin, the Front Line was thoroughly targeted by German artillery and trench-mortars. Many of the waiting fusiliers were injured or killed outright [19.20].

The battalion history records:

> "Such an event has often of itself proved sufficient to crush an attack before it can be launched. But the Fifth (from the Napoleonic times when they were known as the fifth regiment of the line), under the severest ordeal to which troops can be subjected, remained steady."

Thus, reduced but unperturbed, the fusiliers attacked with the aid of a British barrage. However, the enemy put a strong resistance using well placed machine-guns and it took over 45 minutes to take the enemy's front line trench (named Wood Switch).

After a period of consolidation the battalion moved forward to capture a trench system known as Ravine Avenue, where it consolidated and allowed the Royal Fusiliers to take on the attack with the aim of capturing the village of Ribécourt, which they achieved. By 10am, the Northumberlands had been withdrawn from the action to the divisional reserve, west of the Canal du Nord.

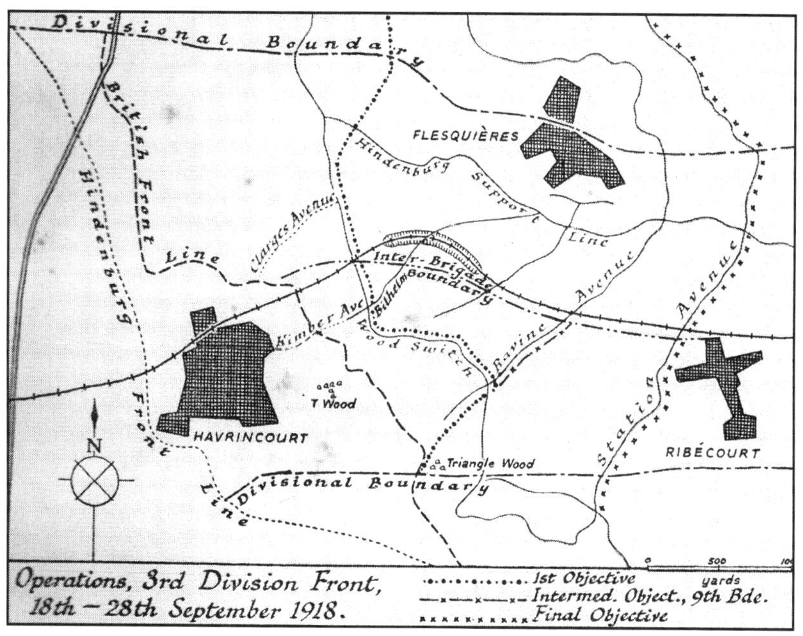


Operations, 3rd Division Front, 18th – 28th September 1918.

The War Diary for 1 October shows:

> "The Battalion was out of the line and records no casualties for the day. Although information records that John died in action, I can only assume that he died of wounds received in the action of the morning 27 September, when figures for casualties were 4 officers killed, 2 wounded, other ranks 26 killed, 134 wounded and 35 missing."

The exploits of the Northumberland Fusiliers and the other battalions of the 3rd Division were reported in many English Newspapers under the heading "The Iron Division". The Times, referring to the attack east of Havrincourt, concluded:

> "It is known as the Iron Division and its iron truly entered into the German soul".

**Private John Henry Milburn, aged 41**
**1st Battalion Northumberland Fusiliers**
**Died 1 October 1918**

John was born in Wark and was the son of James and Margaret Milburn of Woodley Shield East. He worked with his father as a farm labourer. He married a widow, Mary Green, in 1904 and was father to a step daughter and at least three sons. Some time after 1905 the family moved to the Newbrough/Fourstones area, where John was employed as a ploughman. An obituary in the Hexham Courant reported that at the time of John's death the family were living near Morpeth.

**John is buried in Fifteen Ravine British Cemetery, Villers-Plouich.**

## BATTLE OF THE ST QUENTIN CANAL
## 29 SEPTEMBER – 2 OCTOBER

The 1/6th North Staffs (NS) moved in the line on 27 September, relieving the 4th Leicester Regiment. During 28 September 'D' Company was attacked by the Germans, as was the 5th South Staffordshire Regiment on their right, forcing the South Staffs to withdraw. 'D' Company, although practically surrounded, fought with great determination for over six hours inflicting heavy casualties on the enemy using captured ammunition and guns as it was impossible to move supplies to the scene of the attack during daylight. At 9pm the company withdrew from their untenable position. At early dawn of the next day, 29 September, the NS were equipped with life belts, portable bridging materials, scaling ladders and collapsible boats for their attack on the German positions along the St Quentin Canal. At 6.45am the NS had forced a passage across the canal and had entered the Hindenburg Line. 'B' and 'C' companies formed the first wave of the attack, even though they encountered heavy resistance, and 'A' and 'D' companies managed to secure their gains in a furiously defended second line of advance [21,22].

**Private John Reed, aged 32**
**1/6th North Staffordshire Regiment**
**Died 29 September 1918**

John was born in Simonburn, the son of Jane E Reed. The 1901 census shows Jane and her sons living with the boys' grandparents, Edward and Isabella Reed. John, aged fifteen, was working as a shepherd.

**John is commemorated on the**
**Vis-en-Artois Memorial to the missing.**

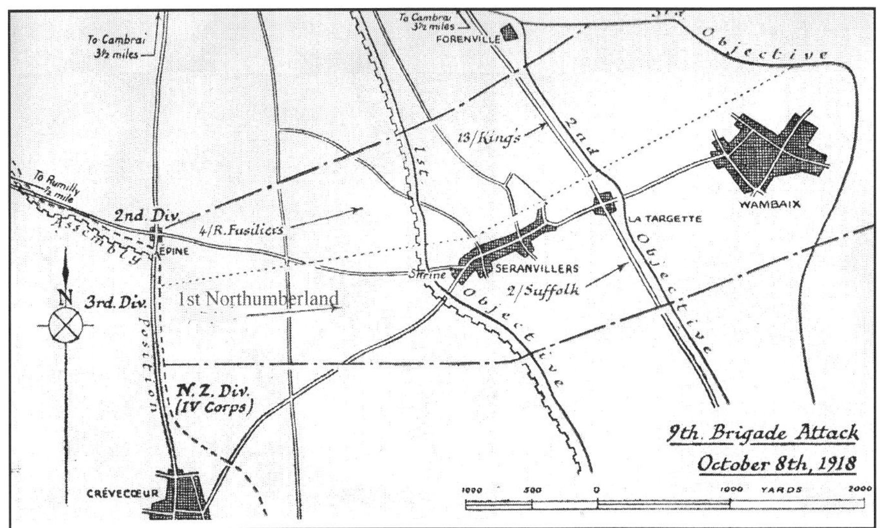


## BATTLE OF CAMBRAI
## 8 - 9 OCTOBER 1918

By early October the pace of the Allied advance had slowed, partly due to German resistance but also due to the exhaustion of the advancing troops. On 7 October the 1st Battalion Northumberland Fusiliers (NF) (part of 9th Brigade) moved forward taking up a position just south of Marcoing.

On 8 October, the opening day of the attack, 9th Brigade was allotted three objectives. One: the capture of a line of trenches running northwest on the west side of Seranvilliers. Two: the capture of Seranvilliers and the line of the La Targette to Forenville Road. Three: the capture of Wambaix and the railway to the north. The NF involvement was initially in the first of these objectives.

The attack began at 4.30am, close behind an advancing barrage, which was planned to advance at 100 yards every 4 minutes. However, an appreciable number of shells fell short, wounding the attackers they were intended to protect. All four of the battalion's companies 'W', 'X', 'Y' and 'Z' were used in the initial attack. Each of these companies came under fire from machine-guns, some of it very intense indeed. After consolidation at around 7.50am, fresh troops passed through the new front line to make their assault on the second objective.

However, the attack on the second objective did not meet with total success. On the right, the Suffolks gained their objective, the line of the Forenville to Esnes road, but they could not overcome the enemy defenders of La Targette. At 9am the Germans began heavily to bombard the position captured by the NF. At 10.30am two platoons from 'W' company were sent forward to reinforce the Suffolks and some time later the remainder of 'W' company were also sent forward to assist in another attack on La Targette at 1pm. Unfortunately, due to a misunderstanding of orders, this attack was not supported by any artillery or reinforcements.

The isolated attack by 'W' Company and 15 men of the Suffolk was repulsed with heavy casualties. By nightfall the NF were no longer involved in this attack. NF casualties for the day were 3 officers killed and 3 wounded, other ranks 22 killed, 111 wounded and 27 missing. As a result of the attacks on 8 October, enemy resistance temporarily gave way and German forces evacuated Cambrai [19,20].

**Private William Turnbull, aged 22**
**1st Battalion Northumberland Fusiliers**
**Died 8 October 1918**

William was born in Humshaugh, the eldest son of Thomas and Rebecca Turnbull of Park Cottage, Humshaugh. The 1911 census show that father Thomas was the village shoemaker and that William was still at school. He was conscripted into the army. His brother John was also a serving in the soldier. The North Tyne Magazine for November 1918 records sympathy for his sister, Mrs Kailifer. His gravestone is inscribed with the following:

**TOO DEARLY LOVED**
**TO BE FORGOTTEN**

**William is buried in Forenville Military Cemetery.**

## THE PURSUIT TO THE RIVER SELLE: 9 - 12 OCTOBER

The 1/7th West Yorkshire Regiment (WY) were part of 146th Brigade 49th Division and in preparation for an attack on the 11 October relieved part of the 4th Canadian Brigade south east of Iwuy. The 149th attack would be initially conducted by 1/6th and 1/7th WY.

Both battalions, which were under strength, assembled during the night of 10/11 October along the Rieux to Iwuy Road with 1/7th WY on the right; 'A' company was on the extreme right of the two-battalion attack. At 9am, following closely behind a heavy barrage described as "magnificent", the troops moved forward.

Initially the advance towards Avenes le Sec was impressive, with the capture of many light and heavy machine guns, but as the morning wore on resistance stiffened. Even so, the attack appeared to have been successful until the appearance of "four German tanks of a light and very mobile type", causing the troops to falter, and then retire across the ridge they had taken earlier. Later in the day the troops rallied, recaptured the ridge and by nightfall were encamped 2 miles in front of their starting point; that night they were relieved by 1/5th WR [23,24].

**Rifleman George Armstrong, aged 31**
**'A' Company 1/7th West Yorkshire Regiment**
**(Prince of Wales's Own)**
**Died 11 October 1917**

George was the eldest son of Thomas and Mary Ann Armstrong of Armstrong Square, Bellingham. He married Beatrice (née Charlton) in April 1915 and they lived at Percy Street, Bellingham. He was the father of one daughter, Gladys. Before enlisting in the army George worked as an assistant in Mr J Allen's, Grocers. He enlisted in the army in November 1915 under Lord Derby's Scheme and was initially posted to the reserve battalion of the 1/4th Northumberland Fusiliers, the same battalion in which his brother Edwin served; Edwin was killed 15 September 1916, (see page 114). George transferred to the West Yorkshire Regiment in August 1918. The Hexham Herald reports that George was found, severely wounded, in a shell hole by another brother, Bob; Bob had George removed to a dressing station but he died there shortly afterwards. His gravestone is inscribed with the following:

**PEACE PERFECT PEACE**
**WITH LOVED ONES**
**FAR AWAY**

**George is buried in Naves Communal Cemetery Extension.**

## FINAL ADVANCE IN FLANDERS
## THE BATTLE OF YPRES 28 SEPTEMBER – 2 OCTOBER

The fourth Battle of Ypres opened at 5.20am on 28 September. The Allied force consisted of twelve Belgian divisions (under King Albert) in the north and ten British and six French divisions in the south. The Front

Line at the start of this advance was where the British Line had been in June 1917 (before *Passchendaele*). On the first day the British captured Wytschaete and advances of six miles were reported in some places along the line of advance. As in 1917, it rained.

On 1 October the 7th Seaforth Highlanders were in position east of the village of Slypscapple (Slijpskapelle) preparing for an attack on the Menin-Roulier railway. At 6.15am, after a brief barrage, 'B' and 'C' companies launched their attack using a smoke barrage. They captured the railway north of Ledeghem and after a brief pause continued their advance, although by now German resistance had strengthened. Intense fire flew in a deadly wave from a line of fortified German pill boxes, which the Germans tried to hold at any cost. Later it was realised that these deadly fortifications were the enemy's last line of defence in the Flanders sector. The Highlanders eventually captured Ledeghem, but any further advance stalled as they came under extremely hostile machine gun and sniper fire.

German pill box at Dadizeele, New British Cemetery, the site of William Baird's grave.

*Photograph A. I. Grint, 2011*

The battalion eventually withdrew to consolidate a position along the railway line. The bill for the day's work was 4 officers and 23 other ranks killed and 4 officers and 69 other ranks wounded [25].

**The Military Medal (MM)** was (until 1993) a military decoration awarded to personnel of the British Army and other services, and formerly also to personnel of other Commonwealth countries, below commissioned rank, for acts of gallantry and devotion to duty under fire on land. The medal was established on 25 March 1916, (back dated to 1914). It was the other ranks' equivalent to the Military Cross (MC), which was awarded to commissioned officers. The MM ranked below the MC and the Distinguished Conduct Medal, which was also awarded to non-commissioned members of the Army, in order of precedence. Recipients of the Military Medal are entitled to use the letters "MM" after their names. In 1993, the Military Medal was discontinued, and since then the Military Cross has been awarded to personnel of all ranks. The circular silver medal is 36mm diameter. The front of the medal bears the effigy of the reigning monarch, whilst the reverse has the inscription "FOR BRAVERY IN THE FIELD" in four lines, surrounded by a laurel wreath, surmounted by the Royal Cypher and Imperial Crown. The suspending bar is of an ornate scroll type. The ribbon is dark blue, 3.2cms wide, with five equal centre stripes of white, red, white, red, and white. Silver, laurelled bars are authorised for subsequent awards.

## Private William Baird, MM, aged 40
## 'C' Company 7th Battalion Seaforth Highlanders
## Died 1 October 1918

William was born in Dumfries, Scotland, the son of Robert and Catherine Baird of Kirton, Dumfries. He was married in early 1914 to Jeanie (née Best) who lived in the Hexham registration area, and he left a son, William, born in late 1914. The Wall Parish Magazine for April 1915, in its Roll of Honour, stated that William Baird of Hallington had been accepted into the 9th Reserve Cavalry Battalion. After the war his wife's address was recorded as Workington Hall, Cumberland. William was originally with the Gordon Highlanders, before being transferred to the Seaforth Highlanders. The Battalion War Diary for October 1918 lists the name of William Baird as a recipient of the Military Medal, presumably posthumously. William's name appears on a number of War Memorials: Hexham, St John Lee and Wall, although details of his life are sketchy.

**William is buried in Dadizeele, New British Cemetery.**

## FINAL ADVANCE IN PICARDY
## BATTLE OF SELLE, 17 - 25 OCTOBER 1918

This action evicted the Germans from their hastily prepared line along the east side of the River Selle after they had been forced out of the Hindenburg Line during late September, early October. The action opened on 17 October along a ten mile Front south of Le Cateau. The attack north of Le Cateau began on the morning of the 20 October. It was in this sector, on 23 October near Solesines, that the 1st Battalion Northumberland Fusiliers, (NF), (9th Brigade, 3rd Division), was involved. The NF began their attack at midday on 23 October, meeting only feeble resistance; by that evening they were to be found on the west bank of the River Écaillon. On 24 October at 4am, under an Artillery Barrage against a German position along the River Écaillon, the NF advanced on the right hand side of the Divisional Front. Initially they met no opposition as they descended into the valley, crossed the stream and climbed the steep wooded slope of the far bank, although there were some casualties from their own barrage. However, as they reached the crest of the far bank they came under fire from machine guns and from five field guns positioned south of Ruesnes which were firing over open sights.

At about lunch time, when the assault was 600 yards short of its objective, the battalion ran into very heavy machine gun fire, which resulted in a significant number of casualties. That night, the NF sent out patrols northwards along the Le Quesnoy to Valenciennes railway, meeting little resistance. The following morning, with the enemy now east of railway, the 9th Brigade was replaced by the 8th Brigade, continuing the relentless pursuit of the retreating Germans [19,20].

**Acting Sergeant George Ridley, aged 27, MM.**
**1st Battalion Northumberland Fusiliers**
**Died 24 October 1918**

George was born in Warden, the fourth son of William and Jane Todd Ridley of Half-Way House Farm, Acomb. Before he worked with his father on the farm, George was employed by Mr T Ellis as a painter. George married Elizabeth Jane Charlton in the last months of 1916 and they had only been married a few weeks before the army separated them. George was called up under the Derby Scheme in February 1916 and embarked to France in the early part of 1917. He was initially with the Durham Light Infantry, but later transferred to the Northumberland Fusiliers.

He was awarded the Military Medal on 24 September 1918. The notification of the award was published in the London Gazette on 13 May 1919 and he died not knowing he had been promoted to full Sergeant. It is recorded that George died of his wounds, in a field ambulance. However, the cemetery in which he was buried was in German hands until the 23 October. With this in mind, I am confident that George must have received his wounds during the *Battle of Selle* (17-25 October 1918), since The Northumberlands were heavily involved in this action.

Elizabeth lived at Town Foot Farm, Acomb. In the late 1980s, at the age of 91, with the help of the Royal British Legion, Elizabeth at last managed to visit her dear husband's grave in France. A newspaper reported Elizabeth's words at the time:

"My love for him is as fresh now as it was then."

**George is buried in Romeries Communal Cemetery Extension.**

On the night of 28 October, the 9th Battalion Northumberland Fusiliers relieved the 11th Suffolks in the Sepmeries sector. The Front was essentially a series of shell holes and depressions scooped out to afford a slight measure of protection. Patrols sent out in the early hours of 29 October found no enemy on the west bank of the River Rhônelle, in front of Maresches. German Artillery sited on the reverse slope, east of the village, bombarded the area and liberally drenched the terrain in gas. On the night of 30/31 October, strong patrols were sent forward in a dash to capture Meresches. However, the Germans anticipated this move and sprang a surprise of their own: they covered the approach to the village with machine-guns and in addition set fire to a thatched cottage, illuminating the whole area. All things considered, casualties for this failed operation were incredibly light, with one man killed and two wounded [26,27].

**Private Robert Newton Famelton, aged 22**
**9th (Service) Battalion Northumberland Fusiliers**
**Died 31 October 1918**

Robert was born in Falstone, the only son of Thomas and Alice Famelton

of Barefoot, Falstone. He initially enlisted with 1/4th Northumberland Fusiliers. The Hexham Courant of 14 October 1916 reported, as did The North Tyne Magazine of November 1916, that Robert had been wounded for the third time on 15 September 1916 during an attack on the Somme (see page 105) and that he was recuperating in hospital in Leeds. On his return to fitness he was redeployed to the 9th Battalion. At the time of his death Robert was serving as a stretcher bearer for the battalion. His gravestone is inscribed with the following:

**TILL THE DAY BREAKS**
**AND THE SHADOWS FLEE AWAY**

**Robert is buried in Vertain Communal Cemetery Extension.**

## FINAL ADVANCE IN ARTOIS: 2 OCTOBER – 11 NOVEMBER

The 1st Battalion Sherwood Foresters were in the Oppy Sector during the early part of October 1918. On 3 October at 5.30am, under an artillery barrage, two platoons of 'B' company led by Lt Clarke and 2/Lt Adams made a determined and successful raid on a post which had been raided without success the previous day, with the aim of occupying a considerable length of the Oppy Support Trench. Three German prisoners were taken, but the raiding party suffered a number of casualties from the retaliatory German barrage [28,29].

**Sergeant John Anthony Charlton, aged 24**
**1st Battalion Sherwood Foresters**
**Nottinghamshire and Derbyshire Regiment**
**Died 3 October 1918**

John was born at Birtley, Northumberland, the youngest son of Anthony and Harriet Charlton. He was a plasterer by trade. The Charltons also had four other sons in the forces. For a number of years John was a Territorial soldier with the Bellingham Company and was a noted marksman, winning the Chipchase Silver Cup at Wark, just before the outbreak of war. At the onset of hostilities he joined up with the Territorials and was engaged for the first two years of the war as a musketry instructor at Barton on Humber

In 1916 he was transferred to the 2/5th Battalion of Sherwood Foresters and was posted to Ireland to help quell the rebellion. By 1917 he was serving in France and on May 4 of that year he was wounded; his battalion had attacked the German strongpoints of Cologne and Malakoff Farms (east of Hargicourt). Although Malakoff Farm was taken, the assault on Cologne Farm had been unsuccessful. On 4 May the Germans counterattacked in considerable force, which is when John was injured.After convalescing in England he returned to France and was allocated to 'B' Company of the 1st Battalion Sherwood Foresters on 17 June 1918, dying in the raid of October 3rd.

**John is commemorated on the Vis-en-Artois Memorial to the missing.**

## REFERENCES

1. Stevenson, D. *With our Backs to the Wall.* Pub: Allen Lane 2011.

2.Farndale, M. Gen. KSO. *History of the Royal Regiment of Artillery, Western Front 1914-18.* Pub: the Royal Artillery Institution, 1986.

3. Bean C. E. W. *Official History of Australia in the War of 1914-1918, Vol. 5.*

4.AWM4 24/1/6. *War Diary 1st Battalion Australian Machine Gun Corps.*

5. AWM4 23/3/34. *War Diary 3rd Infantry Brigade AIF.*

6. Wyrall, E. *East Yorkshire Regiment in the Great War. 1914-1918* Pub: 1928, reprinted Naval and Military Press.

7. WO95/2161. *War Diary 1st Battalion East Yorkshire Regiment.*

8. Simpson, C.R. Maj-Gen. *The History of the Lincolnshire Regiment 1914-1918.* Pub: 1931, reprinted Military and Naval Press 2002.

9. WO95/2154. *War Diary 2nd Battalion Lincolnshire Regiment.*

10. O'Neill, H. C. OBE. *The Royal Fusiliers in the Great War.* Pub: 1922 reprinted Naval and Military Press 2002.

11. *WO95/2539. War Diary 13th Battalion Royal Fusiliers.*

12. WO95/2960. *War Diary 1/2nd Battalion Royal Fusiliers.*

13. Bond, R. C. *The King's Own Yorkshire Light Infantry in the Great War.*
Pub: 1929 reprinted Naval and Military Press 2002.

14. WO95/2402. *War Diary 2nd Battalion King's Own Yorkshire Light Infantry.*

15. WO95/2381. *War Diary 168th Brigade Royal Field Artillery.*

16. Miles, Capt. W. *Durham Forces in the Field.*
Pub: 1920 reprinted Naval and Military Press 2004.

17. WO95/2161. *War Diary 15th Battalion Durham Light Infantry.*

18. WO95/3091. *War Diary 2/4th Battalion King's Own Yorkshire Light Infantry.*

19. Sandilands, Brig. H. R. *The Fifth in the Great War.*
Pub: 1921 reprinted Naval and Military Press 1998.

20. WO95/1430. *War Diary, 1st Battalion Northumberland Fusiliers.*

21. Priestley, R. E. Maj. *Breaking the Hindenburg Line. The story of the 46th (North Midland Division).*
Pub: 1919 reprinted Naval and Military Press 2004.

22. WO95/2685. *War Diary 1/6th Battalion North Staffordshire Regiment.*

23. Wyrall, E. *The West Yorkshire Regiment in the War 1914-1918.*
Pub: 1924-1927 reprinted Naval and Military Press 2002.

24. WO95/2795. *War Diary 1/7th West Yorkshire Regiment.*

25. WO95/1765. *War Diary, 7th Battalion Seaforth Highlanders.*

26. Cooke, C. H. Capt. *Historical Records of the 9th Battalion Northumberland Fusiliers.* Pub: 1928.

27. WO95/2466. *War Diary 9th Battalion Northumberland Fusiliers.*

28. Wylly, H. C. Col. *The 1st and 2nd Battalions. The Sherwood Foresters in the Great War.* Pub: 1925 reprinted Naval and Military Press 2003

29. WO95/1721. *War Diary 1st Battalion Sherwood Foresters.*

# CHAPTER SEVENTEEN

# THOSE WHO DIED AWAY FROM THE FRONT

*Then in the lull of midnight, gentle arms*
*Lifted him slowly down the slopes of death*
*Lest he should hear again the mad alarms*
*Of battle, dying moans, and painful breath.*

From *A Soldier's Grave,* by Francis Ledwidge, died July 1917

## OVERVIEW

The care of wounded soldiers would begin only yards behind the fighting, at Regimental Aid Posts (RAPs), found in either the support or reserve trenches. These aid posts were manned by the Battalion Medical Officer, his orderlies and the battalion's stretcher-bearers (drawn from the battalion's musicians). The facilities were primitive, offering only basic first aid and a drink. From here the wounded were passed down the chain to an Advanced Dressing Station (ADS), usually under the cover of darkness, which may have been many hours after a soldier had suffered his wounds.

Members of the Royal Army Medical Corps (RAMC) were attached to each division and were known as Field Ambulances; they manned the Advanced Dressing Stations. Each division had three Field Ambulances, one to each brigade. Although the ADS were better equipped than the RAP, they still could only provide a limited range of treatments. Wounds could be dressed and a limited range of emergency operations performed. It is unsurprising that many of the ADS's would have an adjacent cemetery, some of whose names still exist today, for example the Duhallow ADS Cemetery, Ypres, which was in operation from July 1917. From the ADS the wounded would be passed down the line to Casualty Clearing Stations (CCS).

Royal Army Medical Corps picking up wounded in a captured village (Mametz, Somme 1916).

Casualty Clearing Stations were large and well-equipped; their role was to retain all serious cases that were unfit to travel further, treat and return minor cases and evacuate all others. A typical CCS could accommodate up to a thousand casualties and would be based as close as possible to a railway line or a canal.

At a CCS, surgeons could perform complex operations such as amputations. Some carried specialist units dealing in nervous disorders, skin diseases and infectious diseases. They could also care for cases of general sickness including trench foot, venereal disease and trench fever. RAMC personnel manned these stations.

From the CCS the wounded would be sent by rail or canal barge to hospitals in France or to an embarkation port for shipment to the UK – an injury that necessitated time back in the UK was known as a *blighty* case. If a soldier managed to get as far as a hospital there was good chance that he would survive. These hospitals were located near the army's principal bases such as Boulogne, Le Havre, Rouen, Le Touquet and Étaples and some were able to accommodate up to 1040 patients. However, in 1917 many were enlarged offering up to 2500 beds. RAMC personnel, including female nurses, staffed the hospitals. Wounded soldiers who were well enough to be moved often travelled to the UK for treatment in British hospitals. If they survived – and after medical board review – they were shipped back to France, sometimes to their original unit, but not always. If a man died in either the CCS or in hospital it is not always a simple matter to find out where he was when he received his fatal wounds.

## 1915

On 24 May the Germans attacked along a four and half mile front, using chlorine gas, and succeeded in capturing Bellewaarde Ridge and 'Mouse Trap' Farm. At the time of the attack, the 1/4th Northumberland Fusiliers were occupying dugouts near Chateau des Trois Tours, near Brielen. They were immediately moved into a reserve position near the canal, three miles from the Front. Even in this position the threat from gas was formidable. Next morning they were moved in to the Line west of the St Jean to Wieltje road. During the evening the fusiliers were instructed to deploy to the right of the road and "to stick to it at all costs". During 25 May the battalion was continuously on the move along the Front in an attempt to stem the German attacks. Although not directly involved in any of the fighting, exposure to non-stop shelling and gas resulted in many casualties, including the death of six fusiliers [1,2].

A letter to the Hexham Courant (17 June 1915) from Private J Moody described the events of the day:

> "The Germans were using those gases so we had to use our respirators. I do not know how we could have come on without them, and we passed a lot of unfortunate soldiers making their way back, some were badly gassed. The effects of gas are too awful for words. The sweat was teeming down the men's faces and they were gasping for breath. Thanks to my respirator I was able to go on although I thought my head was going to split. Once as we advanced towards some trenches a German machine gun opened up on us and a number of fusiliers were wounded. Whenever we crossed a field it was ploughed up by enemy shells."

**Private Joseph William Cowen, aged 21**
**1/4th Battalion Northumberland Fusiliers**
**Died 8 July 1915**

Joseph was born in Midley, near Haltwhistle, and was the eldest son of William and Alice Cowen who after the war resided at West Wharmley, near Hexham. The Cowens were agricultural workers and the various census records show that the family moved from farm to farm. Before going to France in April 1915, with the initial batch of the Territorials, Joseph worked as a farm labourer on Styford Barns Farm, Stocksfield. Joseph was wounded on Whit Monday during the *Battle of Bellewaarde*, (24-25 May 1915). After many weeks in hospital in Rouen, Joseph succumbed to his injuries.

**Joseph is buried in St Sever Cemetery, Rouen.**

The Northumberland Hussars, a Territorial Cavalry Detachment, was brought up to the Front as part of the cavalry contingent which was expected to exploit the planned breakthrough along the Loos battlefront, which did not materialise. On 25 September a patrol from the Hussars was ordered into Gun Trench which was within fifty yards of the German Front Line, and came under intense enemy fire. Charles was wounded in the head on 30 September whilst supervising the burial of forty men just behind Gun Trench (just in front of Cité St-Élie). He was transferred to No 10 Stationary Hospital at St Omer, where after an operation it was reported that he was making good progress. However, a week later Charles was to die of his wounds [3].

**Captain Charles Noel Ridley, aged 30**
**'A' Squadron, Northumberland Hussars**
**Died 7 October 1915**

Charles was born in Ovingham and was the son of John Hilton and Mary Ridley who in 1891 were living in Warden with their elderly parents. By 1901 Charles and his older sister Helen were living back in Ovingham. He was educated at Eton and Jesus College, Cambridge. The 1911 census shows that Charles was a man of private means living at High Park End, Simonburn. He was a married man with at least three children, Nancy, Phyllis and Jean. In 1918 his wife Daphne remarried Lieutenant Colonel Hall Grant Pringle and moved to Brampton in Cumberland. By 1919 Daphne was living in Eastbourne.

Charles was a long serving member of the Northumberland Hussars, serving as 2nd Lieutenant from January 1907 to June 1911 and as Lieutenant from June 1911 until June 1914, after which he was promoted to Captain. He embarked for the Western Front with the Hussars in October 1914 on board the Minneapolis and would have been involved in the desperate fighting around Ypres in 1914 in October, when the Hussars (the first territorial unit to go into action) fought as dismounted troops around Polygon Wood, stemming the German avalanche. He was the proud recipient of the Mons Star. It was reported that Charles suffered from influenza during November 1914. A memorial service was held on 15 October at Simonburn Church which was attended by a large congregation and a troop from the Northumberland Hussars. The service ended with the singing of the National Anthem.

**Charles is buried in Longuenesse Souvenir Cemetery, St Omer.**

## 1916

The following three Northumberland Fusiliers, Bell, Maddison and Dagg, were wounded during the attack by the 1/4th Northumberland Fusiliers against Hook Trench on 15 September 1916, (see page 105) [1,2].

**Lance Corporal John Thomas Bell, aged 21**
**1/4th Battalion Northumberland Fusiliers**
**Died 18 September 1916**

John was born in Wall and was the fourth son of John and Elizabeth Bell. The Wall Parish Roll of Honour records that he was an old boy of Wall School. The 1911 census shows that at the age of fifteen John was working as domestic servant. His medal record shows that he went to France with a draft of Fusiliers after November 1915. He was wounded in action on 15 September and died in either No3 BRCS, otherwise in No2 or No5 Stationary Hospital which were all stationed at Abbeville throughout the war.

**John is buried in Abbeville Communal Cemetery Extension.**

**Private Robert Maddison, aged 22**
**1/4th Battalion Northumberland Fusiliers**
**Died 20 September 1916**

Robert was the son of Robert and Isabella Maddison of Wall. The 1911 census shows that at the age of 16 he was working as a coachman and was living with his widowed father in Wall. He married Hannah (née Robson) in 1914 and was the father of a young girl called Frances, who was born in early 1915; a daughter who would never really know her father. The address given for Hannah Maddison after the war was the Old Lodge, Chesters, Humshaugh. Robert was not one of the original Territorials and was part of a new draft sent to France in 1916. He was wounded in the action on 15 September and died of his wounds at one of the hospitals, near Étaples.

His wife included in his memoriam in the Hexham Herald:

"A loving husband, a faithful friend.
One of the best that God could lend;
His name was good, his friendship sound.

Loved and respected by all around.
There is a link death cannot sever,
Sweet remembrance lasts for ever.
Ever remembered by his wife and child."

The following is found on his headstone:

**UNTIL THE DAY BREAKS &
THE SHADOWS FLEE AWAY**

**Robert is buried at Étaples Military Cemetery.**

**Private Michael Dagg, aged 30
1/4 Battalion Northumberland Fusiliers
Died 25 September 1916**

Michael was born in Elsdon, the son of John and Annie Dagg. Before volunteering Michael worked on his father's farm (Broadgate, West Woodburn) arriving in France on 11 November 1915.

**Michael is buried in Étaples Military Cemetery.**

The 8th Battalion Northumberland Fusiliers (NF) as part of the 11th Division embarked from Liverpool on the SS Aquitania on 2 July 1915 which within two days was attacked by a submarine whose torpedo fortunately missed its target. After further adventures with hostile submarines, the troopship arrived at Lemnos on 10 July. On 6 August they disembarked at Sulva Bay on the Gallipoli Peninsula. Following this disastrous campaign, the NF were evacuated during late December and posted to Egypt in January 1916. They arrived on the Western Front through Marseilles in July 1916.

By the end of September 1916, High Command decided that the heavily defended area around the village of Thiepval, including the heavily fortified Stuff, Zollern and Schwaben redoubts, should be taken. These redoubts had been objectives for the attack on 1 July; since then they had been further strengthened by the Germans. Following three days of intense bombardment using 230 heavy guns and 570 field guns and howitzers, the infantry attack began at 12.35pm on 26 September 1916. The main thrust of the attack was borne by 11th Division and to its left the 18th Division. From the 11th Division, battalions from the 33rd and 34th Brigades (8th Northumberland Fusiliers NF) formed up for the initial attack.

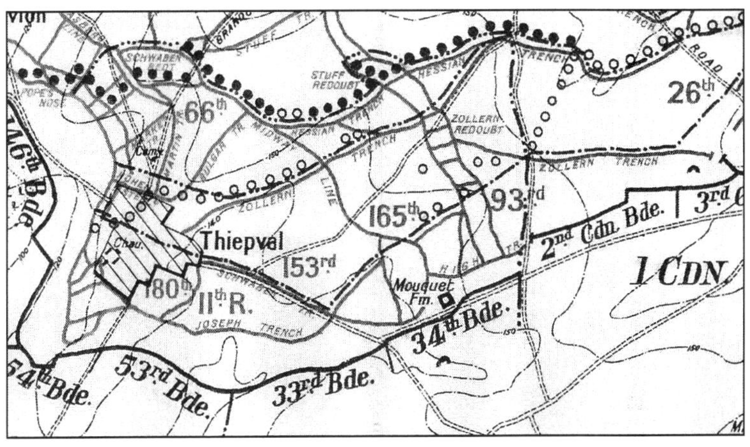


Attack of 8th Northumberland Fusiliers
34th Brigade

The War Diary states that as the Northumberland Fusiliers left their trenches the enemy barrage fell on the battalion's front line causing a significant number of casualties, many within 40 yards of their starting out point. The 8th NF persevered and took very heavy casualties as they moved forward on the first day of the attack, including the loss of most of their officers and sergeants. Casualties (killed and wounded) were 19 officers and 430 other ranks [4].

**Sergeant Walter Dodd, aged 22**
**8th (Service) Battalion Northumberland Fusiliers**
**Died 2 November 1916**

Walter was the son of William and Barbara Dodd of Falstone. The 1911 census shows that he was working as a shepherd for the Murray family at Smale, near Falstone. At the end of May 1914, Walter applied to join the Durham County Constabulary and was commissioned on the 8th June 1914 as PC 977, 3rd Class. After training he was stationed in Stockton, Durham. In mid August Walter resigned from the Police Force and enlisted at Stockton with the Northumberland Fusiliers.

The Hexham Courant reported, complete with his photograph, the news that Walter had been killed outright on the Somme during an attack on Thiepval on the 26 September. We now know that this was incorrect, and that he had been wounded.

The North Tyne Magazine reported that his sister Barbara, on hearing that he had been wounded, left Falstone on 13 October to travel to France to visit her brother and she returned home hopeful that he would recover from his wounds. Alas, this was not to be the case. The following is found on his headstone:

**IN GLORY WRAPPED**
**IN SLEEP HIS WARFARE O'ER**

**Walter is buried in Étaples Military Cemetery.**

Since arriving in France in June 1916, the 22nd Battalion Durham Light Infantry had been working as a Pioneer Battalion, initially for the 19th Division, but latterly for the 8th Division. Their role would have been to supply and consolidate positions that the Divisional Infantry Battalions had occupied.

**Private Edward Crisp, aged 30**
**22nd Battalion Durham Light Infantry**
**Died 25 February 1917**

Edward was the eldest son of Robert and Mary Ann Crisp of Barrasford Crags. Before enlisting he worked at Barrasford Whinstone Quarry. He was called up in April 1916 as part of Group 11 after registering under the Derby Scheme. His enrolment papers show that he had served for two and a half years with the local Territorials before the hostilities began.

Edward was originally posted to the East Yorkshire Regiment and spent the period of April to December 1916 in the United Kingdom. He was transferred to the 22nd Durham Light Infantry in December 1916 and immediately went to join his battalion in France, facing the ordeal of the severe 1916 winter on the Somme. He died of pneumonia in the 5th Casualty Clearing Station in Bray. Three months earlier the death had been confirmed of Edward's younger brother, William John (see page 130) who was serving with the Northumberland Fusiliers.

**Edward is buried in Bray Military Cemetery.**

After the mauling that the 24th Northumberland Fusiliers (NF) received during the first day of the Somme (page 91), it was eventually brought back to full strength and spent the rest of 1916 rotating in and out of Front Line trenches. On 9 April 1917 the 24th Battalion was involved in an attack on the first day of the *Arras offensive*, south of Vimy Ridge. They were back in action on 28 April at *Rouex*. Casualties for both these attacks were pitifully high. During the First World War the area around Étaples was the site for eleven general, one stationary, four Red Cross hospitals and a convalescent depot [5,6].

**Private George James Brown, aged 34**
**24th (Service) Battalion Northumberland Fusiliers**
**Tyneside Irish**
**Died 7 August 1917**

George was born in Rothbury and was the eldest son of Thomas and Margaret Brown of Fountains Square, Bellingham. Before the war he had trained as an upholsterer. The 1911 census shows James living with his mother in Cruddas Terrace and showing his occupation as 'upholsterer'. He married Margaret (née Armstrong) in the spring of 1912 in Newcastle. He was the father of three sons, Ernest, George and Verdun.

He offered his services to the country under the Derby Scheme in late 1915. An additional statement on his medal record card records that he took his own life. After his death his widow, Margaret, continued to live at Fountains Square, Bellingham. The following appeared in the Hexham Herald in August 1918:

> "In loving memory of my dear husband, Pte George James Brown, Northumberland Fusiliers late of Bellingham, who died in France, August 7, 1917."

It is not the tears at the moment shed
But the tears through many long night wept,
And the sad remembrance so fondly kept,
The shock was great, the blow severe,
We little thought his end had come;
T'is only those who have lost can tell
The pain of parting, not saying farewells
Yet again we hope to meet him,
When the day of life is fled;
In Heaven with joy to greet him,
Where no farewell tears are shed.

Ever remembered by his loving wife and three little sons, and his mother.

**George is buried in Étaples Military Cemetery.**

The 15th Battalion Canadian Infantry was part of 3rd Brigade, 1st Division Canadian Expeditionary Force. During the summer of 1917 the 15th Battalion was heavily involved in a number of actions which formed part of the Arras Offensive. These actions include *Vimy Ridge* (9-14 April), *Third Battle of Scarpe and the capture of Fresnoy*, (3-4 May), *the flanking operation towards Lens,* (3 June-26 August) and the *Battle for Hill 70* (15-25 August) [7].

**Private William Little, aged 30**
**15th Battalion (48th Highlanders) Canadian Infantry**
**Died 2 September 1917**

William was born in the summer of 1887 in Greystead, Northumberland, and was the eldest son of John and Annie Little of Smalesmouth. The 1901 census shows that although his parents were still alive, William was living (presumably employed as a farm lad) aged 12 as a boarder with the

Robsons, a farming family at Emmethaugh. William clearly emigrated because his Canadian attestation papers show that at the time he was living with his wife, Bessie, in Toronto and was working as a teamster. It also shows that he had previously spent two and half years with the local militia, whilst living in Toronto. He enlisted into the army in August 1915 and was posted to the 15th Battalion Canadian Infantry which was part of the original Canadian Expeditionary Force to Europe in 1915. The North Tyne Magazine for October 1917 reported that although William had lost a leg he had shown signs of recovery, and that his death in No 7 British General Hospital, St Omer, came as a great shock to the community.

William's wife, Bessie, appears to have returned to England when her husband came over to Europe, and after his death she and their daughter lived in Front Street, Bellingham.

The following was published in the Hexham Herald:

When alone in my sorrow and bitter tears flow,
There stealth sweet dreams of a short time ago;
And unknown to the world he stands by my side,
And whispers the words: Death cannot divide.

Deeply mourned by his wife and little daughter.

**William is buried in Longuenesse Souvenir Cemetery, St Omer.**

The 8th Battalion Northumberland Fusiliers relieved the 6th Yorks and Lancs Regiment during the nights of 14/15 and 15/16 August. For the attack on 16 August at 4.45am, the 8th Northumberland Fusiliers (NF) formed the right sector of the 11th Divisional attacking Front just south of the German-held village of Langermark. On the right of the battalion's

Front, the NF went over the top with very little help from the expected Allied barrage. The attacking troops were met by an intense hail of rifle and machine gun fire. Although the enemy occupied a number of lines of dangerous shell slits, and irrespective of the deficiencies of the barrage, the NF managed to advance using rifle and Lewis Gun fire. During the many stages of the advance the NF engaged the enemy in savage hand-to-hand fighting, during which no prisoners were taken.

**Extracts from a First War Army Training Manual**
Guide rule number 8 for weapons training

The sporting spirit and desire to play for his side or team, or regiment is inherent in every individual of the British race. This should be fostered and made use of by the instructor.

In an assault all ranks go forward to kill and only those who have developed skill and strength by constant and continuous training will be able to kill. If possible the point of the bayonet should be directed against an opponent's throat, as the point will enter easily and make a fatal wound on entering a few inches and, being near the eyes, make an opponent flinch. Other vulnerable and usually exposed parts are the face, chest, lower abdomen and thighs, and in the region of the kidneys when the back is turned. Four to six inches penetration is sufficient to incapacitate and allow for a quick withdrawal, whereas if a bayonet is driven home too far it is often impossible to withdraw it. In such cases a round should be fired to break up the obstruction.

Along the left sector of the battalion's Front the barrage was very effective and the attackers maked good progress, but unfortunately they lost their direction and came under heavy machine gun and sniper fire. The German strong point of Mon de Hibou remained in enemy hands. A further unsuccessful attempt to capture this strongpoint was made on 17 August. That evening, the 8th NF were relieved and retired to Siege Camp. Casualties for this attack were, officers 5 killed and 4 wounded, ordinary ranks were 35 killed, 228 wounded and 39 missing. It is believed that Frank was one of the large number of wounded [4].

**Private Frank Stoker (Stokoe), age 31**
**8th (Service) Battalion Northumberland Fusiliers**
**Died 14 September 1917**

Frank was the son of F Stoker, late of Houghton Mains, and Mrs M J Martin (formerly Stoker) of South Africa. Frank lived in South Africa for about ten years and was employed as a shift boss at the East Rand Gold Mines. Newspapers report that two of Frank's brothers were also fighting with the British Army. One of these had seen action with the South Africans in South West Africa, under General Botha. The St John Lee memorial records the name as 'Stokoe'.

At the onset of war, Frank was visiting his brother J Stoker, who lived in Acomb and was a policeman. He immediately enlisted with 1/4th Northumberland Fusiliers in Hexham and was involved in the fighting on the Somme on 15 September 1916, (see page 105), where he was wounded. Following another spell at the Front, he was subsequently invalided home suffering from appalling trench foot. On his return to France, about two weeks before his death, he was allocated to the 8th Northumberland Fusiliers. Frank died of wounds received in action.

**Frank is buried in Croix-Rouge Military Cemetery, Quaedypre.**

The 65th Army Brigade was made up of four 18-pdr batteries (465, 466, 505 and 507 batteries) The 465th Battery went out to the Western Front on 2 May 1917 and joined the 6th Army Brigade on 6 May 1917. On August 7 the size of these batteries were increased to six guns. From 1 to 4 October these batteries supported the efforts of the 4th Division during the *Battle of Poelcappelle* and later in the same month they supported the attack by 17th Division during the *First Battle of Passchendaele.* (see page 184)

British Artillery Battery

**Gunner William John Foreman, aged 19**
**465th Battery 65th Army Brigade**
**Royal Field Artillery**
**Died 14 October 1917**

William was the eldest son of William and Ellen Foreman of Gate House, Greenhaugh. William died of wounds received in action. As he died in the Étaples area, a centre for the concentration of Military hospitals a significant number of miles away from the Front, it is difficult to pinpoint the date that he was wounded. However, his battery was involved in the intense struggle known as *Passchendaele.*

**William is buried in Étaples Military Cemetery.**

The Siege Batteries of the Royal Garrison Artillery (RGA) were equipped with heavy howitzers, sending large calibre, high explosive shells in a steep trajectory. The usual armaments were 6 inch, 8 inch or 9.2 inch

howitzers, although the RGA was also responsible for the huge railway-mounted and road-mounted 12 inch howitzers. During the course of the war, as British artillery tactics developed, the Siege Batteries were most often employed in destroying or neutralising the enemy artillery, as well as putting destructive fire down on strong points, dumps, stores, roads and railways behind enemy lines. The 191st Siege Battery was part of 77th Brigade and attached to Plumer's Second Army. During 1917 the Second Army saw action at the *Battle of Messines* (see page 161) and was also involved in a large number of the actions making up *Third Ypres* (*Passchendaele* see page 165).

**Gunner John Hunter, aged 32**
**191st Siege Battery, Royal Garrison Artillery**
**Died 19 October 1917**

John was born in Plenmeller, Northumberland, the second son of William and Isabella Hunter of Wark. The 1901 census reports that the Hunter family were living at Cold Coat Hill, Wark, and like his widower father, John was working on a farm. By the time he joined the army at the end

of May 1916, he was working, as was his father, as a shepherd. His battery arrived in France in November 1916 and was equipped with 9.2 inch howitzers.

**John is buried in**
**Wimereux Communal Cemetery.**

From 22 September 1917 the 1st Battalion Northumberland Fusiliers (NF) took up positions on the Front Line near Zonnebeke, and was involved in the action to capture Zonnebeke (*Third Ypres*). After their seven day stint at the Front, casualties for the 1st NF were killed 3 officers and 33 other ranks and wounded 4 officers and 108 other ranks. After this harrowing experience, the battalion was moved to the Bapaume sector [8,9].

**Private Walter Ernest Sisterson, aged 23**
**'W' Company, 1st Battalion Northumberland Fusiliers**
**Died 1 November 1917**

Walter was born in Tynemouth and was the son of John and Elizabeth Sisterson of Yarrow, Falstone. The 1911 census shows that Walter was single and working underground at Falstone coal mine.

Walter had served since July 1911 with the local Territorials. He embarked with them for France on 20 April 1915 and almost immediately saw action at St Julien on 26 April 1915, (see page 35). On 18 May he was wounded in the right foot. After passing through medical establishments at Ballieul and Wimereux, he was transferred to England, where the bullet was removed and he subsequently spent time convalescing at Ripon. Late in January 1916 Walter was certified as fit for overseas service. After spending March at home, he returned to France in late April 1916 and was reassigned to the 1st Battalion Northumberland Fusiliers. The North Tyne Magazine of December 1917 reported that William had again been wounded and had also received injuries caused by barbed wire – a common cause of wounds which frequently become infected. Initially it appeared that he was holding his own, but eventually he died as a result of these injuries. The following is found on his headstone

**FAITHFUL UNTIL DEATH**

**Walter is buried in**
**Bois Guillaume Communal Cemetery Extension.**

## 1918

**Private Robert Middleton Brown, aged 33**
**6th (Service) Battalion Yorkshire Regiment**
**Died 2 January 1918**

Robert was the youngest son of Joseph and Elizabeth Brown of Tynevale House, Acomb. Before he joined the Colours he was employed at Hexham Station goods yard. He was posted to France in November 1917. He died of pneumonia at No1 Casualty Clearing Station in France.

**Robert is buried in**
**Chocques Military Cemetery**

During May, the 1st Battalion Grenadier Guards (GG) occupied a position west of the Ablainzeville–Ayette road. For the whole of May the battalion were either in the front trenches or in reserve. When they were in reserve they inevitably became targets for the German artillery; every day there were men killed, wounded and gassed. On 17 May the area occupied by the battalion was subjected to a severe bombing by aircraft, resulting in an appreciable number of casualties.

**Private William Ernest Hoggard, aged 31**
**1st Battalion Grenadier Guards**
**Died 19 May 1918**

William was born in Harrogate, the eldest son of Charles and Frances Jane Hoggard of Knaresborough, Yorkshire. The 1901 census records his occupation in Knaresborough as 'dairyman'. He married Ada (née Cooke) in Knaresborough in late 1913 and a daughter Frances was born in December 1914. Before he joined the army in December 1915 he worked for the North Eastern Railway as a porter at Fourstone Station. It is interesting to note that his father worked as a guard on the North Eastern Railway. After the war, Ada lived in Moss Cottages, Warden. William initially was posted to the Household Battalion of the Grenadier Guards, in July 1917. William died of his wounds in No 3 Casualty Clearing Station [10,11,12].

**William is buried in Bagneux British Cemetery, Gezaincourt.**

Although John Henry Temple was commissioned into the East Yorkshire Regiment, in early 1918 he was attached to the 2nd Battalion Sherwood Foresters, (SF). The German attack through Flanders (*Georgette Offensive*, see page 242) began on the morning of 9 April and in its first few days met with considerable success. The 2nd SF on 13 April was ordered to take up positions in support of 148th Brigade in the area near Kemmel Hill [13].

The War Diary for the 2nd SF on 17 April reports [14]:

> "Enemy heavily shelled front line trenches with gas shells and 'C' Company was sent to support 'D' Company. Dranoutre was also shelled, and the enemy was said at 11am to be attacking our left; he was repulsed. The enemy bombardment became heavy again at 2pm and he attacked on our right, but was driven back. Remainder of the day was quiet. Casualties for 17 April were 3 men killed, 5 officers including J H Temple and 32 other ranks wounded."

**2nd Lieutenant John Henry Temple, aged 31**
**1/4th Battalion East Yorkshire Regiment**
**Attached 2nd Battalion Sherwood Foresters**
**Died 21 May 1918**

John was born in Liverton, Yorkshire, the eldest son of William and Hannah Temple. The 1891 census shows that the family lived in Liverton near Guisborough and that William's occupation was described as 'farmer and auctioneer'. The 1911 census shows John as single and working as a bank clerk. The electoral roll for 1915 (compiled in the early months of 1915), records that John Henry Temple was a lodger, residing at Hazelhurst in Bellingham, and that his landlord was a Mr George Milburn of the same address. It appears likely that John was a visitor to Bellingham who intended to reside in the town for an extended period. Given his occupation in 1911, it is highly likely that he worked for a bank in Bellingham.

John volunteered to join the forces in early 1916 under the Derby Scheme and after basic training he went as part of a new draft in late August to the Kings Royal Rifle Corps, rising to the rank of Acting Sergeant. He was wounded in the knee on 9 April 1917, and after spending some time at the 6th Stationary Hospital at Le Havre he spent time in hospital in the UK. In August 1917 he attended the Officer Training College at Newmarket.

He was commissioned in late November 1917 and at that stage joined the 1/4th Battalion East Yorkshire Regiment and at some date was attached to the 2nd Sherwood Foresters. On 17 April 1918 John received wounds to his shoulders and left leg whilst in action. He was admitted to the 14th General Hospital, near Boulogne, where he eventually succumbed to his wounds. The North Tyne Magazine for August 1918 records John's death, albeit in reference to the Kings Royal Rifle Corps. The following is found on his headstone:

**HE DIED AS HE LIVED
A SPORTSMAN**

**John is buried in Boulogne Eastern Cemetery.**

On the night of 25/26 September, the 1st Battalion Northumberland Fusiliers had moved into Front Line trenches east and north-east of Havrincourt. Even though enemy artillery fell on these trenches and caused a number of casualties, the attack began at 5.20am on 27 September, in perfect order. Initial resistance by the Germans resulted in heavy casualties to all the attacking companies, (W,X,Y and Z) especially from machine-guns in well-protected emplacements. The advance secured most of the battalion's objectives for the day, including the capture of trench systems known as Ravine and Bilhelm Avenues. As they advanced towards Station

Avenue, they came under intense machine-gun fire from the direction of Ribécourt. During this action on 27 September the battalion casualties were, officers: 4 killed, 2 wounded, other ranks: 26 killed, 134 wounded, and 35 missing [8,9].

**Private John Edward Robson, aged 30 years**
**1st Battalion Northumberland Fusiliers**
**Died 13 October 1918**

John was born in Hexham in 1887 and was the son of William and Mary Robson, who lived at North Terrace, Hexham. John married Alice Tweddle (née Turnbull) in the Summer of 1915 and was the father of two children. His younger brother, Corporal Frederick Robson (10th Battalion Northumberland Fusiliers), died of his wounds on 28 September 1916, and is buried in St Sever Cemetery, Rouen. Before enlisting, John was employed by the Hexham and Acomb Cooperative Society and was the manager of their Acomb Branch.

On 27 September, John was very badly wounded in the stomach, legs, hand and arm and was evacuated to either the 34th, 49th or 56th Casualty Clearing Stations which were based in the area around Grevilliers. During his fight for life John underwent a series of operations, including the amputation of both of his legs.

**John is buried in Grevillers British Cemetery**

**Private Arthur (Arty) Bullock, aged 19**
**10th Battalion Sherwood Foresters**
**Nottinghamshire and Derbyshire Regiment**
**Died 31 October 1918**

Arthur was born in Gunnerton, Barrasford, the son of John and May Jane Bullock of Ridsdale, West Woodburn. Before his conscription, in March 1917, he was employed as a butcher in Colwell. Arthur was closely associated with Chollerton Church and poignantly, in his last letter home, he wrote of his regret at not being able to attend that year's Harvest Festival. He crossed over to France on Easter Monday 1918, and after an interval in a convalescent camp, was posted in August to the Battalion's Lewis Gun Section after a month of treatment. Arthur died in the 20th General Hospital in France of broncho-pneumonia brought on by being badly gassed [15].

The North Tyne Magazine printed a letter in March 1919 from Arthur's Section Leader, Sergeant J A Sturges. He wrote that straight away Arthur had been involved in the 'Great Allied Offensive' and that together they had fought in many localities: Le Transloy, Roequiny, Lechellas Gouzecourt, Guche Wood, Caulery, Montigny and Inchy.

> "On the morning of 20 October we attacked a German position at Neuvilly, near Le Cateau. The attack was a success and our Lewis Gun Section occupied a sunken road east of Neuvilly. During the night the Germans saturated our position with all calibre of gas shells causing us to wear our gas helmets practically all the time. The following morning Arthur reported that his eyes and throat were bad with gas. He was sent immediately to our Regimental Aid Post and was quickly evacuated by one of the Motor Ambulances. His eyes were completely closed and he needed to be led to the

> transport ... when I last saw Arthur he thought he would soon recover, as the remainder of the section had been through exactly the same amount of gas. However, this sinister weapon had various effects on different people and Arthur, being young and of a rather delicate disposition, must have suffered greater injury than most."

The following stirring lines were printed in the Hexham Herald:

Now the foreign grave closes o'er our beloved form.
May the earth lie lightly on him.
May the flowers bloom over his head,
And may the winds sigh softly,
As they herald the coming night.
Peace and respect be with his memory
Farewell, a long farewell.

The following is found on his headstone:

**OH ARTY DEAR DEPARTED SHADE,**
**WHERE IS THY PLACE OF BLISSFUL REST**
**FROM HIS LOVING MOTHER.**

**Arthur is buried in Étaples Military Cemetery.**

**Driver Robert Storey, aged 23**
**Royal Army Service Corps**
**Attached Royal Army Medical Corps,**
**50th Field Ambulance**
**Died 8 November 1918**

Robert was born in Newcastle, the son of Sarah and Thomas Storey of

Bellingham. Before volunteering to join the army in 1915, Robert worked as a farm labourer. He travelled to France in July 1915 and was attached as a driver to the 50th Field Ambulance, as part of the 39th Division. In September 1915 he was awarded 7 days of Field Punishment Number 1, for the use of disrespectful language to his sergeant.

Field Punishment Number 1 was imposed for minor offences such as drunkeness and insoboardination. The convicted man was shackled in irons and secured to a fixed object, often a gun wheel or similar. He could only be fixed for up to 2 hours in 24, and not for more than 3 days in 4, or for more than 21 days in his sentence. This punishment was often known as 'crucifixion' and due to its humiliating nature was viewed by many soldiers as unfair.

Robert was diagnosed with broncho-pneumonia on November 1 and died at No 5 General Hospital in Rouen. His brother Thomas, who was with the Labour Corps, died two days later and is buried in Bellingham Cemetery, (see page 381)

**Robert is buried in St Sever Cemetery extension, Rouen.**

## REFERENCES

1. Wyrall, E. *The Fiftieth Division, 1914-1919.*
Pub: 1939 reprinted Naval and Military Press 2002.

2. WO95/2828. *War Diary, 1/4th Battalion Northumberland Fusiliers.*

3. Pease, H. *The History of the Northumberland (Hussars) Yeomanry.*
Pub: Constable and Company Limited, 1924

4. WO95/1821. *War Diary, 8th Battalion Northumberland Fusiliers.*

5. Stewart, G. and Sheen, J. A. *History of the Tyneside Scottish.* Pub: Pen and Sword, 1999.

6. WO95/2466. *War Diary, 24th Battalion Northumberland Fusiliers.*

7. data4.collections.gc.ca *War Diary 15th Battalion Canadian Infantry Jan – Dec 1917.*

8. Sandilands, Brig. H. R. *The Fifth in the Great War.* Pub: 1921 reprinted Naval and Military Press 1998.

9. WO95/1430. *War Diary, 1st Battalion Northumberland Fusiliers.*

10. Ponsonby F.. Lieut-Col. *The Grenadier Guards in the Great War of 1914-1919.* Pub: 1920 reprinted Naval and military Press 2003.

11. Headlam, C. DSO. *History of the Guards Division in the Great War 1915-1918.* Pub: 1924 reprinted Naval and Military Press 2002.

12. WO95/1233, *War Diary, 1st Battalion Grenadier Guards.*

13. Wylly, H. C. Col. *The 1st and 2nd Battalions. The Sherwood Foresters in the Great War.* Pub: 1925 reprinted Naval and Military Press 2003

14. WO95/1624, *War Diary, 2nd Battalion Sherwood Foresters.*

15. WO95/2008, *War Diary, 10th Battalion Sherwood Foresters.*

# CHAPTER EIGHTEEN

# THOSE WHO DIED ABROAD

*If I should die, think only this of me:*
*That there's some corner of a foreign field*
*That is forever England.*
From Rupert Brooke's *The Soldier*

Apart from fighting relentlessly in France and Belgium during 1914 to 1918, the British were also involved in a number of other conflicts. They fought against Turkish Troops in Gallipoli in 1915 (see page 55) and in Mesopotamia, culminating with the capture of Jerusalem in 1917 and the eventual surrender of the Ottoman Empire. Troops were also stationed in Egypt in order to guard against Turkish infiltration across the Suez Canal. By late 1915 the British and French had established a presence in northern Greece and during the years until the Armistice in October 1918 fought against mainly Bulgarian units. From October 1917 British forces were involved in shoring up the Italians against mainly Austro-Hungarian troops but also some German battalions. In Africa, British troops were involved in the Allied take over of the German colonial territories and in the suppression of the determined resistance in East Africa by Paul Emil von Lettow-Vorbeck's 'Irregulars'. Furthermore, the British continued to maintain a significant military presence in India during the conflict, as its security was seen as vital to a successful conclusion of the war. Further East, a 1,500-man British contingent, consisting of 1,000 soldiers of the 2nd Battalion, the South Wales Borderers later followed by 500 soldiers of the 36th Sikhs, fought alongside the Japanese Army during the Siege of Tsingtao, a German settlement on the Chinese mainland. Closer to home, in 1916 British troops were involved in the suppression of the Irish Uprising.

After the Armistice, between 1919 and 1929, British troops known as the Army of the Rhine were stationed in Germany.

## MESOPOTAMIA

From their pre war base in India, the 14th Hussars were sent to fight against the Turks in Mesopotamia. During 20-21 May 1916, they were involved in a series of actions to capture the Hai Bridge. Early in the morning (3am) of 21 May the Hussars moved forward towards the bridge which spanned a tributary of the Tigris. By this time the Turks were attempting to use a river steamer to tow the bridge from its moorings. As they approached, the Hussars were fired upon from trenches positioned in the angle between the Hai and the Tigris and it could be seen that enemy forces were guarding this position in strength and had no intention of giving up the site. During the morning, Simon Mewburn was hit in the head and killed outright. By 8am the Hussars were ordered to withdraw. Later that night Simon was laid to rest in a desert grave under the shadow of the Sinn Abtar Redoubt, together with Lieutenant Cedric Guy Deakin [1,2].

**Captain Simon Richmond Mewburn, aged 31**
**14th Kings Hussars**
**Died 21 May 1916**

Simon was born in Willesden, Middlesex, the only son of William Richmond and Elizabeth Fanny Mewburn of Acomb House, Acomb and Evelyn Mansions Westminster. He was educated at Eton and was very much a 'wet bob' (an Etonian who is very keen on water sports). He passed directly from Eton into Sandhurst, received his commission in November 1903 and joined the 14$^{th}$ Hussars. He sailed to India with the regiment in September 1906 as Lieutenant and was gazetted Captain in August 1910. Simon was a notable polo player and his regimental team won numerous competitions while it was stationed in India.

At the outbreak of war Simon was at home on leave and was in the first instance ordered to France with the 20$^{th}$ Hussars. Whilst on the Western Front, Simon was involved in a number of battles during 1914, including *Aisne* (12-15 September) and *Gheluvelt* (30-31 October; during April and May of 1915 he was also part of the conflicts known as *Second Ypres*. He rejoined the 14$^{th}$ Hussars in Mesopotamia in November 1915. A fellow officer described Simon as "an affectionate, honest man and a sterling friend".

**Simon is commemorated on the Basra War Memorial to the missing.**

## SALONIKA

**(Eastern Greece/Bulgaria)**

As part of 84$^{th}$ Brigade the 2$^{nd}$ Northumberland Fusiliers were required to co-operate in the attack with the 83$^{rd}$ brigade on 31 October. They were ordered to cover the flanks of the advance as far as Elisan and Haznatar and specifically to capture Dolap Ciftl, a farm situated east of the Dolap stream.

Unlike those on the Western Front, the operations in Salonika demanded the tactics of open warfare. At 7.15am on an overcast day, after the British bombardment had opened, two companies of Fusiliers, 'A' and 'B', attacked using classical fire and movement tactics, each rush giving mutual support. The attack on this subsidiary target met with stiff resistance and as they approached their objective the leading company came under heavy fire from enemy riflemen who had climbed the trees surrounding Dolap Farm.

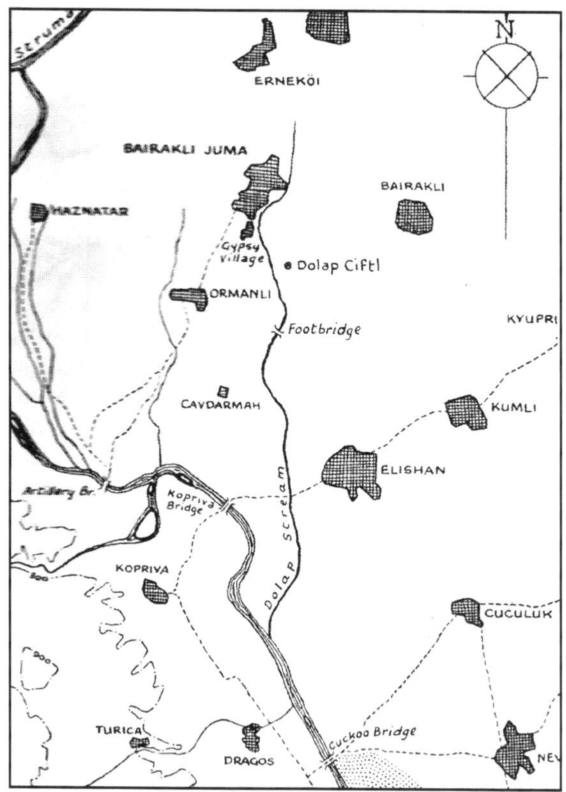


Actions in the Struma Valley
2nd Battalion Northumberland Fusiliers
Scale: 2 miles to the inch

By 8am the Fusiliers had secured a foothold in Dolap Wood, at which point the enemy fled towards Bairakli Juma. By 9am the Fusiliers had passed through Dolap Wood and joined up with the 83rd brigade in Trench 10. During the attack the Northumberland Fusiliers had 3 officers and 11 other ranks killed and 20 other ranks wounded [3,4].

**Private Robert Henry Charlton, aged 34**
**2nd Battalion Northumberland Fusiliers**
**Died 31 October 1916**

Robert was the eldest son of George and Catherine Charlton of Town Foot Farm, Acomb. He was married in Gateshead in the late summer of 1908 to Hannah Maria (née Vipond) and was the father of two children; the family lived at 44 Colston Street, Benwell, Newcastle. Before moving to Benwell he had been employed at Tynedale Colliery in Acomb. He was a keen footballer and played for Acomb United. Just before joining the Colours, he had worked for a short while at the Armstrong Works, hence the family's move to Benwell. He was killed in action.

**Robert is buried in Sturma Military Cemetery.**

## OFF THE COAST OF AFRICA

**Serjeant James Adam Beattie, aged 24**
**2/4th Battalion Northumberland Fusiliers**
**Attached 3/2nd Battalion King's African Rifles**
**Died 14 December 1917**

James was born in Hexham in 1903. He was the son of Adam and Mary Beattie of Walwick Farm, Humshaugh. James was wounded on 15 October at Mtama in German East Africa and was taken to hospital in Dar-es-Saalam. At his own request he was put on the hospital ship, Dunluce Castle, leaving Dar-es-Saalam on the 17 November on its way to

England. He died on 14 December off the coast of Sierre Leone and was buried at sea. His elder brother William, serving with the Royal Army Medical Corps, died in Italy in November 1918 (see page 339).

James' mother received the following letter from Nurse Hilda Flynn, Dunluce Castle:

> "To me was given the privilege of being his day nurse and I must say of all the soldiers that I have nursed your boy was one of the bravest. Although knowing that the chances of his reaching home were remote, the authorities allowed your boy to come on to our hospital ship as he wanted to do so much. Any of us who had to do for your boy just loved him and marvelled at his fortitude as we do not remember once hearing him grumble, or seeing any sign of irritability whatever. His end was most peaceful, the last two days he practically slept away ..."

**James is commemorated on the Mombassa Monument.**

**HMHT Dunluce Castle**

The SS Dunluce Castle was built in 1904 by Harland & Wolff in Belfast with a tonnage of 8114 tons, a length of 475ft, a beam of 56ft and a service speed of 14 knots. In August 1914 she became a troopship and took part in the famous six ship Union-Castle convoy which brought 4000 troops to Europe. She was commissioned as a hospital ship for 755 patients on 6 July 1915 and at Gallipoli and Mudros acted as transfer ship to White Star's Britannic before going to East Africa for duty with the Indian Government. In 1916 she was back in the Mediterranean for service which included voyages from the Adriatic to North Africa with wounded Serbs. On 23 February 1917 she was stopped by a U-boat and after checking that she was complying with the Hague Convention was allowed to proceed. She returned to commercial service on 2 April 1919.

## INDIA

**Private Albert Walton, aged 21**
**1st Battalion Durham Light Infantry**
**Died 10 September 1917**

Albert was born in South Shields in 1896. From an early age, Albert was brought up by his mother's sister, Margaret Fisher of Wall. He was employed as a woodman and he initially enlisted into the 19th Battalion Northumberland Fusiliers. However, he was later transferred to the 1st Battalion Durham Light Infantry, who at the start of hostilities were stationed in India and who stayed there for the duration, seeing action on the North West Frontier. Albert died of enteric fever at Cherat and was buried in Cherat New Cemetery.

**Albert is commemorated on the Delhi Memorial.**

**Private John William Douglas, aged 26**
**1/1st Hertfordshire Yeomanry**
**Died 27 October 1918**

John was born in Elswick, Newcastle, the son of John and Ruth Douglas of Humshaugh Mill. John senior had served as a policeman in the West End of Newcastle, before retiring to Humshaugh.

John was a married in the summer of 1914 to Ethel Christian Coulson. Before answering the call to duty he worked as a grocer's assistant in the Heaton Branch of the Newcastle upon Tyne Cooperative Society. They lived in Heaton with their two children, a boy and a girl. In 1926 Ethel Douglas remarried, becoming Ethel Cowan.

On enlisting John was attached to the Dragoon Guards, undertaking his basic training at Tidworth, in Wiltshire. Following this he was transferred to Hertford Yeomanry as part of the British Reserve Cavalry Regiment, based in Meerut in India. He died of influenza after a short illness; his younger brother Joseph had died not long beforehand, in Hexham.

**John is buried in the Delhi War Cemetery, India.**

## ITALY

The combined Austrian and German Armies launched a crushing bombardment on 24 October 1917, along the Isonzo Front. The infantry attack, spearheaded by the Germans, began at 8am. By late morning the Italians' position had collapsed.

By 27 October the Italian army was routed and had retreated more than 100km (60 miles) to reorganise, stabilizing a new front along the Asiago Plateau, Mount Grappa and the Piave River. More than 700,000 Italian soldiers were lost, with over 90% either captured or deserted. British troops were sent to Italy to help stop the collapse of the Italian Army and to put new heart into their Allies.

This plan was the brainchild of David Lloyd George and it was against the wishes of the 'Westerners' in the High Command. In 1918, the Austro-Hungarians failed to break through, in a series of battles on the Asiago Plateau, finally being decisively defeated in the Battle of Vittorio Veneto in October of that year.

The Austro-Hungarian Army surrendered in the early days of November 1918 [5].

On the morning of 15 June 1918, the 68th Brigade held their sector of the Front Line, using three Battalions, including the 11th Northumberland Fusiliers (NF). One battalion was held in reserve.

At 3am the Austrians opened their attack with a heavy bombardment concentrating on the British first and second line of defence and on a large part of the back area using, primarily, gas shells.

At 6.45am the Austrian infantry attacked along the entire length of the brigade's front line, headed by assault troops with bombers, machine gunners and Flammenwerfer (the infamous flame-throwers). The attack was contained by machine gun and rifle fire. Only in one place did the Austrians enter the front line trench, but they were easily neutralised.

The war diary reports that two patrols on reconnoitring duties were in No Man's Land at the time of the attack. It reports that these soldiers did sterling work in delaying the attack on the 11th NF front and fought hand to hand to their last round before trying to get back when the enemy's barrage lifted. A sergeant was the only unwounded man to reach his lines, which he did at the same time as the enemy.

During the day, the Austrians tried in large numbers and on a number of occasions to break the British Line but were repulsed, suffering exceedingly high casualties. At 8.40am a crisis reared its head as on the 11th Northumberland's left flank, troops of the 48th Division were driven back.

Through a significant effort, the 11th NF managed to establish a defensive flank and the potentially perilous situation was stabilised. All day the Austrians pressed on with their attack, but by early on 16 June the situation was stable, with 48th Division recapturing their original Front Line [6].

**Second Lieutenant Norman Ewart Charlton, aged 20**
**'B' Company**
**11th (Service) Battalion Northumberland Fusiliers**
**Died 15 June 1918**

Norman was born in Wark, the son of John and Mary Charlton of the Black Bull Hotel. Before enlisting Norman worked for Lloyds Bank in Rothbury.

Captain Sterling wrote to his parents from the Italian Front:

> "He was instantaneously killed by a shell on June 15 on returning to the trenches after a very useful patrol across No Man's Land. At the time there was an intense hostile bombardment in progress which was followed by an Austrian attack. There is no doubt that the excellent example of coolness and courage shown by your son had great effect in keeping up the excellent spirits of the men and enable us to withstand and repel the attack."

The North Tyne Magazine for August 1918 reported Norman's death:

> "He died the noblest death a man may die,
> Fighting for God and right and Liberty
> And such a death is immortality."

**Norman is buried at Mognabochi British Cemetery**

**Private William Beattie, aged 29**
**Royal Service Corps**
**Attached 21st Field Ambulance**
**Royal Army Medical Corps**
**Died 2 November 1918**

William Beattie was born in Bardon Mill, the oldest son of Adam and Mary Beattie of Walwick Farm, Humshaugh. He returned from Canada to join the British Forces in July 1915. He left Hexham in August 1915 for France as driver of Dr Stewart's (local charity) Ambulance Car 'North Tyne'. In December 1917, he was transferred to Italy. He contracted pneumonia and died in a Casualty Clearing Station. For his commitment to his work, he had been mentioned in despatches. This family had already faced the death of their son James in late 1917 (see page 333). Another son, George, serving with the Durham Light Infantry, was a prisoner of war in Germany. Coloncl Wright wrote to his mother:

> "Dear Mrs Beattie, with deepest regret … I know well how much he will be missed, both by officers and men with whom he was most popular. He always set a fine example to all ranks and was a splendid example of a true Britisher."

**William is buried in**
**Montecchio Precalcino Communal Cemetery.**

## GERMANY

**Driver Thomas Forrest, aged 25**
**1st Coy Southern Divisional Train**
**Royal Army Service Corps**
**Died 20 March 1919**

Thomas was the oldest son of John and Hannah Forrest of Wood Hall, Barrasford. He was born in North Shields. Thomas had been issued with his demobilisation papers and it was on the eve of his return home that he was accidentally killed in Cologne.

**Thomas is buried in Cologne Southern Cemetery.**

## REFERENCES

1 WO 95/5086. *War Diary of 14th Kings Hussars.*

2 Brigadier Gilbert Browne J, *Historical Record of the 14th (King's) Hussars 1900-1922.* Pub; 1932 reprinted Naval and Military Press 2003.

3 Sandilands, Brig. H. R. *The Fifth in the Great War,*
Pub: 1921 reprinted Naval and Military Press 1998.

4. WO95/2277. *War Diary 2nd Battalion Northumberland Fusiliers.*

5. Thompson, M. *The White War. Life and Death on the Italian Front 1915-1919.* Pub: Faber 2008.

6. WO95/4236. *War Diary 11th Battalion Northumberland Fusiliers.*

# CHAPTER NINETEEN

# THOSE WHO DIED AT SEA

*"We will frighten the British Flag off the face of the waters and starve the British People until they, who have refused peace, will kneel and plead for it."*
Kaiser Wilhelm II, 1 February 1917

In the years leading up to the Great War, Britain's position as a world power was based entirely on the size of her navy, the Senior Service. Kaiser Wilhelm II began to challenge the British position through an aggressive policy of building a great fleet of *capital* ships. The British Government responded by building a navy of a similar number of ships.

When war was declared an untried, untested and highly over-confident British Navy instigated a policy of blockading Germany in an attempt to force the Germans into surrender. It was apparent that a local blockade of each German port would pose a significant danger to the blockading ships who would be subjected to constant bombardment from coastal batteries. Rather, they used a combination of converted merchant ships, Royal Navy vessels and minefields to enforce blockades north and south where the North Sea meets the Atlantic. However, this did allow the German Fleet the freedom to roam the North Sea itself, as shown by the raid made on the North Sea ports of Hartlepool, West Hartlepool, Whitby and Scarbourgh on 16 December 1914, which resulted in 137 deaths.

When war was declared, a number of German capital ships were at large in the oceans of the world, causing disruption to Allied shipping and threatening the supply of troops from the British Empire. Most noteworthy was the SMS Emden which roamed the Indian Ocean sinking or capturing up to 30 Allied merchant ships and bombarding Madras, damaging oil tanks. Eventually, on 9 Nov 1914 the Australian Light Cruiser HMAS Sydney caught up with the Emden, forcing it to ground itself to prevent it from sinking. Similarly, in the Pacific, German ships caused a lot of damage and inflicted the first defeat on the British Navy for over a century (Battle of Coronel, 1 November 1914). This German fleet subsequently fled into the Atlantic and were caught (*Battle of Falklands*, 14 November 1914) and eventually destroyed. The loss of the German ships in the Atlantic effectively terminated the High Seas activity of the German navy. The British navy was also involved in forcing a route through the Dardanelles in 1915, with disastrous and infamous results.

In the North Sea a number of clashes took place between the British and German Fleets, particularly the battles of *Dogger Bank,* 24 January 1915 and *Jutland,* 31 May 1916. At Jutland the Germans sank more British ships than they lost, but left the scene of battle, never to venture from their home ports during the rest of the war, thus allowing the British to claim a "Momentous Victory".

Germany decided to rely on their submarines. At first, during the early stages of the war, submarines attacked merchant ships according to the rules of war: merchant ships were forced to stop and the crew allowed to take to their lifeboats before the ship was sunk. However, from February 1915 the unrestricted sinking of merchant vessels, hospital ships and also the ships of neutral countries thought to be supplying the British war effort, took place. By August 1915, 168,000 tons of Allied merchant shipping had been lost, including the infamous sinking of the *Lusitania* and *Arabic* and the death of American citizens. This led, for a while, to a more considered approach to the sinking of ships on Germany's part.

The Germans realised after the *Battle of Jutland* at the end of May 1916, that their Navy was not strong enough to beat that of the British. Also, the military situation for Germany at the end of 1916 was discouraging; the loss of life on the Somme and at Verdun had been appalling. They concluded that they needed to disrupt the flow of materials to the UK and that the only option was to use the submarine. German Naval Intelligence believed that unrestricted submarine warfare would sink 600,000 tons of shipping per month with the aim of starving Britain into defeat within five months. Germany adopted a policy of unrestricted submarine warfare on 1 February 1917.

In April 1917, German and Austrian submarines inflicted the loss of 860,000 tons of Allied shipping. Britain was in a desperate position. Admiral Sir John Jellicoe said that if this continued in this vein then Britain would have to sue for peace by the summer of 1917. In late 1917, after much pushing by the Prime Minister, the Admiralty finally introduced a convoy system which began to reduce these unsustainable losses. However, not until the middle of 1918 did the level of losses to the merchant fleet fall below 300,000 tons.

## 1914

HMS Bulwark was built at Devonport Dockyard. It was launched in October 1899 and completed three years later, described as a London Class Pre-Dreadnought Battleship. It displaced 15,366 long tons and was capable of 18knots (21mph). Armed with 4x12 inch, 12x6 inch and 16x12 pounders, together with a range of smaller armaments, it cost over £1,000,000 to build.

Initially stationed with the Mediterranean Fleet, it was commissioned in 1907 for service with the Home Fleet, later joining 5$^{th}$ Battle Squadron. From 14 November 1914 it was transferred to Sheerness to guard against

HMS Bulwark

a perceived German invasion of Britain. On 26 November 1914, HMS Bulwark was moored at No. 17 Buoy in Kethole Reach on the River Medway. At 7.50am a powerful, internal explosion ripped apart the Bulwark. All of her officers were killed, and only 12 of 750 sailors survived.

The following is the scene described by an eye witness, who was on board a nearby ship:

> "I was at breakfast when I heard an explosion, and I went on deck. My first impression was that the report was produced by the firing of a salute by one of the ships, but the noise was quite exceptional. When I got on deck I soon saw that something awful had happened. The water and sky were obscured by dense volumes of smoke. We were at once ordered to the scene of the disaster to render what assistance we could. At first we could see nothing, but when the smoke cleared a bit we were horrified to find the battleship Bulwark had gone. She seemed to have entirely vanished from sight, but a little later we detected a portion of the huge vessel showing about 4ft above water. We kept a vigilant look-out for the unfortunate crew, but only saw two men."

HMS Bulwark blows up at Sheerness

The explosion was heard at Whitstable twenty miles away and across the Thames Estuary where Southend Pier was shaken. It was implied at the court of enquiry that the explosion was the result of bad practice, the storage of ammunition in cross passageways which connected her 11 magazines, and that the cause was the overheating of cordite charges stored alongside a boiler room bulkhead.

**Stoker 1st Class John Charles Darcy, aged 22**
**HMS Bulwark, Royal Navy**
**Died 26 November 1914**

John was born in Liverpool in 1892 and was the son of Hannah Darcy. The 1911 census records that John was living at the family home in Toxteth Park, Liverpool, with his remarried mother, Hannah Brown. He was working as a coal miner. He joined the Royal Navy two months later, in June 1911, serving after training on HMS Renown, HMS Pembroke and from June 1912 on the Bulwark. The North Tyne magazine for January 1915 records the death of John Darcy and reports the grief of his grandmother, Mrs Darcy of Bank Top, Falstone and his uncle Charles of the same address. John had been on leave spending time in the North Tyne Valley during the Whitsuntide of 1914.

**John is commemorated on the Portsmouth Naval Memorial.**

## 1917

SS Ivernia

At the outset of war in 1914 the Government hired the Cunard liner SS Ivernia as an auxiliary transport ship. The Ivernia, of 14,038 tons gross, was built in 1900 by Swan and Hunter and Wigham Richardson Ltd of Newcastle upon Tyne. One of its unique features was that it had the largest funnels ever fitted to a ship, measuring 60 feet from top to deck. At the end of December 1916, the Ivernia left Marseilles bound for Alexandria carrying 2,400 troops of the Argyle and Sutherland Highlanders, Royal Scots Fusiliers, Rifle Brigade and some Yeomanry. On New Years Day 1917, whilst sailing off the west of Crete, the Ivernia was torpedoed by UB-47 and had sunk within the hour, 58 miles southeast of Cape Matapan. Of the soldiers on board 3 officers and 82 other ranks were drowned together with the ship's surgeon, chief engineer and 34 of the ship's crew.

The UB-47 was a type UB II submarine and was commanded by Lt Cdr Wolfgang Steinbauer of the German Imperial Navy. Steinbauer was a very successful submariner, recording the sinking of 49 vessels representing a loss of 170,000 tons of Allied shipping. A few days before the sinking of the Ivernia, he had torpedoed the French Battleship, the *Gaulois*. This class of submarine, six in all, had been selected by the Germans for service in the Mediterranean. They were transported in sections by rail and reassembled in Pola (Pula in modern day Croatia).

Swamped by the breakers:
one of the life boats from the transport Ivernia

**Private John George Baty, aged 27**
**1/5th Battalion Royal Scots Fusiliers**
**Died 1 January 1917**

John was born in Acomb, the son of Isaac and Annie Baty of East Salmon Well, Acomb. The 1910 census records that John was working as a groom. He enlisted in the summer of 1916 when the local newspaper recorded that he was employed as a coal carting contractor at Tynedale Colliery in Acomb. He was initially recruited into the Gordon Highlanders and trained at Aberdeen. Subsequently he was transferred to the Royal Scots Fusiliers.

**John was drowned when the Ivernia was torpedoed and is commemorated on the Mikra Memorial, near Thessaloniki, on the mainland of Greece.**

The SS Mordenwood, 3125 tons, was built in 1910 by Roper and Sons Ltd of Stockton and was owned by Joseph Constantine and Pickering SS Co of Middlesbrough. It was torpedoed by the Austro-Hungarian Navy (K.u.K. Kriegsmarine) submarine, U98, commanded by Leo Prasil. The Mordenwood sank 90 miles southeast of Cape Matalan (32.02N, 22.05E). The captain and 20 men of the crew were lost.

**Chief Boatswain Harold Morgan, aged 22**
**SS Mordenwood, Merchant Navy**
**Died 19 May 1917**

Harold, the son of William and Annie Morgan, was born at Dobroyd Castle, Todmorden, West Yorkshire, in 1896. The 1901 census records the Morgan family living in Lower Bebington, Cheshire, with the father working as gardener. Ten years later the family were living in Saltburn, North Yorkshire. Harold, aged 15, was working as a painter and decorator. At the time of their son's death, William and Anne Morgan were working at Chipchase Castle, Wark.

**Harold drowned when the Mordenwood sank and is commemorated on the Tower Hill Memorial.**

# CHAPTER TWENTY

# MAGNIFICENT MEN IN THEIR FLYING MACHINES

*I know that I shall meet my fate*
*Somewhere among the clouds above;*
*Those that I fight I do not hate,*
*Those that I guard I do not love;*
From W B Yeats, *A Irish Airman Forsees His Death,*

At the beginning of the war, both the Army (Royal Flying Corps) and the Navy (Royal Naval Air Service) had their own branches of air service. The army branch was known as the Royal Flying Corps (RFC) and had for its motto *Par Ardua ad Astra* (Through Adversity to the Stars) which remains the motto of the RAF today.

At the start of the war, the RFC consisted of five squadrons: one observation balloon squadron and four aeroplane squadrons. All of its personnel also held ranks in Army regiments. The purpose of the RFC was initially observation, their worth being amply demonstrated in ascertaining German intentions at *Mons* and the *Marne* in 1914. Their efficiency was greatly improved with the optimisation of wireless communications during the *Battle of Aubers Ridge* in May 1915. In March 1915 the RFC was developing techniques for aerial bombardment, especially of enemy rail communications, although payloads were low. Most planes were fitted with guns of one form or the other. For most of the war, RFC pilots faced superior aircraft; German planes were faster and could operate at higher altitudes and also had the advantage of flying with the prevailing westerly wind. In response, the RFC followed a determined and aggressive flying policy; statistics show that British to German losses were about 4 to 1.

At the outbreak of war, the Royal Naval Air Services had 93 aircraft, 6 airships and 2 balloons in service; on the face of it they appeared to have been a lot better prepared to fight a war. Throughout the early years of the war inter service rivalry affected aircraft procurement, with the Navy getting the better deal. With their better planes, the RNAS were pressed into service on the Western Front to help the hard pressed RFC. The RNAS was responsible for fleet reconnaissance, patrolling coasts for enemy ships and submarines and attacking enemy coastal territory. Before techniques were developed for taking off and landing on ships, the RNAS depended on seaplanes to operate at sea.

In August 1917 proposals were made which recommended the formation of an air service on a level with the Army and the Royal Navy. Although not to everyone's liking, the RFC and the RNAS were amalgamated to form the Royal Air Force (RAF) on 1 April 1918 and by the end of the war this new service had over 4,000 combat aircraft and 114,000 personnel.

Beginning on 15 and 16 February 1915, the Royal Naval Air Services attempted bombing raids on Ostend and Zeebrugge using 17 land-based aeroplanes and 7 seaplanes, (this was a large scale raid by 1915 standards). Thirty-seven 20lb bombs were dropped around the harbour and docks at Ostend. The aircraft piloted by Thomas Spencer was involved in the raid on Zeebrugge. It was reported that in this raid, the aircraft involved dropped two bombs which hit the Mole and the lock at Zeebrugge; seven German Marine Artillery men were killed. Three seaplanes and one aeroplane failed to return.

Two of the lost seaplanes that set out from the Dunkirk Naval Air Station on 16 February were piloted by Flight Sub Lieutenants Thomas Spencer and The Hon Desmond O'Brien of Dromoland Castle, Co Clare, (aged 19). The aircraft flown were Short Type C floatplanes (aircraft Nos 813 and 817 were used, but no information is available as to who was flying which plane).

Short Folder Type C Floatplane

The Type C was also known as the 'Short Folder' as its wings could be folded back for storage on board ship if required. It was a two-seater aircraft (but on bombing raids it was piloted by only one person allowing more bombs to be carried). It was powered by a 160hp Gnome 14-cylinder rotary engine and was able to achieve speeds of 78mph. It was also able to carry a 367kg torpedo bomb[1].

**Flight Sub-Lieutenant Thomas Seymour Spencer, aged 20**
**Royal Naval Air Service**
**Died 16 February 1915**

Thomas (Tommy) was the eldest son of Seymour and Ethel Spencer of The Birks, Bellingham; he was born on the 24 December 1894. His younger sister, Nancy, died in September 1914, just after he had left school.

Tommy attended Stonyhurst, the Jesuit College in Lancashire, where he had first attended the Hodder, their preparatory school and then moved on to the college itself, which he left on 25 July 1914, a year in which

he was 'Senior Philosopher'. His father died in 1907, whilst he was school. His younger brother, James, who also attended Stonyhurst College, died in 1967. Tommy was a member of the College Choir and was a regular performer at college events. He was a keen all round sportsman but his real pleasures were shooting and motoring. He was an ardent motor cyclist, winning five events against all comers at the local (Blackburn) motor cycling races. It is believed that it was his interest in mechanics which later led him to join the Air Service [2].

HMS Empress was one of three cross channel steamers taken over from the South East and Chatham Railway on 11 August 1914 and converted into a seaplane carrier. This entailed clearing the deck of all fittings and building canvas aircraft hangers for (initially) three seaplanes. There was no flight deck and the aircraft were launched by being lowered into the sea from where they would take off as normal. After the flight the plane would be landed close to the ship and be retrieved using the same cranes.

Tommy joined the Naval Air Service on 5 October 1914 and gained his Royal Air Corps Certificate (No. 991) on 27 October 1914 at Netheravon, going on to complete his course on the Isle of Grain. He was appointed Flight Sub-Lieutenant on 1 January 1915 with seniority dated back to 5 October 1914, and was appointed to HMS Empress in February 1915.

A fellow RNAS officer who took part in his final raid reported:

> "His engine was blown out by a bomb which refused to be released and his machine was riddled with shot. He was trying to make a forced landing, but the German gunners were concentrating all their guns on him as he came down."

His Squadron Commander, Reginald Bone, wrote to Thomas's mother:

> "Your boy in the first day of the raid (15 February) flew through five snow storms ... and came back as cheery as ever. He did well. He was a born flyer and just cram full of, well I don't know how to describe it in ordinary language: in aviation there is a monosyllabic word signifying capacity to overcome difficulties and he was full of it."

Bone replied to a letter from Thomas' mother:

> "The machines were unsuitable for flying over the highly trained anti aircraft gunners at Zeebrugge, but there is a fearful shortage of seaplanes and will be for months to come..."

**Thomas is commemorated on the
Chatham Naval Memorial to the missing.**

**Lieutenant William Lee, aged 26**
**Royal Air Force**
**5th (Service) Battalion Royal Irish Fusiliers**
**Died 19 August 1918**

William, the only son of Thomas and Mary Lee of Low Brunton, Wall, was born in Wark. Before joining the Colours he was employed as a draughtsman by the North Eastern Railways in their Divisional Goods Manager's Department at Forth Banks, Newcastle. He was a talented artist and spent much of leisure time at Armstrong College. The contemporary Roll of Honour for Wall, Bingfield and Hallington recorded that in early 1915, William had enlisted in the Officers' Training Corps at Armstrong College. After receiving his commission with the Royal Irish Fusiliers, he was sent to Egypt in the spring of 1916. Later that year the Irish were sent to Salonika and he saw service in the Sturma Valley. It is reported that William was employed in reconnoitring the Bulgarian lines at which time, in a letter home, he wrote that:

> "Johnny Bulgar was a decent fellow, who might often have fired at [us] when he did not."

In September 1917, the Irish Rifles returned to Egypt and in the October were part of the force destined to capture Jerusalem from the Turks in early December. William later joined the RAF and was acting as an instructor in Egypt when he met his death in a flying accident.

**William is buried in Suez War Memorial Cemetery.**

## REFERENCES

1. Private Communication, *Gareth Morgan Great War Forum, 1914-1918 invisionzone.com/forum*

2. Private Communication. *Archivist Stoneyhurst School.*

# CHAPTER TWENTY ONE

# DIED IN PRISONER OF WAR CAMPS

*"On the way we passed several POW camps and at one camp I will always remember the sight of about twenty 'Englanders' being driven out to work, the guards having long whips beside their rifles and lashing out at any men who lagged behind. It was enough to make your blood boil to see men treated like a lot of cattle, just because they were unfortunate enough to be prisoners of war and in their power."*

Baron Richard Racey, Canadian Army, 1915 POW Diary

During the Great War, over 190,000 British and Empire soldiers were taken prisoner by the Germans. Some of these fellows were captured in the earliest days of the war and spent over fifty months in captivity in camps all over Germany. There is a misconception that the life of prisoner of war was simply boring and frustrating; however, many diaries

and records show that, for all ranks, captivity under the Germans was a real test of endurance and physical survival. Oral and written testimonies bear witness to ill-treatment, starvation, hard labour and death, indeed it has been calculated that one in eight of the British and Empire soldiers captured on the Western Front died in captivity. After the war, a committee was set up to investigate the treatment of Allied soldiers in captivity in Germany; it collected data from debriefing interviews of escapees and returning prisoners.

On 8 May 1915 during the desperate days of the Second Battle of Ypres (See Chapter 5) the 2nd Battalion Northumberland Fusiliers were positioned near Mousetrap Farm and found that they were surrounded on three sides by the enemy. Lieutenant-Colonel H S Enderby (Acomb) and his Adjutant Captain R Auld were taken prisoner. In captivity, both men were subjected to physical and mental torture. For example, in their prison camp at Augustabad in Neu Brandenburg Province, Lieutenant-Colonel Enderby was forced to run the gauntlet along a hail of German rifle fire. A similar fate was meted out to Captain Auld. Both men survived the war.

On 21 December 1918, an article appeared in the Hexham Herald entitled **Murdered by Germans.** The article outlined the experiences of Lance-Corporal J Holyoak of Sunderland who had been repatriated after four years of internment in German Prisoner of War Camps. He had been serving with the 1st Battalion Northumberland Fusiliers and was taken prisoner on 25 August 1914.

He described two cases of British soldiers being murdered by their German Guards.

**Case 1**

> In February 1918, Private Hughie Gault of the 2nd Battalion Irish Rifles, a Belfast man, was waiting in a canteen for hot water and was ordered away by a German sentry. After a short while, Gault was bayoneted through the right shoulder and after a scuffle he was bayoneted in the right arm. After falling to the floor he was bayoneted in the chest, later dying of his wounds. Holyoak states that the German guard was later promoted.

The CWGC site reports the death of Rifleman H Gault Royal Irish Rifles who died 1 April 1918 and is buried in Cologne Southern Cemetery.

**Case 2**

> In September 1917 'Tiddler' Richardson, a private in the Northumberland Fusiliers, refused to load a wagon of barbed wire destined for the Front. As a result, Richardson was immediately shot by a German corporal, who was not punished for his brutality.

The CWGC site reports the death of Private H Richardson, 1st Battalion Northumberland Fusiliers who died 25 September 1917 and is buried in Cologne Southern Cemetery.

A large number of prisoners taken in the Spring offensive were held behind the lines (contrary to agreements) working on unloading trains, burying the dead, digging trenches, moving munitions etc. Many of them were killed or died as a result of shelling or starvation.

## EXTRACT FROM THE BRISBANE COURIER, SUNDAY 1 FEBRUARY 1919

The paper reported the story of Kenneth Murphy under the headline,

**Hun Treatment of Prisoners Held Behind the Lines**

> Kenneth reported that he and his mates were compelled to give their address as 'Gustrav' (i.e. Gustrow, which is near Mecklenberg). He said, "The Huns starved and beat a lot of the lads to death; we never got to Germany. We were just behind the Line digging trenches, building roads and dugouts for the Huns. Every man had to work; if they refused they were beaten with the butt end of a rifle and put down a dark dugout and had no rations for days. We had to march five or six miles to work and back every day, Sunday included … I have seen men faint from sheer weakness and fatigue, and a big Hun would pick up a shovel and belt him back to his senses. The party I was working for were about 180 in June 1918; at the Armistice we were just 80 odd …. We buried some where they died.
>
> We never went near Germany, but when writing home we were forced to give an address in Germany. During the German retreat we were kept on the move as the British made a push. We moved closer to Germany. We were somewhere near Namur when the Armistice was declared."

At noon on 22 April 1918 the 2/5th Lincolnshire Battalion (LR) and 4th Leicestershire Regiment were ordered to occupy the second system trenches near Bullecourt. As they advanced they were confronted by the enemy who had already overrun the Ecoust Ridge and were occupying the second system of trenches. Before the LR could extend their line, three companies were cut off. The Regimental History reports, "What happened to these companies is not known as they were never seen again" [1].

It is highly likely that Walter Forster was wounded in this action and was taken prisoner by the Germans and later died in a German Military Hospital.

**Pte Walter Forster, aged 20**
**2/5th Battalion Lincolnshire Regiment**
**Died 14 April 1918**

Walter, son of Robert and Helen Foster, was born in Slaley. The 1911 census records the family living at Errington, Wall on Tyne. The father worked as a shepherd. Although not commemorated on either of Wall's Memorials, the Bingfield and Wall Parish Magazine for August 1916 recorded his name in its Roll of Honour. In April 1918, the town of Denain was a German Hospital Centre and the Communal Cemetery was used to bury British prisoners.

**Walter is buried in Denain Communal Cemetery.**

At the time of Thomas Wright's death, in August 1918, the city of Lille was in the hands of the Germans and would remain so until its reoccupation on 17 October 1918. From this it can be ascertained that Thomas died a prisoner of war.

**Private Thomas Wright, aged 29**
**736th Area Employment Company, Labour Corps**
**Died 28 August 1918**

Thomas, the son of Elizabeth Wright, was born in Falstone. The 1891 census shows that at the age of one he was living with his grandparents, Robert and Jane Thompson. The 1901 census shows Thomas, aged 11, still living with his grandparents, but working on the railway. By the age of 21 he was living at Billerby, Wark, and working as a farm labourer.

Thomas joined the army under the Derby Scheme in November 1915 and was allotted to the 3rd Reserve Battalion of the Yorkshire Regiment. In June 1917 Thomas was transferred to the Labour Corps, and in late July was sent to France. He was posted missing during the fighting around Lavantie on 9 April 1918 (see Operation Georgette page 242). Later it was confirmed he was being held as a prisoner of war at Gardologen Camp, in Altmark Province, Germany. However, it was subsequently reported that Thomas had died in the War Hospital in Lille; the cause of death was not reported. This curious geographical gap between the assumed place of imprisonment and death, and the burial of the body, raises the suspicion that Thomas was not in Germany but was in fact working behind the German lines, within the battle zone, as part of a German enforced labour contingent, see page 358 for an explanation of this.

**Thomas is buried in Lille Southern Cemetery.**

The 1st Lincolnshire Regiment (LR) as part of the 21st Division was involved in the fighting associated with all three German advances against British positions during the early months of 1918. They were in action trying to stem the German advance in late March on the Somme, (Operation Michael) and in early April near Ypres (Operation Georgette). Later in the year (May-June) they were also involved in the fighting in the Ainse (Operation Blücher). During one of these intense attacks by superior German forces, John Southern was wounded and imprisoned. In captivity he died of his wounds [1].

**Private John George Southern, aged 19**
**1st Battalion Lincolnshire Regiment**
**Died 11 September 1918**

John, the son of Joseph and Elizabeth Southern, was born in Falstone. He was educated at the Reed School, Bellingham. The 1911 census shows the family living at Buteland, Bellingham. He apparently died from his wounds in a German hospital at Giessen.

**John is buried in Niederzwehren Cemetery**

The 7th Field Company, Royal Engineers, was attached to 50th (Northumbrian) Division from June 1915. The Northumbrian Division was involved in stemming the German advance of 27 May 1918. See below and section on Operation Blücher (page 251) [2].

**Sapper Thomas Robson, aged 24**
**7th Field Company, Royal Engineers**
**Died 16 September 1918**

Thomas, the eldest son of Thomas and Florence Robson, was born at

Lanehead, Northumberland. He enlisted into the army in Newcastle. Before he enlisted he worked as a carpenter.

**Thomas is buried in Niederzwehren Cemetery.**

On 27 May 1918 the Germans launched a massive attack called Operation Blücher in the Chemin Des Dames region. On this day Robert Leathard was captured, suffering from a broken arm and leg; he was imprisoned in a camp near Cassel in Germany. In letters home, the last dated September 1918, Robert told his parents that he was getting on well, but was disappointed that he was not receiving any parcels from home, although his parents confirmed that they sent parcels regularly. A letter dated 4 October from the British Mission, Prisoners of War Camp, Cassel, stated that Robert had suddenly developed septic poisoning, which caused his death.

**Private Robert Leathard, aged, 26**
**14th (Service) Battalion Northumberland Fusiliers**
**Died 2 October 1918**

Robert, the eldest son of George and Matilda Leathard of the Leazes Head, Humshaugh, was born in Sunderland. Robert was one of four sons who had served with the forces; one of these had already been discharged from service. The 1911 census reports that Robert was working as a farm labourer with his father. Before enlisting in February 1916 he was working for Mr Preston of White House, North Shields. After undergoing basic training at Rugeley, Robert embarked for France in June 1916. It was reported that Robert was seriously wounded in October 1917, when the 14th Battalion Northumberland Fusiliers were the Pioneer Battalion for the 21st Division. Soldiers from this Division were involved in a number of the battles of *Third Ypres (Passchendaele)*, including *Polygon Wood* (26 September - 3 October) *Broodeindse* (4 October) and *Second Battle of Passchendaele* (26 October - 10 November). When and how Robert was captured by the Germans is unknown.

**Robert is buried in Niederzwehren Cemetery.**

In April 1918 Thomas Hall's parents, Michael and Elizabeth Hall, were notified that their son was missing in action. Over a year later, the North Tyne Magazine for August 1919 reported that word had been now been received that Thomas had died in hospital at Antwerp, although no particulars of his death were disclosed.

**Private Thomas John Hall, aged 23**
**1st Battalion Northumberland Fusiliers**
**Died 25 October 1918**

Thomas was born in West Woodburn and was the eldest son of Michael and Elizabeth Hall of Hair Walls West. The 1911 census recorded that Thomas, aged 15, was working on his father's farm.

**Thomas is buried in Schoonselhof Cemetery**

The 1/4th Battalion Northumberland Fusiliers (NF) as described above and in the section on Operation Blücher (see page 251) were completely overwhelmed on the 27 May 1918 and the battalion ceased to exist as a fighting force after this date. It is highly likely that Corporal Weir was wounded and captured at this time [2].

**Corporal John Robert Weir, aged 40**
**1/4th Battalion Northumberland Fusiliers**
**Died 11 November 1918**

John, the son of Mary Weir, was born in Carlisle, Cumberland. The 1891 census shows that John, aged 13, was an inmate of a Carlisle Workhouse, but by 1901 the census records that he was boarding with Edward and Elizabeth Pearson in Humshaugh and working as a station porter. John married Elizabeth Prudhoe Coulson, from Chollerton, in the summer of 1903 and was the father of at least two sons and three daughters. By 1911 the family had moved to Wark and were living at High Parksend. John was working as a cartman. Officially, John died of wounds whilst a prisoner of war.

**Robert is buried in Cologne Southern Cemetery.**

## REFERENCES

1. Simpson, C.R. Maj-Gen. *The History of the Lincolnshire Regiment 1914-1918.* Pub: 1931, reprinted Military and Naval Press 2002.

2. Wyrall, E. *The Fiftieth Division,* 1914-1919.
Pub: 1939, reprinted Naval and Military Press 2002.

.

# CHAPTER TWENTY TWO

# DIED AT HOME

*Shall they return to beatings of great bells*
*In wild train loads?*
*A few, a few, too few for drums and yells*
From Wilfred Edward Salter Owen's *The send off*

During the Great War, nearly ten million men served in the British Army, the Royal Navy, the Merchant Navy and the Air Force. No repatriation took place of the dead, regardless of where they fought; they were buried where they fell or near to the sites to which they had been admitted for medical attention. The vast majority of their deaths are recorded in official data bases such as the Commonwealth War Grave lists, but not everyone to be found on our War Memorials died on the various battlefields in Europe or in the Middle East; some men had joined up and were in training, but died before they ever reached the battlefield. This was the case with Private W Bullock, of Chollerton.

Throughout the country, on gravestones and on War Memorials, the names can be found of fallen soldiers whose names are not recorded in the official databases. Some died after the official cut off date for the Commonwealth War Grave Commission lists, at the end of 1921; this happened in the case of George Dalton of Humshaugh, who died on the day the village unveiled its War Memorial. The knowledge of his sacrifice for his country comes to light only from a plaque in St Peter's Church, Humshaugh.

Others returned home, injured and traumatised from the battle; often, they were considered to be unfit for further duty and were honourably discharged, but many died within a few months, their names were lost to the authorities and they were not remembered on any official data base. However, their memories would live on, because their names were included on their local war memorials.

All along the North Tyne Valley there are memorials to valiant men whose deaths are not nationally recorded; combatants who were medically discharged from the services but who went on to die while the war was still in progress: Gunner J W Conkleton, Acomb; Private Walter Rutherford, Wark; Private John English Urwin, Chollerton and others are examples of this.

Today, more and more deaths are at last being officially catalogued through the excellent work of a number of dedicated workers under the banner of *In from the Cold*. Some, like Able Seaman John Rae of Bellingham, have been honoured as the result of work by this group. Well done to them. I hope that my studies will be instrumental in honouring more of the men who marched away.

## 1915

**James Robert Clapperton, aged 27**
**1/4th Battalion Northumberland Fusiliers**
**Died 22 February 1915**

James was born in Corsenside, the eldest son of Robert and Jane Clapperton. The 1911 census shows that James lived at Wood Head, Bellingham and worked as a gamekeeper. On enlisting he worked on the Hesleyside Estate, as did his father. He married Edith (née Hardy) in May 1914 and was the father of a small son. He had been with the Territorials for only six weeks, undergoing basic training, when he died at the Military Depot in Battle Hill, Hexham.

James was buried on the 27 February, with full military honours including the firing of three volleys over his grave. Sergeant Instructor Wilkie was in charge of the guard of honour. The Hexham Herald recorded this event with the headline "Last rites performed in tempestuous gale".

**James is buried in Bellingham Cemetery.**

**Private John James Welton, aged 19**
**1/4th Northumberland Fusiliers**
**Died 21 April 1915**

John was born in Chollerton, the second son of William and Eleanor Welton. They lived at the Crags, Barrasford. After the war they lived at Bavington Mires, Capheaton. The 1911 census records that John, aged 15, was working along with his father in the local whinstone quarries as a stone breaker. John died at home on the same day as his battalion was finding its feet in France. John, a Catholic, was interred with full military honours and the customary three volleys were fired over his grave. Drum-Major J W Robson sounded *The Last Post* at the end of the service. His brother Robert, also a member of the local Territorials, was wounded during the fighting around Ypres in early 1915 (see page 220).

**John is buried in Chollerton (St Giles) Churchyard.**

On the night of 15 June 1915, Zeppelin L10, under the command of Kapitänleutnant Hirsch, crossed the English coast north of Blyth and headed south towards Wallsend. Above Palmer's Works in Jarrow it dropped 12 bombs which killed 17 men and injured another 75. After this, the zeppelin crossed back over the Tyne and dropped bombs on Willington Quay, where Cookson's Antimony and Pochin's Chemical Works were damaged, together with a number of houses. During this raid a policeman died. After further attacks on Haxton Colliery and South Shields, the raider escaped across the North Sea [1,2,3,4].

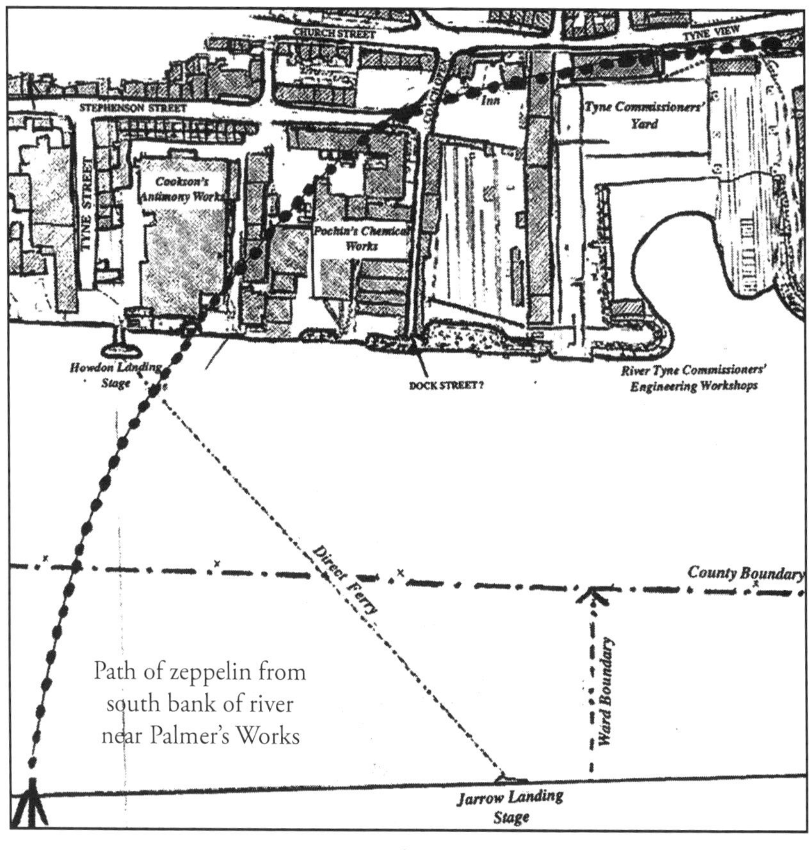


Courtesy of Philip Strong
Great War Forum

**Police Constable Robert Telford, aged 21**
**Northumberland Police Constabulary**
**Died 15 June 1915**

Robert was born in 1892 at Gilesgate Bank, Hexham, the son of John and Margaret Telford. A single man, before joining the Police Force he had worked as a farm labourer, a quarry labourer and from April 1913 on the roads for Northumberland County Council in the Chollerton district. He was also a member of the local Territorial Battalion until he resigned in 1911. He joined the Northumberland County Constabulary in March 1914 as PC 73 and trained at its headquarters in Morpeth until the end of April. From the Beginning of May he was stationed at Willington Quay, part of the Wallsend Division. He appears to have been less than content with his position as a policeman and after a number of requests the Constabulary agreed he could leave the force and enlist in the Northumberland Fusiliers. He attested into the forces on 31 May 1915 and was awaiting his call up papers when he was killed.

At the inquest on the 18 June, evidence was given that the zeppelin bomb was dropped close to where PC Telford was on duty outside the Co-op butcher's shop at Willington Quay. It was reported that death was instantaneous; his injuries included a wound to the back (of ten inches by nine), his ribs and shoulder blade were completely shattered and one of his lungs badly damaged. His funeral, which took place on the afternoon of 19 June, was attended by the Chief Constable of Northumberland.

**PC Robert Telford is buried in St Giles' Churchyard, Chollerton, where a memorial was erected in August 1927 by Northumberland County Constabulary.**

**Private John Johnstone, aged 30**
**1/4th Battalion Northumberland Fusiliers**
**Died 21 December 1915**

John was born in Bellingham, the son of George and Agnes Johnstone. The 1911 census records that John was working as a horseman and living at Hareshaw House, Bellingham. During his basic training at Hexham, John was suddenly taken ill and died shortly after at the Royal Victorian Infirmary in Newcastle. He was afforded a full military funeral with the military band and over 40 soldiers attending from Hexham.

**John is buried in St Cuthbert's Churchyard, Corsenside.**

## 1916

**Private Frank (Francis) Hunter, aged 21**
**1/4th Northumberland Fusiliers**
**Died 28 May 1916**

Frank was born in Melkridge, Northumberland, the son of William and Isabella Hunter of Shillahaugh, Wark. Two of his brothers were also serving with the forces: John and Thomas, who served with the Royal Garrison Artillery. The 1911 census shows Frank working as labourer at Town Shields, Haydon Bridge. He landed in France on 20 April 1915 (see page 35) and was wounded in the right arm on 26 April, during the attack on St Julien In February 1916 he was wounded again, in the left arm and right leg. Frank died of a pulmonary disease in the Military Hospital, Tooting.

The North Tyne magazine for July 1916 reports Frank's death:

"… who died in hospital after a severe illness. He had been wounded twice previously – but it was not permitted for him to give his life the country in the way which he would have wished."

**Frank is buried in Wandsworth, (Earlsfield) Cemetery, London.**

As the war progressed with an increasing number of casualties, lots of new soldiers were needed as replacements. New Canadian Battalions were formed with men initially trained in Canada and then sent to England in great haste. After arriving in England these reserve battalions were centred in Shorncliffe in Kent. These fresh troops were absorbed as replacements into the 1st and 2nd Canadian Divisions already serving in France, or into the newly formed 3rd and 4th Divisions. Shorncliffe was also the home for a least two Canadian Military Hospitals. On three occasions Canadian soldiers were killed during air raids on Shorncliffe. The 82nd Battalion of the Canadian Expeditionary Force (CEF) was based in Calgary and began recruiting in the late summer of 1915. After sailing to England in May 1916 the 82nd Battalion was absorbed into the 9th Battalion CEF on 18 July 1916. Private Ridley died within days of reaching the UK.

**Private Walter Ridley, aged 43**
**82nd Battalion Canadian Infantry**
**Died 21 June 1916**

Walter was born in Netherton, Northumberland, the son of Walter and Mary Ridley of Acomb. Walter married Emily Hannah (née Cowing) in the summer of 1895. The 1901 census shows that Walter was the father of four children and was working as a self employed carrier, probably hauling coal from the local mine at Acomb. Some time before 1911 he and his family emigrated to Canada, eventually living in Calgary. Shipping papers for Emily and four children show that they arrived in Canada in April

1906. Walter's attestation papers, dated the 28 September 1915, records that his wife, Emily was his next of kin and that they were living at 1215, 15th Avenue West, Calgary. His occupation is recorded as 'broker'.

**Walter is buried at Shorncliffe Military Cemetery, Kent.**

**Private John Rutter, aged 20**
**1/4th Northumberland Fusiliers**
**Died 3 October 1916**

John was the youngest son of Christopher and Elizabeth Rutter. The 1911 census shows that at the age of fourteen, like his brothers and sisters, John was working as a farm labourer. John joined the army in the summer of 1915. Whilst he was undergoing basic training at Redcar he had a reoccurrence of an illness from which he had suffered a few years previously. He died whilst receiving attention in North Ormesby Hospital, Middlesbrough. A full military burial took place at Chollerton. Robert, his older brother, was killed in 1917 (see page 191).

**John is buried in Chollerton (St Giles) Churchyard.**

## 1917

**Corporal Joseph Patrick Murphy, aged 25**
**1/7th Battalion Northumberland Fusiliers**
**Died 5 February 1917**

Joseph was born in 1891 at Biddlestone, near Rothbury. He was the eldest son of Michael and Elizabeth Murphy. The 1911 census records that Joseph was living with his widowed father and three sisters in Biddlestone and working as an estate gardener. At the time of enlistment in April 1915 he was living at Hesleyside, Bellingham. He spent all of his military service in the UK and was discharged as being 'no longer physically fit for war service' in late December 1916. A few weeks later, Joseph died at home.

**Joseph is buried in an unmarked grave in All Saints Churchyard, Thropton**

Anno1917 die 5° mensis Februaii.
*In the year 1917 on the 5th day of the month of February*
Josephus Patricus Murphy ex Biddlestone
*Joseph Patrick Murphy from Biddlestone*
Aetatis 25 ano in comunione Matris Ecclesiae
*Aged 25, in communion with Mother Church*
Animam Deo reddidit sacramentis
*With sacraments I return his soul to God*
Mundus cujus corpus die 8° mensis eiusdem sepultum est in caemeterio apud Thropton
*His clean body was buried on the 8th day of the same month in the cemetery at Thropton.*

Josephus Fitzsimons
[From the register of burials of All Saints RC Church]

**Private Walter Rutherford, aged 20**
**1/4th Battalion Northumberland Fusiliers**
**Died 28 April 1917**

Walter was the grandson of Richard and Annie Rutherford of East Whygate, Wark. Before enlisting in the army in May 1915, he worked as a farm labourer. He served in France from November 1915 until March 1916, when he returned to England and was admitted to North Staffs Infirmary.

He was initially diagnosed with bronchitis and was unable to speak; this developed into tuberculosis. His illness was attributed to exposure to bad weather and damp trenches. Walter was discharged as being 'no longer physically fit for active service' in July 1916 and died at home at the end of April 1917. A letter from the local doctor to the Army Medical Board, received 18 April, explained that Walter was suffering from pulmonary infection which would be 'lethal'. Walter died ten days later.

**Walter is buried in an unmarked grave in St Michael's Churchyard, Wark.**

**Private Robert Smith, aged 32**
**1/4th Battalion Northumberland Fusiliers**
**Died 2 July 1917**

Robert was the third son of Robert and Mary Smith of Woodbine Terrace, Hexham. He was born in Nether Warden. The 1911 census reports Robert, aged 25, single and working as a gardener. He married Constance Lonsdale in late 1914 and was the father of a small child; they lived in St Andrew's Road, Hexham. He was a member of the Hexham Territorials who were mobilised in August 1914, but due to his health he did not go out to France with the first draft of fusiliers. He spent a substantial part of the early years of the war on garrison duties on the Isle of Man, but he died a matter of weeks before he was due to go out to France. On his journey from the Isle of Man to Catterick Barracks, Yorkshire, he became seriously ill. He died two weeks later in Catterick Bridge Hospital. His body was transported back to Hexham.

**John is buried in St Michael's Churchyard, Warden.**

**Driver William Armstrong, aged 20**
**Royal Field Artillery**
**Died 2 August 1917**

William was born in Falstone, the son of William and Mary Armstrong. The registration district for William's death was Bellingham so it is likely that he died at home. The following is found on his headstone:

**LOOKING UNTO JESUS**
**HEB 12.2**

**William is buried in Falstone Cemetery.**

**Private John English Urwin, aged 26**
**Army Veterinary Corps (Northern Division)**
**Died 4 October 1917**

John was born in Wall in the summer of 1891, the son of Smith and Mary Jane Urwin of Wall and later of Stocksfield. He enlisted in May 1915 and appears to have spent his entire military career in the UK. He was discharged as being 'no longer physically fit for service' on the 21 June 1916. After his discharge he lived with his mother at Kimberley Gardens in Stocksfield, until he died in October 1917.

**John is buried in St Giles' Churchyard, Chollerton.**

## 1918

**Private Robert Thomas Curry, aged 18**
**51st Graduating Battalion Durham Light Infantry**
**1 March 1918**

Robert was the only son of Robert and Isabella, of Brunton Banks, Wall. He had been in the army for only a few months when he died. He was educated at Wall Church of England Day School. While stationed at Durham he contacted pleurisy and was transferred to a military hospital in Newcastle, where sadly his illness developed into pneumonia. Even though an operation was carried out, Robert succumbed to his illness.

The funeral conducted by Reverend WW London was attended by a large gathering, including the teachers and pupils of Wall School. He was laid to rest to the firing of three volleys over the grave and the sounding of *The Last Post.*

**Robert is buried in St Oswald's (Heavenfield) Churchyard, Wall.**

**Private William Bullock, aged 28**
**East Yorkshire Regiment**
**9 March 1918**

William was the son of William and Annie Jane Bullock of Camp Hill, Barrasford. Before the war he worked on his father's farm. William was married to Maggie Burns (née Hunter) on 15 June 1914. He enlisted in 1916 and was attached to the East Yorkshire Regiment, even though it was recognised that he had a delicate constitution, indeed many people who knew him well believed that military service would be a strain on his health. In 1917, it was reported that during his basic training, William's

health deteriorated, with the development of a lung disease. Subsequently he was discharged and allowed to return home, where eventually he died after a prolonged illness. At the same time his parents received notification that his younger brother John, had been killed in France whilst serving with the Coldstream Guards, (see page 218). The Hexham Herald (23 March 1918) records the burial of William and the tragedy of the Bullock Family. Their youngest son, Thomas, was also serving with the forces.

**William is buried in St Giles' Churchyard, Chollerton.**

**Private Thomas Horne, aged 27**
**1/4th Battalion Northumberland Fusiliers**
**Died 12 July 1918**

Thomas was born in Frizington, Cumberland, the eldest son of William and Alice Horne of the Barracks, Acomb. The 1901 census shows the Horne family living in Netherton, Northumberland, where the father, William, worked in the local coal mine. The 1911 census shows the family living in Acomb with the father and both sons, Thomas and John, working underground at a local coal mine.

Thomas was a serving Territorial and was involved in the action of 26 April 1915 (see page 35) and although previously wounded he served until his death with the 1/4th Northumberland Fusiliers. The Hexham Herald records that Thomas was well known as a playing member of Acomb

AFC. Thomas's younger brother, Sergeant John Horne, was awarded the Military Medal for gallantry on 15 September 1916 (see page 105).

The Hexham Herald reported that Thomas was in the 1st General Hospital, London, suffering from wounds to the head, from which he died. This was the second time that Thomas had been wounded.

**Thomas is buried in St John Lee Churchyard, Acomb.**

**Private Joseph Collinson Hedley, aged 20**
**1st Battalion Northamptonshire Regiment**
**Died 11 October 1918**

Joseph is the son of George and Jane Hedley of Broomhill Cottages, West Woodburn. When he died he had been in hospital for a long time suffering from the effects of frostbite and trench foot, which had crippled him. In January 1918, The North Tyne Magazine reported that Joseph had had his toes removed. In June 1918 it was noted that Joseph was in hospital near St Alban's where he had undergone a further operation to remove a bone from his foot, and that he was recovering slowly. Whilst in hospital he developed phthisis pulmonalis a form of tuberculosis (consumption) and was discharged from hospital to die 'amongst his friends'.

He eventually died on 11 October at the home of his aunt, Mrs Hudson. Joseph was the third of the Hedley's sons to die during the War: Edward (see page 82) and James (see page 88) both died in France during 1916. Joseph's funeral was with full military honours and concluded with the firing of three volleys over the grave, together with the sounding of *The Last Post.*

**Joseph is buried in St Cuthbert's Churchyard, Corsenside.**

The 9th Battalion Canadian Infantry was the official name for a reserve battalion based in the United Kingdom. The initial core for this battalion was recruited in Edmonton and sailed for Europe from Quebec on 30 September 1914. On arrival in the UK approximately half the men were drafted into various 1st Canadian Brigade Battalions to fill vacancies left by wounded and dead comrades. Many of this new draft saw action during Second *Ypres* (April-May 1915) where a huge number suffered horrendously from the effects of gas. By the end of April 1915 the calls for new drafts had used up virtually all of the original 9th Battalion.

James Daley was eventually drafted to the 49th Battalion, part of the 3rd Canadian Division which was formed in France in December 1915, and saw action at *Mount Sorrel* in June 1916. During this time James received injuries which saw him repatriated to Edmonton, where he died of pneumonia in a military hospital.

**Sergeant James Daley, aged 35**
**General List Canadian Army**
**Died 28 October 1918**

**A Day's Funerals**

Mrs. J. C. Hudson, 10526 106th avenue, who died October 26th, will be interred today (Friday) at Mt. Pleasant cemetery. Funeral from Connelly & McKinley's parlors at 1 o'clock.

The funeral of Miss. Katie Allen will take place today (Friday) at 3 p. m. from Connelly & McKinley's. Interment at Beechmount Cemetery.

The remains of Corp. Robert Pretty are at Connelly & McKinley's parlors. Funeral arrangements are not yet made.

The funeral of Private Daly takes place at 2 p. m. today (Friday) from Connelly & McKinley's. Interment at the Catholic cemetery.

An extract from the
Edmonton Daily Bulletin
1 November 1918

James was born in Newcastle, the son of John and Mary Daly of Bellingham. His Canadian attestation papers show that he enlisted on September 1914 at Valcartier in Quebec and was assigned to the 9th Battalion Canadian Infantry. Later he was transferred to the 49th Battalion. He was married to Edith Maud (née Clark) and they lived at 2079 34th Street, Edmonton. It also shows that before volunteering he was employed as a policeman and had served with the Royal Canadian Regiment, the 101st Edmonton Fusiliers, the equivalent of the British Territorials. He died of pneumonia in Edmonton Military Hospital. A picture of his headstone in Edmonton shows that James served with the Canadian Infantry 49th Battalion.

**James is buried in**
**St Joachim's Roman Catholic Cemetery, Edmonton, Canada**

The Army Services Corps, Motor Transport Training Depot, was initially based at the Greenwich Workhouse in Grove Park, London. However, later, as the war effort expanded, numerous sites around London were used, including those in Camberwell, Catford, Sydenham and Twickenham.

**Private George Edward Cattermole, aged 23**
**Motor Transport Training Depot**
**Army Service Corps**
**Died 5 November 1918**

George was born in Clerkenwell, London, in 1896. He was the eldest son of Edward George and Ann Elizabeth Cattermole, later of Chollerton Vicarage. George was less well known in the district than his two brothers who were serving with the Royal Navy, probably because for most of his working life George had lived in Newcastle and served his time with Armstrong, Whitworth and Company. Early in the course of the war George volunteered to join the army, but his employers refused to grant him permission owing to his work being of importance to the war effort. He worked at Armstrong's until June 1918, when a considerable number of employees were called up. He joined the ASC and was posted to Osterley Park and then to Sydenham where he was employed on motor transport work. In early October he contracted influenza which developed into acute pneumonia. He died in Horton War Hospital, Epsom. His burial took place on Saturday 9 November at Chollerton.

**George is buried in St Giles' Churchyard, Chollerton.**

Thomas Storey had been transferred to the Northern Command Labour Centre based in Ripon in Yorkshire. This was a receiving centre for men enlisted into the Labour Corps, transferring from an existing unit or returning from service overseas.

**Private Thomas William Storey, aged 30**
**South Staffordshire Regiment**
**852 Agricultural Company, Labour Corps**
**Died 10 November 1918**

Thomas was born in Hexham, the eldest son of Thomas and Sarah Storey. Before joining the army he was employed as a farm labourer by Henry Snaith of Dudlees, Otterburn. Having served for over two and a half years in the army, he died in Langport, Somerset, of influenza. At this time a huge number of soldiers were dying of this terrible disease, which was ravaging the populations of Europe.

Thomas's brother Robert died two days earlier of pneumonia in France, (see page 326). Thomas was buried on Thursday 14 November with a contingent of local volunteers forming a military escort.

**Thomas is buried in Bellingham Cemetery**

The 4th Lancashire Fusiliers (LF) was a home based battalion which did not see action abroad during the war (seriously wounded and recuperating soldiers, including Thomas Harrison, could be allocated to this battalion on their return to England). Thomas Harrison's service number 39254 suggests strongly that whilst on active duty he was serving with the 16$^{th}$ Battalion Lancashire Fusiliers (LF). During 1918 the LF served on the Somme, when the Germans renewed their drive for Amiens on 4 April [5].

For 4 April 1918, the war diary for the 16$^{th}$ Battalion Lancashire Fusiliers records [6]:

> "Sector was shelled heavily from 5am to 11am. Shelling appeared to be the fringe of a heavy bombardment on the corps to the right. Mainly 5.9 and 4.2 inch shells with a high proportion of gas shells. Casualties were 13 killed, 64 wounded and 46 gassed."

**Private Thomas Harrison, aged 24**
**4$^{th}$ Battalion Lancashire Fusiliers**
**Died 11 November 1918**

Thomas was the eldest son of Joseph and Elizabeth Harrison of Railway Cottages, Warden. He worked as a casual gangman for the North-Eastern Railways. The Hexham Herald of 20 April 1918 records that Thomas had been gassed in early April 1918 and that he was in hospital in Kent. A further newspaper article reported that he was seriously ill, suffering from pneumonia. The Roll of Honour in the Hexham Herald stated that he died in the Albany Hospital, Cardiff.

**Thomas is buried in**
**St Michael's Churchyard, Warden.**

**Sapper Joseph John Laidler, aged 32**
**344th Road Construction Company**
**Royal Engineers**
**Died 27 November 1918**

Joseph was born at Swinton, Berwickshire, the eldest son of Thomas and Isabella Laidler. He was the husband of Christina Laidler (née Morton) of Shincliffe. His obituary in the Hexham Herald states that Joseph died in 4th Northern Hospital, Lincoln, of wounds received in France. The report states that Joseph was late of Acomb, Hexham and the North. The following is found on his headstone:

**GREATER LOVE**
**HATH NO MAN THAN THIS**
**THAT HE GIVETH HIS LIFE**
**FOR HIS FRIENDS**

**Joseph is buried in St Mary's Churchyard, Shincliffe, Durham.**

**Able Seaman John Rae, aged 24**
**Hawke Battalion, Royal Naval Division**
**Died 28 November 1918**

John was born in Canobie, Dumfriesshire, the son of Thomas and Isabella Rae of Pinchmenear, Bellingham. He was educated at the Reed School, Bellingham. Like his father, John worked on the railway as a goods clerk before he joined the Colours. He joined the army reserve in December 1915 and was drafted for France in July 1917, joining the Hawke Battalion. He spent some time away from the Front in early 1918, as a result of arthritis in the right knee. He rejoined his battalion in February 1918.

During February 1918, the Hawke Battalion (188th Brigade) made up part of 63rd Division's three brigade [188th (left), 189th (centre) and 190th (right)] defending the Flesquières Salient (see page 203). On 12 March the Germans began to drench the whole of the salient with gas shells. The official figure was that over 200,000 shells were fired by the enemy, the majority containing mustard gas. John was a casualty of this action [7,8,9].

The History of the Royal Naval Division states:

> "The gas used was chiefly Yellow Cross (mustard gas), and its greatest tactical value was that the results were not, as a rule instantaneous; it hung round every trench, every dug out, every headquarter for an indeterminate period, and no amount of gas discipline could prevent a growing casualty list among troops bound to remain in the infected area and to carry on their ordinary and laborious duties."

During this time at the Front the Hawke Battalion lost 15 officers and 582 men from gas poisoning between 12 and 21 March.

John was invalided to the UK in early April 1918; he was diagnosed with pulmonary tuberculosis as a result of gas inhalation and was discharged. He died at home of Phithisis Pulmonalis.

### John is buried in Bellingham Cemetery

After extensive research by the people of Bellingham to provide the necessary evidence, the Commonwealth War Grave Commission has agreed to mark his grave with an official CWGC headstone. This is a small victory in the struggle to have acknowledged the burial sites of men who died after being discharged.

## 1919

**John James Rome, aged 19**
**3rd (Reserve) Battalion Northumberland Fusiliers**
**4 July 1919**

John was born in Dumfriesshire, the eldest son of David and Janet Rome. After the war his mother lived at Donkley Wood, Falstone. His death was registered in Newcastle upon Tyne. It is very likely that John died from the effects of the influenza which was endemic in 1919. The 3rd Reserve Battalion was a training unit that remained in the United Kingdom for the duration of the war, based in Sunderland. The following is found on his headstone:

**FAITH IS LOST IN SIGHT**
**AND DEATHLESS HOPE IS**
**CROWNED**

**John is buried in Falstone Cemetery**

## 1920

In late August 1918 the 2nd Battalion, The Loyal North Lancashire Regiment (LNL) (34th Division), received orders to move towards the Front Line near La Clytte. During the 28 and 29 August the battalion's position came under artillery fire which caused a large number of casualties, including a number who were affected by gas [10].

**Private George Errington, aged 24**
**2$^{nd}$ Battalion The Loyal North Lancashire Regiment**
**Died 15 January 1920**

George was born in Acomb, the son of William and Elizabeth Errington, who lived at 15 Morrison Terrace, Acomb. Before joining up he worked as a labourer in the local brickyard. Initially he served with the Border Regiment, but later transferred to the North Lancashire Regiment. George died in Queen Mary's Hospital, Whalley, Lancashire, of wounds received on 28 August 1918. His older brother William was also in the army and was killed in September 1916 (see page 122).

**George is buried in Farlam Churchyard, Brampton.**

**Driver (Gunner) John William Conkleton, aged 39**
**Royal Field Artillery**
**Died March 1920**

John was born in Sunderland, the eldest son of William and Jane Conkleton. The family moved to Acomb in the 1880s and both the father and son were employed as cart men around the district. He enlisted in the services in December 1914 and was discharged in March 1916 from 51 Reserve Battery Royal Field Artillery. He died in the Royal Victoria Infirmary, Newcastle.

**John was buried in an unmarked grave in St John Lee Churchyard, on 31 March 1920.**

**Corporal George Dalton, aged 22**
**Northumberland Fusiliers**
**Died 4 April 1920**

George was born in Bingfield, the son of George and Margaret Dalton of Cowper Hill, Humshaugh. Before joining up George was employed by Mrs Clayton of Chesters. George was initially on the strength of the 2/4$^{th}$ the Reserve Battalion of the Northumberland Fusiliers. Standing orders show that he was granted leave with rations allowance, from 25-28 November 1917, before proceeding to Southampton for embarkation to Italy on 4 December.

The 1/4$^{th}$ Northumberland Fusiliers did not serve on the Italian Front, however the 10$^{th}$ and 11$^{th}$ Battalion of the Northumberland Fusiliers were involved in this campaign, (see page 336). George was transferred to one of these two battalions. The North Tyne Magazine reports that George died of heart disease contracted on active service during the Great War.

**George is buried in St Peter's Churchyard, Humshaugh.**

## 1921

**Private Watson Eddy, aged 24**
**Northumberland Fusiliers**
**Died 10 April 1921**

Watson was born in Acomb in 1896 and was living with his grandmother Mary in 1901. Before he enlisted in the army he was employed by Miss Allgood of the Hermitage as an under-gardener. He was initially reported missing on 21 March 1918. At this time his brother Joseph was reported as being severely wounded. However, his mother, Mrs Savage of Acomb, eventually received a card from Watson stating that he was a prisoner of war at Reserve Lazerette, Verden Afuller, in the province of Hanover and that he was in good health. He clearly returned home to Acomb, but the cause of his death in 1921 is not recorded.

**Watson is buried in an unmarked grave in St John Lee's Churchyard extension, Acomb.**

## 1922

**ABS Frederick Adam Lyons, MM aged 27**
**Anson Battalion, Royal Naval Division**
**Died 14 February 1922**

Frederick was born in Gateshead in October 1894, the son of Frederick and Dorothy Lyons. Before the war he worked as a miner and at the outset of hostilities he enlisted with the Northumberland Fusiliers, but within a short time he was transferred to the Royal Naval Volunteer Reserve and joined the Howe Battalion. He served in *Gallipoli* until he was invalided home with gun shot wounds to his left leg and back, in June 1915. The Howe Battalion was part of the 2nd Naval Brigade attack at the *Third Battle of Krithia* (4-6 June 1915). After a short and ineffectual thirty minute bombardment the Howe, Hood and Anson advanced only to be mowed down by Turkish rifle and machine gun fire. After convalescence Lyons was posted to France to the Howe Battalion [7,11].

On 26 October 1917, during the *Passchendaele* conflict, he was again wounded during an attack on German pill boxes, known as Berks Houses, Bray Farm, Banff House, Sourd Farm and Varlet Farm. However, it is reported that Frederick remained on duty, despite his injury. During

February 1918 he was transferred to the Anson Battalion and was honourably discharged early in 1919 [12]. Frederick was awarded the Military Medal for his actions at *Miraumont* on 17 February 1917 which was published in the London Gazette (17 April 1917).

**Frederick is buried in an unmarked grave in St John Lee Churchyard extension, Acomb.**

**Robert Bowman, aged 35**
**1/4th Battalion Northumberland Fusiliers**
**Died October 1922**

Robert was born in Hexham, the second son of John and Margaret Bowman of Acomb. The 1911 census shows that he had been newly married to Lizzie (née Hodgson); at this time they had a son, also named Robert, and lived in Forge Cottage, Acomb. John worked as a miner. In June 1915 he enlisted with the Territorials' training battalion (3/4th Northumberland Fusiliers) and proceeded to France with a draft of new recruits in early November 1915. Robert appears eventually to have been the father of seven children. It is reported that his last child, Sarah Ann, who was born in the summer of 1922, was buried in February 1929 in the same grave as her father.

**Robert is buried in an unmarked grave in St John Lee's Churchyard extension, Acomb.**

## REFERENCES

1. Private Communication. *Philip Strong, Great War Forum 1914-1918 invisionzone.com/forums*

2. Morris, J. Capt. *German Air Raids on Britain*. Pub: Sampson Low and Marston, 1925.

3. Private Communication. *RAF_Louvert. Great War Forum 1914-1918 invisionzone.com/forums*

4. Raleigh. Sir W. A. and Jones H. A. *The War in the Air. Being the part played by the Royal Air Force.* Pub: 1922-1937.

5. Private Communication. *Melpack. Great War Forum 1914-1918 invisionzone.com/forums*

6. WO95/2397. *War Diary 16th Battalion Lancashire Fusiliers.*

7. Jerrold, J *The Royal Naval Division.* Reprinted Naval and Military Press

8. Jerrold, J. *The Hawke Battalion.* Pub: 1925, reprinted Naval and Military Press

*9. WO95/3114. War Diary Hawke Battalion.*

10. WO95/4465. *War Diary 2nd Battalion Loyal North Lancashire Regiment.*

*11. WO95/3111. War Diary Howe Battalion.*

*12. WO95/3111. War Diary Anson Battalion.*

# CHAPTER TWENTY THREE

# ENIGMA

## David Jackson

Throughout the northern part of the North Tyne Valley, 'David Jackson' is commemorated on a large number of war memorials. His name can also be found on his parents' gravestone in Kielder Churchyard.

> In loving memory of John Jackson husbsnd of Mary Jackson
> who died at Bakethin August 1st 1920 aged 58
> and also their dear and only son Private David Jackson of the
> 4th MGC section who fell in action in France July 1st 1917.

However, on the Presbyterian Memorial now sited in the United Reform Church in Falstone, the name of David Jackson appears *twice*, first as a Northumberland Fusilier and secondly as a member of the Machine Gun Corps, who died 1 July 1917 (see page 168).

My extensive searches could not find any record of a David Jackson being killed whilst serving in, or dying after discharge from, the Northumberland Fusiliers. However, I was fortunate enough to be given a picture of a David Jackson who died July 1917 whilst serving with the Machine Gun Corps, but it shows him wearing a cap with a *Northumberland Fusiliers* badge. I therefore believe that the two commemorations 0f David Jackson on the Presbyterian Memorial are to the same man: David Jackson's service record reports that he was allotted to the reserve army as a Fusilier before transferring to the Machine Gun Corps.

## Ernest Johnson

On two of Bellingham's memorials the name of E. Johnson is to be found: The E. Johnson on the cemetery's lych-gate memorial is clearly the Ernest Johnson found on St Cuthbert's Church memorial, but the name E. Johnson is not present on any of the other memorials in Bellingham. Extensive research has not allowed me to identify this person. There appears to be no connection with William Armstrong Johnson who is commemorated only in St Oswald's Roman Catholic Church. The Roll of Honour for Bellingham was published in the North Tyne Magazine for February 1918 and did not list an E. Johnson.

It is my belief that the Ernest was not a resident of Bellingham but his name was accepted for inclusion through a link with the community which I am unable to confirm.

It is possible that our mysterious E. Johnson is in some way connected to the well-known Mr Edwin Johnson who attempted to enrol into the army under the Derby Scheme but who was rejected on health grounds. He spent the war years organising charity events to support the soldiers at the Front, to help soldiers' widows and their families and to make sure that the community was prepared for the support of returning combatants.

**Kielder**

Plaque: United Reform Church

**Plashetts**

Plaque 1914-1918: Methodist and United Reform Chapel Bellingham

Roll of Honour: Methodist and United Reform Chapel Bellingham

**Falstone**

Plaque: Presbyterian Church

Roll of Honour: St Peter's Church

Cross: Falstone Cemetery

**Greystead**

Plaque to the Fallen: St Luke's Church

Plaque to those who served: St Luke's Church

**Thorneyburn**

Plaque: St Aidan's Church

Plaque: St Aidan's Church

**Bellingham**

Lych-gate Memorial: Bellingham Cemetery

Plaque: St Cuthbert's Church

White Stained glass window: St Cuthbert's Church

Plaque 1914-1918: St Oswald's Church

Plaque Spencer: St Oswald's Church

Plaque 1914-1918 Presbyterian: Methodist and United Reform Chapel

Roll of Honour Presbyterian: Methodist and United Reform Chapel

Plaque 1914-1918 Methodists: Methodist and United Reform Chapel

Reed Charity School: Heritage Centre

**West Woodburn**

Obelisk 1914-1918: Roadside

**Birtley**

Cross 1914-1918: Roadside

Robson Plaque: St Giles' Church

Hutchinson Plaque: St Giles' Church

Hutchinson Stained glass window: St Giles' Church

Allgood Grave marker: St Giles' Churchyard

**Wark**

Cross: Village Green

Plaque 1914-1918: St Michael's Church

Roll of Honour: Mechanical Institute

**Simonburn**

Allgood Plaque: ; St Mungo's Church

Ridley C N Plaque: St Mungo's Church

Ridley C N Stained Glass Window: St Mungo's Church

Ridley H Q Plaque: St Mungo's Church

Plaque 1914-1918: St Mungo's Church

Hutchinson Stained Glass Window: St Mungo's Church

**Humshaugh**

Obelisk 1914-1918: Roadside

Plaque 1914-1918: St Peter's Church

Plaque Methodists 1914-1918: now in St Peter's Church

**Chollerton**

Cross: Roadside

**Wall**

Cross; Village Green

Roll of honour: Village Hall

**Acomb**

Plaque 1914-1918 Methodist Church

**St John Lee Church**

Cross: Churchyard

Walton Plaque: Church

Mewburn Stained glass window: Church

Mewburn Effigy Mewburn: Church

Cuthbert Plaque: Church

**Warden**

Cupboard 1914-1918: St Michael's Church

Harrison Cross: St Michael's Churchyard

Leadbitter Cross St Michael's Churchyard

# INDEX OF SOLDIERS

INDEX OF SOLIERS